MW01027929

LOEB CLASSICAL LIBRARY

FOUNDED BY JAMES LOEB 1911

EDITED BY

JEFFREY HENDERSON

PINDAR

I

LCL 56

PINDAR

OLYMPIAN ODES
PYTHIAN ODES

EDITED AND TRANSLATED BY

WILLIAM H. RACE

HARVARD UNIVERSITY PRESS
CAMBRIDGE, MASSACHUSETTS
LONDON, ENGLAND

Copyright © 1997 by the President and Fellows
of Harvard College
All rights reserved

First published 1997
Revised 2012

LOEB CLASSICAL LIBRARY® is a registered trademark
of the President and Fellows of Harvard College

Library of Congress Control Number 95-42927
CIP data available from the Library of Congress

ISBN 978-0-674-99564-2

Composed in ZephGreek and ZephText by
Technologies 'N Typography, Merrimac, Massachusetts.
Printed on acid-free paper and bound by
The Maple-Vail Book Manufacturing Group

CONTENTS

CONTENTS OF VOLUME II

PREFACE

My aim has been to produce a readable, clear translation that reflects the grammar of the original Greek, while following the lineation of the Greek text as closely as normal English word order allows. When enjambment of a word is natural to the English, I have imitated the Greek by preserving it; when not, I have maintained the Greek grammatical structure. In the present edition Greek proper names appear in their common Latinized spellings.

This edition does not provide the alternate verse numbering of Heyne's edition, whose sole purpose is to facilitate reference to the scholia. It also is very sparing in its citation of secondary literature for two reasons: such references quickly become outdated and students of Pindar are fortunate to have an excellent historical survey of Pindaric scholarship by D. C. Young and annotated bibliographies by D. E. Gerber and others.

I have greatly profited from the generous help of four outstanding Pindarists: Christopher Carey, Douglas Gerber, Sir Hugh Lloyd-Jones, and Andrew Miller, none of whom can be held accountable for my inevitable slips. In addition, Margaretta Fulton, George Goold, Robert Rust, and Jeffrey Rusten have been of great assistance. On points of detail I also wish to thank Bruce Braswell, Adolph

Köhnken, Herwig Maehler, Ian Rutherford, and Zeph
Stewart. The University Research Council of Vanderbilt
assisted with a grant in the summer 1994, and my wife,
Diane, aided me throughout with good advice and improvements of style.

INTRODUCTION

"Of the nine Greek lyric poets Pindar is by far the greatest for the magnificence of his inspiration, his precepts, figures of language, lavish abundance of matter and words, and river (so to speak) of eloquence." This assessment by Quintilian in his survey of Greek poets (*Inst. Or.* 10.1.61) was the standard evaluation of Pindar in antiquity and helps to explain why nearly one fourth of his odes are well preserved in manuscripts, whereas the works of the other lyric poets have survived only in bits and pieces.

The ancient editors divided Pindar's poems into seventeen books (papyrus rolls) by genres: 1 book of hymns to various gods; 1 of paeans (hymns addressed mainly to Apollo); 2 of dithyrambs (hymns addressed mainly to Dionysus); 2 of prosodia (hymns for approaching a god's shrine); 3 of partheneia (hymns sung by maidens); 2 of hyporchemata (dancing hymns); 1 of encomia (songs in praise of men at banquets); 1 of threnoi (songs of lament); and 4 of epinicia (victory songs). Although numerous fragments of his paeans and other poems have survived on papyrus or through quotation by ancient authors, only the four books of epinicia, comprising forty-five odes in celebration of athletic victors, have been preserved almost intact in a continuous manuscript tradition, and it is upon them that his reputation has largely rested as Greece's greatest poet of praise.

The victory odes are, however, notoriously difficult to understand. They are complex mixtures of praise (and blame), mythical narratives, prayers and hymns, advice, athletic triumphs (and failures), and even current events, conveyed in a highly artificial language in often very complicated poetic meters, all designed to be sung and danced to the accompaniment of lyres and pipes. They represent the apex of their genre, in much the same way that Bach's works are a culmination of baroque music. Pindar's art, like Bach's, presents a constant tension between the constraints of form and the freedom of innovation; it too exhibits tremendous energy, great variety within its genres, and reveals ever-new depths upon repeated hearings.

Our understanding of Pindar's odes has been complicated by what Hugh Lloyd-Jones has called a "fatal conjunction of nineteenth-century historicism with nineteenth-century Romanticism."[1] The former, already employed by ancient commentators, seeks to explain details in the odes as reflections of historical (and all too often pseudo-historical) events. The latter interprets the poems as expressions of the poet's personal opinions and subjective feelings. There is no doubt that the odes refer to historical persons and events (indeed every ode has an actual

[1] Lloyd-Jones, "Pindar," *Proceedings of the British Academy* 68 (1982) 145; the entire address provides an excellent assessment of Pindar's qualities. For a good, brief overview of trends in Pindaric scholarship, see the same author's "Modern Interpretation of Pindar: The Second Pythian and Seventh Nemean Odes," *Journal of Hellenic Studies* 93 (1973) 109–117.

victory as its occasion) and that Pindar presents a distinctive personality, but these aspects of the poems are subsidiary to their generic function of praising men within the religious and ethical norms of aristocratic fifth-century Greece. In E. L. Bundy's formulation, they constitute "an oral, public, epideictic literature dedicated to the single purpose of eulogizing men and communities."[2]

Pindar's poetry expresses the conservative, so-called "archaic," mores of the sixth and early fifth century. His thought is ethically cautionary and contains frequent reminders of man's limitations, his dependence on the gods and nature, and the brevity of life's joys. He espouses moderation (μέτρον, καιρός), the aristocratic ("Doric") values of civic order (εὐνομία) and peaceful concord (ἡσυχία), and reverence for the gods (εὐσέβεια).[3] His gaze is primarily backwards toward the models of the past, as they are exemplified in the legends from Hellenic myth, and it is against these that the victors' achievements are measured. To help guide the reader, I provide some key terms that point to recurring themes in the epinicia.[4]

ἀρετά the realization of human excellence in achievements

φυά one's inborn nature (also σύγγονος/συγγενής)

θεός the divine component of all human achievement (also δαίμων, πότμος, etc.)

[2] Bundy, *Studia. Pindarica* (Berkeley 1962; repr. 1986) 35.

[3] See E. Thummer, *Die Religiosität Pindars* (Innsbruck 1957).

[4] Often these positive elements are set in contrast to the envy (φθόνος) of ill-wishers and the darkness (σκότος) and silence (σιγά) that attend failure.

πόνος   the hard work required for success (also δα-
πάνα, expense)

ἀγλαΐα   the splendor of success (also one of the Graces)

χάρις   the joy of celebration and charm of poetry (also
personified as the Graces)

κλέος   the renown which rewards hard-earned success
(also δόξα and κῦδος)

σοφία   the poet's wisdom, including poetic skill, inspi-
ration, and ethical knowledge

χρέος   the poet's obligation to praise ἀρετά (also χρή)

φιλία   the bond among good men (also ξενία, guest-
friendship)

Pindar's Life and Career

What little we know about Pindar comes from the po-
ems themselves and from five brief accounts of his life.[5]
Although they contain much fanciful material and numer-

---

[5] A brief life preserved on a papyrus dating from about 200
A.D. (P. Oxy. 2438) was first published in 1961. The other sources
are the *Vita Ambrosiana* (preserved in the Ambrosian MS), *Vita
Thomana* (attributed to Thomas Magister), *Vita Metrica* (31 hex-
ameters perhaps composed in the 4th or 5th cent. A.D.), and the
notice in the *Suda*. Sections 25–33 in Eustathius' *Praefatio* rely
heavily on the other lives and provide little new information. The
texts of the vitae in the MSS and Eustathius' *Praefatio* can be
found in A. B. Drachmann, *Scholia Vetera in Pindari Carmina*
(Leipzig 1903,1927) 1.1–9 and 3.296–303. For a translation of the
Vita Ambrosiana, see M. R. Lefkowitz, *The Lives of the Greek
Poets* (Baltimore 2012) 145–147; for a text and translation of the
papyrus life, see I. Gallo, *Una nuova biografia di Pindaro* (POxy.
2438). *Introduzione, testo critico e commentario* (Salerno 1968).

4

ous contradictions, one can, by careful sifting, arrive at the following probable information. Pindar was born in Cynoscephalae, a village on the outskirts of Thebes (the chief city in Boeotia). His father was probably Daïphantus and his mother Cleodice. If a first-person statement in one poem (*Pyth.* 5) refers to the poet himself, Pindar belonged to the clan of the Aegeidae, prominent in Thebes and Sparta. If the quotation in the *Vita Ambrosiana* indicating that Pindar was born during a Pythian festival (*fr.* 193) is combined with the statement in the *Suda* that he was born in the 65th Olympiad (520–516 B.C.), the most likely date for his birth becomes 518. He studied pipe-playing with Scopelinus (perhaps his uncle), choral direction in Athens with Apollodorus (or Agathocles), and possibly music with Lasus of Hermione. The earliest victory ode for which dates are given in the ancient sources is *Pyth.* 10, composed in 498 when Pindar would have been about twenty. The papyrus life reports that he won the dithyrambic contest in Athens in the following year (497/6), and if the scholiastic date of 446 is correct for *Pyth.* 8, it is the latest extant epinicion. We can be confident, however, that Pindar was composing until at least 452, the date of *Ol.* 4, confirmed by both the papyrus life and a papyrus victory list.[6] Since the life span of 80 years given in the *Vita Metrica* is the only one long enough to encompass the dated odes (the other lives give 55 and 66), his death can arbitrarily be put at 438.

A number of anecdotes preserved in ancient sources, although of little or no historical value, serve to illustrate

[6] P. Oxy. 222, dating from about 250 A.D., lists Olympic victors for the years 480–468 and 456–448.

aspects of Pindar's career and poetic art. Two reported in the *Vita Ambrosiana* point to his poetic precociousness. One, attributed to the early Hellenistic biographer Chamaeleon, tells that when Pindar was a boy hunting near Helicon, he fell asleep and a bee built a honeycomb on his mouth. While the honey points to the sweetness of his song (cf. *Ol.* 11.4 and *Pyth.* 3.64), the site of Helicon links Pindar with his Boeotian predecessor Hesiod (c. 750 B.C.), who received his poetic commission while shepherding sheep at the foot of that mountain. The other relates that when his Athenian instructor Apollodorus had to be out of town and turned over the training of a chorus to the young Pindar, he did so well that he became immediately famous. Plutarch informs us that the Boeotian poet Corinna criticized the young Pindar for priding himself on stylistic embellishments rather than on mythical topics. He then composed the hymn that begins, "Shall it be Ismenus, or Melia of the golden spindle, or Cadmus . . . that we shall hymn?" (*fr.* 29). When he showed it to her, she laughed and said, "One should sow with the hand, not the whole sack."[7] The story illustrates Pindar's generous use of mythical catalogs, especially to introduce poems (cf. *Nem.* 10 and *Isth.* 7), and the frequent references to myths and legends throughout his works.

Three anecdotes in the *Vita Ambrosiana* point to Pindar's close relationship with the gods. We are told that Pan was once heard singing one of Pindar's paeans between the two Boeotian mountains of Cithaeron and Helicon, and

[7] Plut. *de glor. Ath.* 4.347F–348A. Corinna may, however, actually belong to the 3rd cent. B.C.; see M. West, "Dating Corinna," *Classical Quarterly* 84 (1990) 553–557.

that in a dream Demeter blamed him for neglecting her in his hymns, whereupon he composed a poem in her honor. It is also reported that the priest at Apollo's temple in Delphi announced upon closing each day, "Let the poet Pindar join the god at supper." The 2nd century A.D. traveler Pausanias claims to have seen the iron chair at Delphi upon which Pindar sat to sing his poems to Apollo (10.24.5). All these anecdotes reflect the deeply religious nature of his poetry and his special devotion to Apollo, who figures so prominently in his works.

Finally, there is the famous story of Pindar's house being spared when Alexander the Great razed Thebes in 335 B.C.,[8] familiar to English readers from Milton's lines in Sonnet 8: "The great Emathian conquerer bid spare | The house of Pindarus, when temple and tow'r | Went to the ground." Although some have rightly questioned the historical validity of the story,[9] it serves to illustrate the Panhellenic reputation Pindar enjoyed in the century following his death.

The most important historical event during Pindar's career was the Persian invasion under Xerxes that culminated in two decisive battles, one at sea near Salamis in 480 and the other on land at Plataea in 479. There are three references in the epinicia to these Greek victories. In *Pyth.*

---

[8] The story is mentioned in numerous places besides the lives and the *Suda*: Plutarch, *Alexander* 11; Arrian, *History of Alexander* 1.9.10; Pliny, *Natural History* 7.29; and Dio Chrysostom 2.33. Some sources mention a previous sparing by the Lacedaemonians.

[9] See W. J. Slater, "Pindar's House," *Greek, Roman, and Byzantine Studies* 12 (1971) 146–52.

1 Pindar mentions the Athenian and Spartan pride in the battles of Salamis and Plataea, in *Isth.* 5 he praises the Aeginetan sailors for the part they played at Salamis, and in *Isth.* 8 he expresses his relief at being free from the Persian threat, which he calls the "rock of Tantalus, that unbearable labor for Hellas." His own city of Thebes had unfortunately sided with the invaders and actually fought against the Athenians at the battle of Plataea. We have no way of knowing Pindar's private reaction to his city's policy, but he publicly lauded the victors, even going so far as to call Athens the "bulwark of Hellas" (*fr.* 76) for her part in the war effort.[10] The story in the *Vita Thomana* that tells of his being fined by his own city for praising Athens reflects what must have been a sensitive issue for him, but the evidence of his poetry shows that he remained a Panhellenic poet, consistent with his wish at the end of *Ol.* 1 to be "foremost in wisdom among Hellenes everywhere."

While the mainland Greeks were confronting the Persians, the Greeks in Sicily were facing a Carthaginian threat. In 480 Gelon of Syracuse (whose younger brother Hieron succeeded him two years later as tyrant of Syracuse) joined forces with Theron of Acragas to defeat a Carthaginian army numbering 100,000 at the battle of Himera, spoils from which greatly enriched both cities. At *Pyth.* 1.75–80 Pindar ranks this battle on the same level as Salamis and Plataea.

The 76th Olympiad in 476, the first following these three great battles, marks a high point in Pindar's career as

[10] In *fr.* 77 he also praised the Athenians for their naval action at Artemisium earlier in 480, where they "laid the bright foundation of freedom."

an epinician poet. Five of the fourteen Olympian odes are
to victors in that Olympiad, including two of his major
poems, *Ol.* 1 to Hieron of Syracuse (whose horse Phereni-
cus won the single-horse race) and *Ol.* 2 to Theron of
Acragas (who won the chariot race). In 476/5 Hieron
founded the city of Aetna and in 474 his ships defeated an
Etruscan fleet at Cyme near the Bay of Naples. The poets
who enjoyed his patronage included Aeschylus, who wrote
the *Aetnaeae* (*Women of Aetna*) to celebrate the founding
of that city, Simonides, Bacchylides, who wrote three epi-
nicia (3, 4, 5) and an encomium (*fr.* 20C) for him, and, of
course, Pindar, who honored him with *Ol.* 1, *Pyth.* 1, 2, 3,
a hyporchema (*fr.* 105), and an encomium (*fr.* 124d). In
Pyth. 1 Pindar compares Hieron to Philoctetes and praises
him for his victory at Cyme, in which he "delivered Hellas
from grievous slavery." In *Pyth.* 2 he mentions the grati-
tude of the Western Locrians for Hieron's deliverance of
them from war; the scholia claim that Hieron intervened
to stop Anaxilas of Rhegium (d. 476) from attacking Locri
(probably in 477), but the date and circumstances of the
poem remain uncertain. In addition, Pindar wrote odes
for Theron's brother Xenocrates and nephew Thrasybulus
(*Pyth.* 6 and *Isth.* 2), for Hieron's general, Chromius (*Nem.*
1 and 9), and for his fellow Syracusan, Hagesias (*Ol.* 6).

The geographical dispersion of the victors celebrated
by Pindar indicates how broadly his reputation and associa-
tions had spread. Of the 45 odes, only five are to Thebans.
Seventeen are for victors from cities in Sicily and southern
Italy (Syracuse, Acragas, Camarina, Himera, and Western
Locri), eleven for victors from the island of Aegina (the
most by far for a single city), seven for victors from cities on
mainland Greece (Corinth, Opus, Orchomenus, Pelinna,

Athens, Acharnae, and Argos), three for victors from
Cyrene on the coast of north Africa, and one each for
victors from the islands of Rhodes and Tenedos. Victors
mentioned in the epinician fragments are from Rhodes,
Aegina, and Megara; paeans are composed for the peo-
ple of Thebes, Abdera, Ceos, Delphi, Naxos, Aegina, and
Argos; dithyrambs for Argos, Thebes, and Athens; and
encomia for individuals from Acragas, Macedonia,
Corinth, Tenedos, and Syracuse.

Other than anecdotal comments in the scholia, we have
no details about how contracts were arranged,[11] whether
Pindar was present at the athletic contests (although at *Ol.*
10.100 he says that he saw the victor win at Olympia), or
whether he oversaw any of the performances (at *Ol.* 6.88,
however, he addresses one Aeneas, identified by the
scholia as the chorus trainer). Even when there is a state-
ment in an ode such as "I have come," it is not always cer-
tain that this is meant literally. For example, *Nem.* 3 opens
as if the poet were present at the celebration, but at line 77
he says, "I am sending" (πέμπω) the song. At *Pyth.* 2.4–5
the poet says, "I come bearing the song" (φέρων μέλος

[11] The scholia provide two fanciful attempts to explain the
opening of an ode in terms of contractual arrangements. Inscr. a to
Pyth. 1 reports: "According to the historian Artemon, Pindar be-
gins with 'golden lyre' because Hieron had promised him a golden
cithara." Schol. 1a on *Nem.* 5 recounts: "They say that Pytheas'
relatives approached Pindar to write an epinicion for him, but
when he asked for three thousand drachmas, they said that for
the same price it was better to have a statue made; later they
changed their minds and paid the sum; to chide them he began
with 'I am not a sculptor.'"

ἔρχομαι), while at line 68 he says, "the song is being sent" (μέλος πέμπεται).

The dating of most of the Olympian and many Pythian odes is relatively sound, thanks to the discovery of the Oxyrhynchus list of Olympic victors (P. Oxy. 222) and to the fact that Aristotle had compiled a list of Pythian victors upon which the ancient commentators drew.[12] The dates of the Nemeans and Isthmians are another matter. Occasionally there is a clear historical reference in the poem (e.g., the allusion to the battle of Salamis in *Isth.* 5), but the dates given in the manuscripts are often inaccurate or contradictory.[13]

The Epinician Genre and Greek Athletics

The brief but brilliant flowering of epinician poetry spans the careers of three poets. Simonides began the practice of composing elaborate odes in honor of athletic victors in the generation before Pindar, while Bacchylides, Simonides' nephew, appears to have continued writing epinicia somewhat later. The three poets moved in the same circles and praised the same men. Simonides' most famous patrons were Thessalian nobility, for one of whose members Pindar composed his first dated ode in 498

---

[12] The list of Olympic victors (cf. note 6, above) perhaps derives from one the 5th cent sophist Hippias compiled (cf. Plut. *Numa* 1.4). An inscription at Delphi thanks Aristotle for compiling a list of Pythian victors; cf. M. N. Tod, *A Selection of Greek Historical Inscriptions* (Oxford 1948) 2.246–248.

[13] For an extensive treatment, see C. Gaspar, *Essai de chronologie pindarique* (Brussels 1900).

(*Pyth.* 10). Like Pindar, Simonides wrote an ode for Xeno-crates of Acragas (*fr.* 513 Campbell), while Bacchylides composed odes for Hieron (3, 4, 5) and Pytheas of Aegina (13). Although a few victory odes from the later fifth century are mentioned, by 440 the genre seems to have been moribund.

The apex of dozens of athletic contests throughout the Greek world were the four major Panhellenic festivals established at Olympia (776), Delphi (582), the Isthmus (c. 581), and Nemea (c. 573). They were called crown games because the victors received crowns of wild olive, laurel, dry parsley (or pine), and green parsley, respectively.[14] The Olympic and Pythian games (the latter held at Delphi) were celebrated every four years, the Isthmian and Nemean every two, all staggered so as to produce a continuous succession of contests. Thus the 76th Olympiad would have included the following crown games: 476, Olympic (August); 475, Nemean (July); 474, Isthmian (April), Pythian (August); 473, Nemean (July); 472, Isthmian (April). The 77th Olympiad then began in August 472.

During Pindar's time the non-equestrian events at Olympia consisted of the stadion (200 meter race), diaulos

[14] The prizes awarded at lesser games included silver cups at Sicyon and Marathon, bronze shields at Argos, woolen coats at Pellana, and prizes of money, bulls, and olive oil at the Panathenaic games. According to the calculations of D. C. Young, *The Olympic Myth of Greek Amateur Athletics* (Chicago 1984) 115–127, the prizes at the Panathenaea would have been very valuable in purely monetary terms. In addition, home towns awarded victorious athletes money, free meals, and other honors.

(one-lap 400 meter race), dolichos (4,800 meter race), hoplites dromos (400 meter race in armor), pentathlon (consisting of stadion, discus throw, javelin throw, long jump, and wrestling), wrestling, boxing, pancratium (combination of wrestling and boxing), and boys' stadion, wrestling, and boxing. The equestrian events were the mule car race (*apene*), bareback single-horse race (*keles*), and four-horse chariot race (*tethrippon*). P. Oxy. 222 lists the following winners for the 76th Olympiad:

[76th. Sca]mandrus of Mitylene, stadion
[Da]ndis of Argos, diaulos
[. . . . . .]of Sparta, dolichos
[. . . . .] of Taras, pentathlon
[. . . . . . of Ma]roneia, wrestling
[Euthymus of Loc]ri in Italy, boxing
[Theagenes of Th]asos, pancratium
[. . . . .] of Sparta, boys' stadion
[Theognetus of Aegi]na, boys' wrestling
[Hag]esi[da]mus of Locri in Italy, boys' boxing
[Ast]ylus of Syracuse, hoplites
[Ther]on of Acragas, owner, tethrippon
[Hier]on of Syracuse, owner, keles

The list omits the mule car race, perhaps because it was included in the Olympic program for some fifty years only (c. 500–444) and was of inferior status (cf. Paus. 5.9.1–2). Naturally, great men like Hieron and Theron hired jockeys and drivers to do the actual driving that won them their victories. Only one victor is praised for driving his own chariot, Herodotus of Thebes (*Isth.* 1). Three drivers are mentioned by name: Phintis, Hagesias' mule car driver (*Ol.* 6), Nicomachus, Xenocrates' charioteer (*Isth.* 2), and

Carrhotus, Arcesilas' charioteer (*Pyth.* 5). The chariot
races consisted of twelve laps around the hippodrome (cf.
Ol. 2.50, 3.33, and *Pyth.* 5.33).

Whereas the Olympic games had only divisions of men
and boys in certain events, the Nemean and Isthmian
games had a third, intermediate category for youths.
Trainers played an important role in the formation of
young athletes and four are mentioned in the epinicia:
Melesias (*Ol.* 8, *Nem.* 4 and 6), Menander (*Nem.* 5), Ilas
(*Ol.* 10), and Orseas (*Isth.* 4). The victory of Alcimedon
in the boys' wrestling at Olympia (*Ol.* 8) was the thirtieth
won by the trainees of Melesias, who had himself been a
victorious pancratiast at Nemea. Many families and clans
were devoted to athletic competitions, and some domi-
nated certain events. Three sons and two grandsons of the
boxer Diagoras of Rhodes, celebrated in *Ol.* 7, won Olym-
pic crowns. Alcimidas of Aegina won his clan's twenty-fifth
crown victory (*Nem.* 6), while the clan of Xenophon of
Corinth boasted a total of sixty Nemean and Isthmian vic-
tories (*Ol.* 13).

Clear notions of the music, dance, and performance
of the victory odes were already lost by the time of the
scholia; what little we know about their performance must
be inferred from internal evidence. Pindar speaks of his
odes as hymns (ὕμνοι), revels (κῶμοι), and songs (ἀοιδαί,
μέλη); he mentions accompaniment by lyres (φόρμιγγες,
λύραι) and pipes (αὐλοί); he occasionally refers to the
celebrants as men (ἄνδρες), young men (νέοι), or boys
(παῖδες). The relationship between the revel and the ac-
tual performance of the ode is not clear, and there has
been considerable controversy over whether the epinicia
were sung by a chorus or by a soloist. The fact that Pindar

never refers directly to the performance of his epinicia by a chorus (χορός) has led some scholars to question whether a chorus performed them at all. The evidence for choral or solo performance is not conclusive either way,[15] but given the fact that other Pindaric genres such as paeans, dithyrambs, partheneia, and hyporchemata were performed by choruses and that the formal features of the epinicia are similar to those of tragic choruses, it seems probable that at least some of the epinicia were performed by a choir that sang in unison and danced to the accompaniment of lyres or *auloi* or both combined. Late sources say that choruses danced the strophe ("turn") in one direction, reversed the steps for the antistrophe ("counterturn"), and stood in place for the epode ("after song"), but even that must remain a conjecture.[16]

The location of the performance is often indicated by the deictic article ὅδε "this" and is usually at the hometown of the victor (e.g., "this island" at *Nem.* 3.68 and 6.46). It is often claimed that shorter epinicia (e.g., *Ol.* 11 and *Pyth.* 7) were improvisations performed at the site of the victory and that monostrophic odes (e.g., *Pyth.* 6 and *Nem.* 2) were processional, but there is no conclusive evidence for such assumptions.

[15] For a review of the evidence and positions, see M. Heath and M. Lefkowitz, "Epinician Performance," *Classical Philology* 86 (1991) 173–191 and C. Carey, "The Victory Ode in Performance: The Case for the Chorus," *Classical Philology* 86 (1991) 192–200.

[16] The evidence is collected and translated in W. Mullen, *Choreia: Pindar and Dance* (Princeton 1982) 225–230.

INTRODUCTION

Elements of the Epinicia

In generic terms, the epinicia are occasional poems that invoke shared social values to praise victors and offer them immortality in verse. For this task there is no set prescription, and each ode is a unique blend of praise, myth, and argumentation. Certain elements, however, are bound to recur, and a fundamental understanding of any ode must begin with them.

An epigram attributed to Simonides succinctly sets forth the basic facts of an athletic victory (A.P. 16.23):

εἶπον, τίς, τίνος ἐσσί, τίνος πατρίδος, τί δ᾽
    ἐνίκης.
Κασμύλος, Εὐαγόρου, Πύθια πύξ, Ῥόδιος.

Tell your name, your father's, your city, your victory.
    Casmylus, son of Euagoras, boxing at the Pythia,
    Rhodes.

These elements, three identifying the victor (name, father, city) and two the victory (games, event), are, with the occasional exception of the patronymic, normally given in each epinicion; they ultimately derive from the herald's proclamation at the games and were preserved on papyrus and in stone inscriptions.[17]

---

[17] An inscription from the first half of the 4th cent. B.C. from Ioulis on Ceos (IG XII 5.608) which lists Ceans who won victories at the Panhellenic games is quoted and discussed by H. Maehler, *Die Lieder des Bakchylides II* (Leiden 1982) 1–3. For a detailed treatment of verse inscriptions for athletes, see J. Ebert, *Griechische Epigramme auf Sieger an gymnischen und hippischen Agonen* (Berlin 1972).

Pindar shows great ingenuity in incorporating such facts into his grand-style verse. One way is to vary the timing and placement of the information. In *Pyth.* 9, for example, all the facts of victory (except the father's name, which comes at 71) are provided in the first sentence, which reserves the name of the city until the last word, thus forming a bridge to the narrative. In *Ol.* 11 the information comes in the middle of the ode (lines 11–15) and concludes with the city, whose people are then praised in the final lines of the poem. *Ol.* 13 reserves the event for emphatic last place (at line 30) because Xenophon had achieved an unprecedented double victory in the stadion and pentathlon.

Another means of varying the presentation of the basic information is by allusive references. In *Pyth.* 9 the victor is called "bronze-shielded" (1), indicating that he won the race in armor. In *Ol.* 12 only the word "feet" (15) alludes to the fact that the victor was a runner. Pindar uses many circumlocutions for places, especially game sites. References to the Olympic games are made in terms of: Pisa (the town nearest Olympia), Alpheus (the river at Olympia), the hill of Cronus (the adjacent hill), or such phrases as "Zeus' greatest games." The Pythian games are signified by the mention of Delphi or Pytho (the site), Crisa or Cirrha (nearby towns), Parnassus (the adjacent mountain), Castalia (the spring), the "navel of the earth," or the "games of Apollo." The "valley of the lion" invokes Nemea (where Heracles slew the Nemean lion), and "the bridge at Corinth" denotes the Isthmus. Alternatively, the mention of the patron god or the type of crown won may indicate the place of victory.

Pindar often refers to his poems as hymns, and there is not a single ode without some reference to divinity. Both hymns and prayers underscore the essentially religious nature of the athletic contests and of the celebrations associated with them. Pindar draws upon a long tradition of hymns and masterfully adapts both cultic and rhapsodic elements to his poems.[18] Some begin with elaborate hymns to various minor gods: Olympia (*Ol.* 8), Fortune (*Ol.* 12), the Graces (*Ol.* 14), Peace (*Pyth.* 8), Eleithyia (*Nem.* 7), Hora (*Nem.* 8), Theia (*Isth.* 5), and Thebe (*Isth.* 7). Although the major Olympian gods are continually mentioned, there is, surprisingly, no opening hymn to any of them.

Prayers abound in the odes, and their function is invariably transitional: they conclude a topic, introduce a new one, or pass from one to another. The poet often prays for continued blessings for the athlete and his city or asks for assistance in his task of praising adequately. Many prayers are expressed negatively, asking that something bad may not happen, especially in the wake of the present success.

Pindar also draws upon the earlier didactic tradition, represented by Hesiod, Theognis, Phocylides, and a collection of the "Sayings of Chiron." A hallmark of epinician style is its frequent use of maxims, which are often among Pindar's most memorable verses.[19] Examples include "great risk does not take hold of a cowardly man" (*Ol.* 1.81), "wise is he who knows many things by nature" (*Ol.* 2.86), "trial is the test of mortals" (*Ol.* 4.18), "about the minds of humans hang numberless errors" (*Ol.* 7.24–25),

[18] For the features of cultic and rhapsodic hymns, see W. H. Race, "How Greek Poems Begin," *Yale Classical Studies* 29 (1992) 19–34.

[19] Cf. H. Bishoff, *Gnomen Pindars* (Diss. Wurzburg 1938).

"one cannot conceal the character that is inborn" (*Ol.* 13.13), "even wisdom is enthralled to gain" (*Pyth.* 3.54), and "the word lives longer than deeds" (*Nem.* 4.6).

Pindar's debt to the epic tradition represented by Homer, Hesiod, and the Homeric Hymns is most apparent in his narratives, loosely called "myths," which are taken from the great store of Hellenic legend. He normally selects an episode from a larger story, which he elaborates with striking details. Often the narratives concern heroes connected with the victor's city, like those telling of the birth and colonization of Rhodes in *Ol.* 7, the origins of Opus and its heroes in *Ol.* 9, and Corinthian heroes in *Ol.* 13. Sometimes the narrative tells about an ancestor of the victor (Iamus in *Ol.* 6 and Alexidamus in *Pyth.* 9). Eight of the eleven odes to Aeginetans relate episodes from the sagas of Aeacus and his descendants, heroes closely associated with that island. Heracles is a frequent subject, especially in his role as founder of the Olympic festival (*Ol.* 3 and 10) and as exemplar of one who has reached the limits of human success (*Nem.* 3); his whole life from infancy to apotheosis is briefly sketched in *Nem.* 1. At times a short narrative makes a specific point: Erginus succeeds in spite of his appearance (*Ol.* 4); Philoctetes' situation resembles that of Hieron (*Pyth.* 1); Antilochus, in dying to save his father, is a model of filial piety (*Pyth.* 6); and Ajax receives posthumous fame after disgrace (*Isth.* 4). Occasionally narratives depict examples of behavior to be avoided: Tantalus (*Ol.* 1), Ixion (*Pyth.* 2), Coronis and Asclepius (*Pyth.* 3), Clytaemestra (*Pyth.* 11), and Bellerophon (*Isth.* 7).

Especially memorable scenes or tableaux in the narratives include Pelops praying to Poseidon for assistance in defeating Oenomaus (*Ol.* 1), the birth of Iamus in a thicket

19

(*Ol.* 6), the first Olympic competitors (*Ol.* 10), Typhos' eruptions from beneath Mt. Aetna (*Pyth.* 1), Apollo's love for Cyrene (*Pyth.* 9), the festivities of the Hyperboreans (*Pyth.* 10), the panic of Alcmene when the snakes attack Heracles (*Nem.* 1), the exploits of youthful Achilles (*Nem.* 3), Peleus' resistance to the blandishments of Hippolyta (*Nem.* 5), the expedition of the Seven against Thebes (*Nem.* 9), Polydeuces' decision to share his immortality with Castor (*Nem.* 10), Heracles' visit to Telamon (*Isth.* 6), and the quarrel of Zeus and Poseidon over marrying Thetis (*Isth.* 8). By far the most complex and extensive narrative (of almost two hundred verses) is the depiction of Jason's career in *Pyth.* 4.

Many myths are demarcated by ring composition, a technique common in epic.[20] By means of a summary statement (κεφάλαιον) or brief allusion (often in relative or temporal clauses) the poet sketches the coming narrative. He then takes up the topics in greater detail, usually in reverse chronological order. After retracing his steps to the initial point, often with echoing vocabulary, he may add an epilogue. For example, in *Ol.* 1.24–27 Pindar briefly mentions Pelops, Poseidon's love for him, his being taken from a cauldron, and his ivory shoulder. In lines 37–87 he gives his own version of Tantalus' feast and relates at greater length Poseidon's love for Pelops, which culminates in his helping Pelops win Hippodameia. A brief epilogue (88–96) tells of Pelops' success and glorification at Olympia. The beginning of *Pyth.* 3 offers a more elaborate

---

[20] The pioneering work on ring composition in Pindar is by L. Illig, *Zur Form der pindarischen Erzählung* (Berlin 1932) 55–67, who cites the story of Niobe at *Il.* 24.601–619 as a model.

example of ring composition. In lines 1–11 the poet makes the following points: he wishes Chiron were still alive; it was Chiron who raised Asclepius to be a doctor; Asclepius' mother Coronis died before he was born. After relating the stories of Coronis' love affair and death (12–42) and Asclepius' career as a doctor (43–58), he returns to his wish that Chiron were still alive (63–67). Other examples include *Ol.* 3.13–34 (Heracles' bringing the olive tree to Olympia); *Ol.* 7.27–80 (history of Rhodes); *Ol.* 13.63–90 (story of Bellerophon); *Pyth.* 6.28–42 (Antilochus' rescue of his father); *Pyth.* 9.5–69 (story of Cyrene); *Pyth.* 10.31–48 (Perseus' visit to the Hyperboreans); *Pyth.* 11.17–37 (Orestes' revenge on his father's murderers); *Pyth.* 12.6–24 (Athena's invention of the pipe); and *Nem.* 10.55–90 (Polydeuces' decision to share his immortality with his brother Castor).

Most narratives occur in the middle of their odes between initial and concluding treatments of the occasion (ABA structure). No ode opens immediately with a mythical narrative, but in two striking cases (*Nem.* 1 and 10) the myths begin in the middle and continue to the very end, while *Pyth.* 9 concludes with an additional narrative about an ancestor of the victor. The transition to the myth is sometimes elaborately executed, but often it is effected, with varying degrees of abruptness, by a relative pronoun or adverb, as in the Homeric Hymns.

Catalogs are common in archaic poetry, whether as lists of epithets or places in hymns, contingents in the *Iliad*, or women in Hesiod's *Ehoiai*. Lists of victories (e.g., *Ol.* 7.80–87), heroes (e.g., *Pyth.* 4.171–183), places (e.g., *Ol.* 9.67–68), legendary exploits (e.g., *Nem.* 10.4–18), and virtuous attributes (e.g., *Pyth.* 6.45–54) abound in the odes. Pindar

21

skillfully adapts them to his complex meters and varies them by means of circumlocutions, allusive references, metaphors, negative expressions, and digressions.

Another distinctive aspect of Pindar's composition is the sudden, sometimes startling, curtailment or outright rejection of a topic. Often labeled *Abbruchsformeln* or *recusationes*, such interjections by the poet give a sense of spontaneity, as if allowing us to witness him in the process of deciding which topic to treat or how to treat it. Often he provides justifications for his decision, thus giving such passages an apologetic tone. Examples of break-offs from and rejections of narratives include *Ol.* 1.28–35 (rejection of the popular story of Tantalus' feast), *Ol.* 9.35–41 (rejection of Heracles' battles against gods as an unsuitable theme), *Ol.* 13.91–92 (refusal to treat Bellerophon's death), *Pyth.* 4.247–248 (abridgment of the narrative), *Pyth.* 10.48–54 (curtailment of Perseus' deeds), *Pyth.* 11.38–40 (turning from the narrative to praise of the victor), *Nem.* 3.26–32 (turning from Heracles to more relevant heroes), *Nem.* 4.69–72 (curtailment of stories about the Aeacidae), and *Nem.* 5.14–21 (refusal to tell why Peleus and Telamon were exiled). A similar technique is used to terminate catalogs, as at *Ol.* 13.40–48, *Nem.* 7.50–53, *Nem.* 10.19–20, and *Isth.* 1.60–63.

Twentieth-century scholars have identified and studied a poetic device widespread in Greek and Latin poetry called a priamel.[21] The form consists of two parts: foil and

[21] F. Dornseiff, *Pindars Stil* (Berlin 1921) 97–102 provides the initial treatment of priamels in Pindar. For an overview, see W. H. Race, *The Classical Priamel from Homer to Boethius* (Leiden 1982).

climax. The purpose of the foil is to lead up to and highlight the climactic element by adducing other examples, which yield to that element with varying degrees of contrast or analogy. The foil may consist of two or more items, even a full catalog, or it may be summarized by such words as "many" (πολύς) or "various" (ἄλλοτ᾽ ἀλλοῖος). Priamels may occur at the beginning of an ode, as in *Ol.* 1, where water and gold (both supreme in their realms) yield to the item of real interest, the Olympic games, supreme among athletic contests, and in *Ol.* 11, where the need for winds or rains is capped by the need for song to celebrate great achievements; but priamels occur throughout the extant works whenever the poet wishes to introduce or emphasize a particular subject. For example, at *Ol.* 9.67–70 a list of places from which foreign settlers have come to Opus culminates in its most distinguished immigrant, Menoetius.

Meter, Form, Dialect, and Style

There are three basic meters in the poetry of Pindar. By far the most frequent are dactylo-epitritic and Aeolic; the third, derived from an iambic base, is represented only by *Ol.* 2 and *frr.* 75, 105, and 108. The dactylo-epitritic combines the dactyl (– ᴗ ᴗ), often in the larger unit of the hemiepes (– ᴗ ᴗ – ᴗ ᴗ –), with the epitrite (– ᴗ – –). It is a stately rhythm (called "Doric" by Pindar), and although used in all the genres, it is especially frequent in those celebrating humans: epinicia, encomia, and threnoi. The dactylo-epitritic epinicia are: *Ol.* 3, 6, 7, 8, 11, 12, 13;[22]

---

[22] *Ol.* 13 is the only epinicion to have strophes and antistrophes in Aeolic, epodes in dactylo-epitritic.

Pyth. 1, 3, 4, 9, 12; *Nem.* 1, 5, 8, 9, 10, 11; *Isth.* 1, 2, 3/4, 5, and 6. The major dactylo-epitritic fragments are: *Isth.* 9; *Hymn.* 1; *Pae.* 5; *Dith.* 2; *Thren.* 7; *frr.* 42, 43, 122, 123, 124, 131b, and 133. The Aeolic rhythm permits greater variety and is composed mainly of iambs (∪ –) and choriambs (– ∪ ∪ –). It is especially frequent in the paeans. The Aeolic epinicia are: *Ol.* 1, 4, 5, 9, 10, 13, 14; *Pyth.* 2, 5, 6, 7, 8, 10, 11; *Nem.* 2, 3, 4, 6, 7; *Isth.* 7, and 8. The major Aeolic fragments are: *Pae.* 1, 2, 4, 6, 8, 9; *Parth.* 1, 2; and *fr.* 169a.

The odes are built of stanzas called strophes, antistrophes, and epodes. The first stanza, varying in length from three to twenty lines, is called a strophe. Seven epinicia (*Ol.* 14; *Pyth.* 6, 12; *Nem.* 2, 4, 9; and *Isth.* 8) and a few fragments (*Pae.* 5, *frr.* 122 and 124ab) repeat the metrical pattern of the strophe two to twelve times and are called "monostrophic." The remaining thirty-eight epinicia, most paeans, *Dith.* 2, *Parth.* 1 and 2, *frr.* 123, 140a, and 169a are "triadic," in that the strophe is followed by a metrically identical stanza called an antistrophe, which in turn is followed by a metrically distinct stanza called an epode, the three forming a unit called a triad. Each successive triad is metrically identical. Five epinicia consist of one triad (*Ol.* 4, 11, 12; *Pyth.* 7; and *Isth.* 3); most have three to five triads, except for the exceptionally long *Pyth.* 4, which has thirteen.

Pindar's dialect is a highly artificial idiom which contains such a complex mixture of epic, Doric, and Aeolic forms that only a very superficial sketch can be given here.[23] Epic vocabulary and forms familiar from Homeric

[23] For more details see the introductions to the editions of Gildersleeve and Fennell and B. Forssman, *Untersuchungen zur Sprache Pindars* (Wiesbaden 1966).

verse are evident throughout (although Pindar avoids
forms in -φι). The most obvious feature of the Doric dia-
lect is a long α for Ionic η (e.g., ἀρετά for ἀρετή and
Κυράνα for Κυρήνη) and -ᾶν for -ῶν in genitive plurals
of the first declension (e.g., τᾶν ἀρετᾶν πασᾶν for τῶν
ἀρετῶν πασῶν). Aeolic forms are most apparent in the
use of οι instead of ου in some nouns (e.g., Μοῖσα for
Μοῦσα), verbs (e.g., τρέφοισι for τρέφουσι), and aorist
participles (e.g., ἰδοῖσα for ἰδοῦσα).

In his discussion of the austere style (whose practi-
tioners include Aeschylus, Pindar, Antiphon, and Thu-
cydides), Dionysius of Halicarnassus makes many ob-
servations applicable to Pindar's style (*de Compositione*
22).

[The austere style] is not loath to use frequent harsh
and dissonant collocations, like stones put together
in building that are not squared or polished, but
rough and improvised. It generally likes expansion
with big, long words,[24] for it is averse to being con-
strained to few syllables unless compelled to do
so . . . In its clauses it chooses stately and grand
rhythms; it does not like clauses of equal length, of
similar sound, or slaves to a necessary order,[25] but
ones that are noble, brilliant, and free; it wishes
them to resemble nature rather than art and to re-
flect emotion rather than character . . . The austere

[24] Particularly compound epithets.
[25] Reading οὔτε ἀναγκαίᾳ δουλεύοντα ἀκολουθίᾳ, ἀλλ'
εὐγενῆ. Dionysius probably has in mind the smoothly balanced
clauses of Isocrates' Gorgianic style.

25

style is further marked by flexibility of cases, variety
of figures, use of few connectives and no articles,
and frequent disregard for normal sequence. Far
from being polished, it is high-minded, outspoken,
blunt—its beauty being the patina of old-fashion-
edness.

The best known characterization of Pindar's style is
by Horace in *Odes* 4.2.5–12: "Like a river rushing down
a mountain which rains have swollen above its normal
banks, the deep-voiced Pindar seethes and floods far and
wide, sure to win Apollo's laurels when he tumbles new
words through his daring dithyrambs, and is carried along
by rhythms freed from rules." From these descriptions we
can isolate the following general characteristics of Pindar's
style: it is abundant, creative of new words and expres-
sions, bold, passionate, old-fashioned, tinged with aristo-
cratic bluntness, disdainful of the ordinary, and displays a
rough strength typical of nature rather than of balanced
art.

Perhaps the most pervasive aspect of Pindar's style is
ποικιλία (variety), a term he himself applies to his poetry
(e.g., *Ol.* 6.87 and *Pyth.* 9.77). His verse gives the impres-
sion of ever new creativity. In the epinicia, a genre which
requires that similar points be repeated, he is especially
adept at finding alternate wordings, different metaphors,
allusive references, synonyms, circumlocutions, or nega-
tive expressions to vary the idiom. For example, on nine
occasions he mentions the relationship between some-
one's performance and his appearance; ten times he states
that an individual has reached the limits of human success.
Yet by variations of wording, rhythm, and emphasis, he

avoids exact repetition and produces strikingly new for-
mulations.[26]

A major component of Pindar's ποικιλία is what J. E.
Sandys called "a constant and habitual use of metaphor."[27]
There are hundreds of metaphorical expressions, some so
slight as to be barely perceptible, others extremely bold.
Pindar is not averse to mixing metaphors and occasionally
piles them up at a confusing rate. For example, at *Ol.* 6.90–
91 he calls his chorus trainer "a true messenger, a message
stick of the Muses, a sweet mixing bowl of songs." In order
to express the exaltation of being celebrated in poetry, he
describes the victor as "lifted on the splendid wings of the
melodious Pierians" (*Isth.* 1.64–65). This expression con-
tains three perceptual categories—height, brightness, and
sound—from which Pindar constantly draws metaphors to
designate the joy and celebration of victory, while, con-
versely, images of depth, darkness, and silence are used to
characterize the disappointment of defeat. To describe his
poetic art, he draws metaphors from farming, sailing, char-
iot driving, archery, flying, wrestling, building, sculpture,
weaving, javelin throwing, and business. The song can be
a crown, mirror, building, storehouse, drink, toast, wave,
flame, breeze, doctor, remedy, or charm.

Stated comparisons are frequent in the poems. Gold
shines "like fire blazing in the night" (*Ol.* 1.1–2), mere

[26] For an analysis of these two topics, see "Appendix 3" in
W. H. Race, *Style and Rhetoric in Pindar's Odes* (Atlanta 1990)
187–195.

[27] In the previous Loeb edition of *Pindar* (1915) xviii. For
many examples, see D. Steiner, *The Crown of Song: Metaphor in
Pindar* (Oxford 1986).

27

learners are "like a pair of crows" (*Ol.* 2.87), the poet is
"like a cork" (*Pyth.* 2.80) or a "wolf" (*Pyth.* 2.84), and his
song "flits like a bee" (*Pyth.* 10.54). Pindar opens three
odes with similes that compare his poetry to a splendid
palace (*Ol.* 6.1–4), to the toast given by a father to his son-
in-law (*Ol.* 7.1–10), and to libations at a symposium (*Isth.*
6.1–9). At *Ol.* 10.86–90 he compares his late-arriving
poem to a son finally born to an aged man. Often, however,
the comparison is left implicit or unstated.[28] For example,
at *Nem.* 6.26 he acts like (ὥτ') an archer, but at *Ol.* 2.83
and *Ol.* 9.5 he simply appears as one; at *Ol.* 13.93 he is a
javelin thrower, whereas at *Pyth.* 1.44 the ὡσείτ' makes
the comparison explicit.

Pindar is much more sparing than authors such as Ae-
schylus or Lucretius in the use of alliteration. One place,
however, where he uses it to obvious effect is in the de-
scription of the eruption of Mt. Aetna at *Pyth.* 1.23–24,
which ends with ἀλλ' ἐν ὄρφναισιν πέτρας | φοίνισσα
κυλινδομένα φλὸξ ἐς βαθεῖαν φέρει πόντου πλάκα σὺν
πατάγῳ ("but in times of darkness a rolling red flame car-
ries rocks into the deep expanse of the sea with a crash"),
in which the φ's and π's imitate the sound of the crashing
rocks (and perhaps the σ's echo the hissing of the flames).
At times there appears to be an intentional correspon-
dence between rhythm and sense, as in *Ol.* 1, where there
is an unusually long string of seven short syllables in
the eighth verse of each strophe and antistrophe, in three
of which the word "swift" (ταχυ-) occurs: μετὰ τὸ

---

[28] F. Dornseiff, *Pindars Stil* (Berlin 1921) 97 labels this phe-
nomenon "Vergleich ohne wie."

ταχύποτμον (66), ἐμὲ δ' ἐπὶ ταχυτάτων (77), Πέλοπος, ἵνα ταχυτάς (95).

There are a number of puns on names, such as Iamus and ἴων (violets) at *Ol.* 6.55, Ajax and αἰετόν (eagle) at *Isth.* 6.50, Orion and ὀρειᾶν (mountain) at *Nem.* 2.11, Hieron and ἱερῶν (temples) at *fr.* 105a2, and perhaps Athens and ἀεθληταῖσιν (athletes) at *Nem.* 5.49. In *Isth.* 2 the recurrence of the word ξένος (24, 39, 48) in an ode praising Xenocrates for his lavish hospitality seems deliberate. Pindar sometimes employs riddles or kennings; for example, a honeycomb is "the perforated labor of bees" (*Pyth.* 6.54) and Panathenaic amphoras are "richly wrought containers of earth baked in fire" (*Nem.* 10.36).

Certain images, themes, or related words are particularly prevalent in some odes: for example, words related to eating in *Ol.* 1; an unusual number of pairs in *Ol.* 6; gold, plants, and weather in *Ol.* 7; time in *Ol.* 10; music in *Pyth.* 1; numerous words pertaining to knowledge and the mind in *Pyth.* 3; references to medicine in *Pyth.* 3 and *Pyth.* 4; and courtship and athletics in *Pyth.* 9. Nautical imagery occurs throughout the odes.[29]

The odes are also rich textures of verbal echoes, and scholars have carefully listed many occurrences of repeated words and sounds, especially in metrically equivalent parts of an ode. But while the frequency of recurrent

[29] For the imagery of *Ol.* 7, see D. C. Young, *Three Odes of Pindar* (Leiden 1968) 69–105; for nautical imagery, see J. Péron, *Les images maritimes de Pindar* (Paris 1974); in general, see C. M. Bowra, "The Scope of Imagery," in *Pindar* (Oxford 1964) 239–277 and M. S. Silk, *Interaction in Poetic Imagery* (Cambridge 1974) 179–190.

words is indisputable—Fennell lists over sixty words recurring one or more times in *Ol.* 1 alone—there is considerable disagreement about the significance of individual cases, and attempts to discover meaning in them often create ingenious but implausible interpretations.

Because of the pliability of Greek as an inflected language and the requirements of intricate metrical patterns, Pindar often places great strains on word order. As a result, many sentences must be pieced together like puzzles (e.g., *Isth.* 4.18–18a).[30] Hyperbaton, a lengthy separation of two grammatically connected words, occurs frequently. Two extreme examples are at *Pyth.* 4.106–108, where ἀρχαίαν is separated from its noun τιμάν by fifteen words, and at *Ol.* 12.5–6a, where the article αἱ is separated from its noun ἐλπίδες by thirteen words. Often, important words are withheld for climactic effect until the end of a sentence, or are enjambed at the beginning of a line or stanza.[31]

Enallage (hypallage) or transferred epithet, by which an attribute belonging logically to one thing is grammatically given to another, is very common.[32] Some examples are so slight as to be barely noticeable, such as "the tawny herds of cattle" (*Pyth.* 4.149); others are much bolder, such as "your honor of feet" (="the honor of your feet," *Ol.* 12.13) and "fearless seed of Heracles" (="the seed of fearless Heracles," *Nem.* 10.17). The so-called *schema Pin-*

---

[30] See A.-I. Sulzer, *Zur Wortstellung und Satzbildung bei Pindar* (Bern 1970).

[31] See R. Nierhaus, *Strophe und Inhalt im pindarischen Epinikion* (Diss. Leipzig 1936).

[32] See V. Bers, *Enallage and Greek Style* (Leiden 1974) 45–48 and the Index Locorum s.v. Pindar.

daricum, in which a singular verb is used with a masculine or feminine plural subject, is infrequent in the epinicia, but particularly noticeable in *Dith.* 2, where there are three instances in the first thirteen verses. There are also striking examples of zeugma (the use of one verb with differing meanings for two objects) as at *Ol.* 1.88, where Pelops took (i.e. defeated) Oenomaus and took (i.e. won) Hippodameia as a bride (cf. also *Pyth.* 1.40).

Other figures include hendiadys, two nouns that express a single thought, (e.g., *Pyth.* 1.37: στεφάνοισι ἵπποις τε, "crowns and horses" = "victorious horses"), and various kinds of brachylogy or ellipsis, in which connecting elements have been omitted. A complex example of brachylogy occurs at *Ol.* 12.13–15: "truly would the honor of [i.e. won by] your feet, like [that of] a fighting cock . . . have [like a tree or wreath] dropped its leaves ingloriously." Finally, Pindar scrupulously avoids precise grammatical symmetry of terms in pairs or series. For example, instead of a simple "day and night" we find ἀμέραισιν μὲν . . . ἀλλ' ἐν ὄρφναισιν (*Pyth.* 1.22–23), ἇμαρ ἢ νύκτες (*Pyth.* 4. 256), and ἐφαμερίαν . . . μετὰ νύκτας (*Nem.* 6.6).

Pindar's Legacy

Since choral epinician poetry ceased to be written soon after Pindar's death, his style and subject matter exerted more influence on subsequent Greek and Roman authors than did his genre. In the 4th century Isocrates adapted many Pindaric poetic strategies and topics to his prose works, particularly those praising individuals (e.g., *Evagoras*) or advising them (e.g., *To Demonicus, To*

31

Nicocles, and *To Philip*).[33] In the Hellenistic period Callimachus (in his *Hymns*) and Theocritus (in his *Idylls*) exhibit Pindaric influence, especially the latter in his panegyric of Hieron II (*Id.* 16) and in his portrayal of the infant Heracles' fight with the snakes sent by Hera (*Id.* 24), an episode treated by Pindar in *Nem.* 1.

The Roman poet most indebted to Pindar was Horace, whose eulogy of Augustus (*Odes* 1.12) opens with a quotation from Pindar's *Ol.* 2: "What man, what hero do you undertake to celebrate on the lyre or shrill pipe, Clio, and what god?" His hymn to Calliope (*Odes* 3.4) is to a considerable extent modeled on *Pyth.* 1. Horace's greatest tribute to Pindar, however, is in *Odes* 4.2, which opens with Pindar's name and describes the dangers of trying to emulate him: "Whoever strives to rival Pindar, Julus, relies on wings waxed by Daedalus' craft and will give his name to a transparent sea." In the next five stanzas Horace describes Pindar's poetry in terms of its power, range, and grandeur, and compares it to a rushing river. He then goes on to contrast Pindar, "the Swan of Dirce," soaring among the clouds, with himself, the small "Bee of Matinus," staying low to the ground and laboriously gathering thyme. This exaggerated characterization of these two styles provided the Renaissance with its distinction between the "greater" Pindaric and the "lesser" Horatian odes.

Soon after Pindar's epinicia were published in Europe in the early 16th century, the French poet Ronsard, who

[33] For an examination of Isocrates' adaptations, see W. H. Race, "Pindaric Encomium and Isokrates' *Evagoras*," *Transactions of the American Philological Association* 117 (1987) 131–155.

aspired to become the "French Pindar," published a collection of fourteen Pindaric odes in praise of contemporaries in 1550.[34] The first important Pindaric adaptation in English poetry is Ben Jonson's "To the Immortal Memory and Friendship of that Noble Pair, Sir Lucius Cary and Sir H. Morison" (1630), which imitates Pindar's triadic structure with "Turns," "Counter-Turns," and "Stands." In 1656 Abraham Cowley published his "Pindarique Odes." He began his preface with the famous statement: "If a man should undertake to translate Pindar word for word, it would be thought that one mad-man had translated another." Taking as his point of departure Horace's description of Pindar in *Odes* 4.2, Cowley emphasized Pindar's "enthusiastical manner" and produced irregular verse without regard for triadic structure.

After Cowley, "Pindaric" became a label for any poem of irregular form with pretensions of grandeur. Boileau's "Ode sur la Prise de Namur" (1693) and Dryden's "Alexander's Feast" (1697) are examples, as are Gray's "Progress of Poesy" and "The Bard" (1757). The early German Romantics admired Pindar (especially Hölderlin, who translated a number of his epinicia), but afterwards his influence began to diminish. Although English Romantic poems such as Wordsworth's "Ode: Intimations of Immortality" (1807) and later poems such as G. M. Hopkins' "The Wreck of the Deutschland" (1875) are sometimes called Pindaric odes, they bear little resemblance in form or content to Pindar's poems.

[34] See T. Schmitz, *Pindar in der französischen Renaissance* (Göttingen 1993).

INTRODUCTION

History of the Text

The most important early editor of Pindar's works was Aristophanes of Byzantium, head librarian in Alexandria c. 194–180 B.C., who divided the individual poems into short lines based on metrical cola and the entire corpus into seventeen books. The numerous epinicia were separated into manageable rolls according to the four major games at which the victories were won. Within each roll the odes were ordered by the categories of events, beginning with the equestrian (in the order of chariot race, horse race, mule car race) followed by the gymnastic (in the order of pancratium, wrestling, boxing, pentathlon, and foot races).[35]

Since only the wealthy could afford to raise and train horses of the caliber to win at the great games, this arrangement favored Pindar's powerful patrons and placed more impressive odes at the beginning of each roll. Deviations from this system are instructive. If strict order were followed, *Ol.* 2 and 3 celebrating Theron's chariot victory should precede *Ol.* 1 celebrating Hieron's single-horse victory, but we are told that Aristophanes placed the latter first because it contained praise of the Olympic games. The eminence of Hieron and the scale of the ode must have been factors in this reversal as well, because *Ol.* 3 also tells of the establishment of the Olympic games. It is questionable whether *Pyth.* 2 celebrates a Pythian victory at all, while *Pyth.* 3, not an epinicion in any strict sense,

[35] Simonides' epinicia were arranged by events won; apart from the fact that odes for the same victor are grouped together, no particular order is apparent among Bacchylides' epinicia.

34

merely refers in passing to a previous single-horse victory
at Pytho. Yet these two poems were placed ahead of *Pyth.*
4 and 5 that celebrate Arcesilas' chariot victory, presum-
ably to form a group of odes to Pindar's greatest patron.
Anomalous odes were placed at the end of books. The final
Pythian ode, *Pyth.* 12, celebrates a victory in pipe-playing,
and the last three Nemeans were not composed for
Nemean victories. *Nem.* 9 celebrates a chariot victory in
the Sicyonian games, *Nem.* 10 a wrestling victory in the
Argive games (although previous victories in the crown
games are mentioned), and *Nem.* 11 celebrates the instal-
lation of a former athlete as a magistrate in Tenedos.

Two Pindaric scholars of note who followed Aristoph-
anes of Byzantium were Aristarchus of Samothrace
(c. 217–145 B.C.) and Didymus (c. 80–10 B.C.), the latter
of whom composed lengthy commentaries, bits of which
have come down to us as scholia (marginal notes) in our
MSS. In the 3rd century A.D. the other books began to
drop out of circulation and only the four books of epinicia
continued to be read.[36] About this time they were trans-
ferred from papyrus rolls to codices, apparently in the
order of the founding of the games: Olympian, Pythian,
Isthmian, and Nemean. At some point the last two books
were interchanged and some of the final pages of the Isth-
mian odes were lost.

In the 4th and 5th century A.D. two recensions of

---

[36] See J. Irigoin, *Histoire du texte de Pindare* (Paris 1952).
Eustathius, *Praefatio* 34 reports that the epinicia were especially
popular because they were more concerned with human affairs
(ἀνθρωπικώτεροι), contained fewer myths, and were not as diffi-
cult as the other genres.

the epinicia took shape: the Ambrosian recension, represented by a single MS in the Ambrosian Library in Milan (end of 13th cent.), and the Vatican recension, best represented by two MSS, one in the Vatican Library (end of 12th cent.)[37] and the other in the Laurentian Library in Florence (early 14th cent.). Although both recensions derive from the same source (probably a 2nd cent. edition), they differ, especially in their scholia. Two lesser recensions are the Parisina, best represented by a MS in Paris (late 13th cent.), and the Gottingensis, by a MS in Göttingen (mid-13th cent.).

The late Byzantine period saw a revival of editorial work on Pindar. Eustathius (d. c. 1194) wrote a commentary, but only the preface has survived. A century later editions were prepared by Thomas Magister (c. 1280–1350), Manuel Moschopulus (fl. 1300), and Demetrius Triclinius (c. 1280–1340). Modern editors have adopted many of their readings, and many of the more than 180 extant MSS exhibit their editorial work.

The following table provides the sigla for the principal MSS.

Recensio Ambrosiana

A	Ambrosianus C 222 inf.	c. 1280	*Ol.* 1–12

Recensio Parisina (= ζ)

C	Parisinus graecus 2774	c. 1300	*Ol.* 1– *Pyth.* 5.51
N	Ambrosianus E 103 sup.	late 13th cent.	*Ol.* 1–14
O	Leidensis Q 4 B	c. 1300	*Ol.* 1–13

[37] For a facsimile of the Olympian odes in this MS, see J. Irigoin, *Pindare Olympiques* (Vatican 1974).

| U | Vindobonensis graecus 130 | early 14th cent. | *Ol.* 1– *Nem.* 2 |
| V | Parisinus graecus 2403 | late 13th cent. | *Ol.* 1– *Nem.* 4.68; 6.38–44 |

Recensio Vaticana (= v)

B	Vaticanus graecus 1312	late 12th cent.	*Ol.* 1– *Isth.* 8.53 (with some lacunae)
D	Laurentianus 32, 52	early 14th cent.	*Ol.* 1– *Isth.* 9.8
E	Laurentianus 32, 37	c. 1300	*Ol.* 1– *Pyth.* 12.25
F	Laurentianus 32, 33	late 13th cent.	*Ol.* 1– *Pyth.* 12.32
L	Vaticanus graecus 902	early 14th cent.	*Ol.* 1–10

Recensio Gottingensis (= γ)

| G | Gottingensis philologus 29 | mid-13th cent. | *Ol.* 1– *Nem.* 3 |
| H | Vaticanus graecus 41 | early 14th cent. | *Ol.* 1– *Pyth.* 12 |

In addition, α = ζ + v; β = EFL + γ; Σ = scholion; Π = papyrus; paraphr. = scholiastic paraphrase; Byz. = readings in the Byzantine interpolated MSS. The most important papyri are P. Oxy. 408 (*fr.* 140a-b), 659 (*Parth.* 1-2), 841 (*Pae.* 1-10), 1604 (*Dith.* 1-3), 1792 (*frr.* of paeans), and 2450 (*fr.* 169a). Those cited in the critical apparatus of the epinicia are:

37

Π^1 P. Oxy. 13.1614
Π^2 P. Oxy. 17.2092
Π^{22} PSI 1277
Π^{24} P. Oxy. 26.2439
Π^{39} P. Ant. 2.76 + 3.212
Π^{41} P. Berol. 16367
Π^{42} P. Oxy. 31.2536

The editio princeps is the Aldine (Venice 1513). The first Latin translation is by Lonicerus (Basel 1535). Erasmus Schmid's edition (Wittenberg 1616) is a landmark of Renaissance scholarship on Pindar, notable for its rhetorical schemata of each ode and many sound emendations. It was closely followed by Iohannes Benedictus' text (Saumur 1620), the most widely used edition in the 17th century (John Milton owned and annotated a copy). The next edition of note was C. G. Heyne's (Göttingen 1798), soon superseded by the monumental edition of August Boeckh (Leipzig 1811–1821), which first set forth the division of Pindar's verse into periods rather than cola and provided extensive commentaries (those on the Nemeans and Isthmians were written by Ludwig Dissen). Dissen soon followed with his own edition (Gotha 1830). Tycho Mommsen (Berlin 1864) provided the first systematic examination of the Byzantine MSS. Otto Schroeder produced an important critical edition (Leipzig 1900). Alexander Turyn's edition (Cracow 1948; Oxford 1952) is notable for its scrupulous examination of manuscripts and copious testimonia. Although differing in many details and numerous readings adopted, the present text is based primarily on the eighth edition of Snell-Maehler's Epinicia (1987) and H. Maehler's Fragmenta

(1989), to which the reader is referred for additional
details.

SELECT BIBLIOGRAPHY

Scholia, Lexical and Bibliographical Aids,
History of Scholarship

A. B. Drachmann, *Scholia Vetera in Pindari Carmina*, 3
vols. (Leipzig 1903, 1910, 1927).

C. Gaspar, *Essai de chronologie pindarique* (Brussels
1900).

D. E. Gerber, *A Bibliography of Pindar*, 1513–1966 (Cleveland 1969); *Pindar and Bacchylides 1934–1987*, in
Lustrum 31 (1989) 97–269 and *Lustrum* 32 (1990) 7–67;
Emendations in Pindar 1513–1972 (Amsterdam 1976).

P. Hummel, *La syntaxe de Pindare* (Louvain 1993).

J. Irigoin, *Histoire du texte de Pindare* (Paris 1952).

M. Rico, *Ensayo de bibliografía pindárica* (Madrid 1969).

W. J. Slater, *A Lexicon to Pindar* (Berlin 1969).

E. Thummer, "Pindaros," *Anzeiger für die Altertumswissenschaft, hrsg. von der Österreichischen Humanistischen Gesellschaft, Innsbruck* 11 (1958) 65–88; 19
(1966) 289–322; 27 (1974) 1–34; and 35 (1982) 129–164.

D. C. Young, "Pindaric Criticism," in *Pindaros und Bakchylides*, ed. W. Calder III & J. Stern (Darmstadt 1970)
1–95.

Commentaries

A. Boeckh, *Pindari opera quae supersunt*, 2.2 (Leipzig
1821).

B. K. Braswell, *A Commentary on the Fourth Pythian Ode of Pindar* (Berlin 1988); *A Commentary on Pindar Nemean One* (Fribourg 1992); *A Commentary on Pindar Nemean Nine* (Berlin 1998).

J. B. Bury, *The Nemean Odes of Pindar* (London 1890); *The Isthmian Odes of Pindar* (London 1892).

M. Cannatà Fera, *Pindarus: Threnorum Fragmenta* (Rome 1990).

C. Carey, *A Commentary on Five Odes of Pindar* (New York 1981).

L. Dissen, *Pindari Carmina quae supersunt* (Gotha 1830).

L. R. Farnell, *The Works of Pindar II* (London 1932).

C. A. M. Fennell, *Pindar: The Olympian and Pythian Odes*^{2} (Cambridge 1893); *Pindar: The Nemean and Isthmian Odes*^{2} (Cambridge 1899).

M. Fernández-Galiano, *Píndaro, Olímpicas. Texto, introducción y notas* (Madrid 1944).

P. J. Finglass, *Pindar Pythian Eleven* (Cambridge 2007).

B. Gentili, P. A. Bernardini, E. Cingano, and P. Giannini, *Pindaro: Le Pitiche* (Verona 1995).

D. E. Gerber, *Pindar's Olympian One: A Commentary* (Toronto 1982).

B. L. Gildersleeve, *Pindar: The Olympian and Pythian Odes*^{2} (New York 1890).

L. Lehnus, *Pindaro, Olimpiche: Traduzione, commento, note e lettura critica* (Milano 1981).

I. L. Pfeijffer, *Three Aeginetan Odes of Pindar: A Commentary on Nemean V, Nemean III, & Pythian VIII* (Leiden 1999).

G. A. Privitera, *Pindaro, Le Istmiche* (Milano 1982).

S. L. Radt, *Pindars zweiter und sechster Paian* (Amsterdam 1958).

INTRODUCTION

I. C. Rutherford, *Pindar's Paeans* (Oxford 2001).

O. Schroeder, *Pindars Pythien* (Leipzig 1922).

E. Thummer, *Pindar. Die Isthmischen Gedichte*, 2 vols. (Heidelberg 1968–1969).

M. J. H. Van Der Weiden, *The Dithyrambs of Pindar: Introduction, Text and Commentary* (Amsterdam 1991).

W. J. Verdenius, *Commentaries on Pindar*, 2 vols. (Leiden 1987, 1988).

M. M. Willcock, *Pindar: Victory Odes* (Cambridge 1995).

Selected Studies

E. L. Bundy, *Studia Pindarica* (Berkeley 1962; repr. 1986).

R. W. B. Burton, *Pindar's Pythian Odes* (Oxford 1962).

B. Currie, *Pindar and the Cult of Heroes* (Oxford 2005).

F. Dornseiff, *Pindars Stil* (Berlin 1921).

H. Gundert, *Pindar und sein Dichterberuf* (Frankfurt 1935).

R. Hamilton, *Epinikion: General Form in the Odes of Pindar* (The Hague 1974).

A. Köhnken, *Die Funktion des Mythos bei Pindar* (Berlin 1971).

L. Kurke, *The Traffic in Praise: Pindar and the Poetics of Social Economy* (Ithaca 1991).

W. H. Race, *Pindar* (Boston 1986); *Style and Rhetoric in Pindar's Odes* (Atlanta 1990).

W. Schadewaldt, *Der Aufbau des pindarischen Epinikion* (Halle 1928).

D. C. Young, *Three Odes of Pindar: A Literary Study of Pythian 11, Pythian 3, and Olympian 7* (Leiden 1968); *Pindar Isthmian 7: Myth and Exempla* (Leiden 1971).

41

ΟΛΥΜΠΙΟΝΙΚΑΙ

OLYMPIAN ODES

OLYMPIAN 1

Olympian 1 celebrates Hieron's victory in the single-horse race (*keles*) in 476 (confirmed by P. Oxy. 222). The more prestigious four-horse chariot race (*tethrippon*) was won by Theron of Acragas and celebrated by Pindar in *Olympians* 2 and 3. In the normal order established by the Alexandrian editors, it would have followed the odes to Theron, but the *Vita Thomana* reports (1.7 Dr.) that Aristophanes of Byzantium placed *Olympian* 1 first in the collection because it "contained praise of the Olympic games and told of Pelops, the first to compete in Elis."

The ode opens with a priamel, in which water and gold, best in their respective realms, serve as foil for the greatest of games, the Olympics (1–7). Hieron is briefly praised for his wealth, hospitality, political power, achievements celebrated in song (8–17), and in particular for the Olympic victory of his horse Pherenicus (17–23).

The central portion of the poem contains Pindar's re-fashioning of the story of Pelops. Little is known about this myth before Pindar, but a former version (cf. 36) seems to have been that Tantalus served his dismembered son Pelops at a banquet for the gods, who, upon discovering this, resurrected him from the cauldron, replaced part of his shoulder (supposedly eaten by Demeter) with ivory, and punished Tantalus in Hades. Pindar attributes the ap-

peal of such a tale to the charm of exaggerated story telling
(28–32) and its details to the gossip of an envious neighbor
(46–51). In Pindar's version, Pelops was born with an ivory
shoulder (26–27) and Tantalus gave a most proper feast
(38), at which Poseidon fell in love with Pelops and took
him to Olympus as Zeus later did with Ganymede (37–45).
Tantalus' punishment resulted from stealing nectar and
ambrosia from the gods and sharing them with his human
companions (55–64). As a consequence, Pelops was re-
turned to earth (65–66). When he grew to young manhood,
he desired to win Hippodameia in the contest contrived
by her father Oenomaus, who killed all suitors unable to
beat him in a chariot race. He called upon his former lover
Poseidon for help and the god gave him a golden chariot
and winged horses, with which he defeated Oenomaus,
thereby winning Hippodameia, by whom he had six sons
(67–89). Pelops' tomb now stands beside the altar of Zeus
at Olympia (90–93).

Pindar mentions the fame and satisfaction belonging
to Olympic victors (93–99), praises Hieron as the most
knowledgeable and powerful host of his time (100–108),
and hopes that he will be able to celebrate a future char-
iot victory (108–111). In a brief priamel, he declares that
kings occupy the apex of greatness, and concludes by pray-
ing that Hieron may enjoy his high status for the rest of his
life and that he himself may celebrate victors as the fore-
most Panhellenic poet (111–116).

1. ΙΕΡΩΝΙ ΣΤΡΑΚΟΣΙΩΙ

ΚΕΛΗΤΙ

Α΄ Ἄριστον μὲν ὕδωρ, ὁ δὲ χρυσὸς αἰθόμενον πῦρ
ἅτε διαπρέπει νυκτὶ μεγάνορος ἔξοχα πλούτου·
εἰ δ' ἄεθλα γαρύεν
ἔλδεαι, φίλον ἦτορ,
5 μηκέτ' ἀελίου σκόπει
ἄλλο θαλπνότερον ἐν ἀμέρα φαεν-
νὸν ἄστρον ἐρήμας δι' αἰθέρος,
μηδ' Ὀλυμπίας ἀγῶνα φέρτερον αὐδάσομεν·
ὅθεν ὁ πολύφατος ὕμνος ἀμφιβάλλεται
σοφῶν μητίεσσι, κελαδεῖν
10 Κρόνου παῖδ' ἐς ἀφνεὰν ἱκομένους
μάκαιραν Ἱέρωνος ἑστίαν,

θεμιστεῖον ὃς ἀμφέπει σκᾶπτον ἐν πολυμήλῳ
Σικελίᾳ, δρέπων μὲν κορυφὰς ἀρετᾶν ἄπο πασᾶν,
ἀγλαΐζεται δὲ καί

12 πολυμήλῳ A^sC^sH: πολυμάλῳ rell.

---

[1] Pindar regularly addresses himself or uses the first person

46

1. FOR HIERON OF SYRACUSE

WINNER, SINGLE-HORSE RACE, 476 B.C.

Best is water, while gold, like fire blazing	Str. 1
in the night, shines preeminent amid lordly wealth.	
But if you wish to sing	
of athletic games, my heart,[1]	
look no further than the sun	5
for another star shining more warmly by day	
through the empty sky,	
nor let us proclaim a contest greater than Olympia.	
From there comes the famous hymn that encompasses	
the thoughts of wise men, who have come	
in celebration of Cronus' son[2] to the rich	10
and blessed hearth of Hieron,	

who wields the rightful scepter[3] in flock-rich	Ant. 1
Sicily. He culls the summits of all achievements	
and is also glorified	

(often an emphatic pronoun) at climactic or transitional points in
an ode (e.g., 17, 36, 52, 100, 111, and 115b). His addresses to
Pelops (36) and Hieron (107, 115) also signal climactic passages.

  [2] Zeus, patron god of the Olympic games.

  [3] Or *scepter of law* (cf. *Il.* 9.99: σκῆπτρόν τ᾿ ἠδὲ θέμιστας).

15 μουσικᾶς ἐν ἀώτῳ,
    οἷα παίζομεν φίλαν
    ἄνδρες ἀμφὶ θαμὰ τράπεζαν. ἀλλὰ Δω-
        ρίαν ἀπὸ φόρμιγγα πασσάλου
    λάμβαν', εἴ τί τοι Πίσας τε καὶ Φερενίκου χάρις
    νόον ὑπὸ γλυκυτάταις ἔθηκε φροντίσιν,
20 ὅτε παρ' Ἀλφεῷ σύτο δέμας
    ἀκέντητον ἐν δρόμοισι παρέχων,
    κράτει δὲ προσέμειξε δεσπόταν,

    Συρακόσιον ἱπποχάρ-
        μαν βασιλῆα· λάμπει δέ οἱ κλέος
    ἐν εὐάνορι Λυδοῦ Πέλοπος ἀποικίᾳ·
25 τοῦ μεγασθενὴς ἐράσσατο Γαιάοχος
    Ποσειδάν, ἐπεί νιν καθαροῦ λέβη-
        τος ἔξελε Κλωθώ,
    ἐλέφαντι φαίδιμον ὦμον κεκαδμένον.
    ἦ θαύματα πολλά, καί πού τι καὶ βροτῶν
28b φάτις ὑπὲρ τὸν ἀλαθῆ λόγον
    δεδαιδαλμένοι ψεύδεσι ποικίλοις
    ἐξαπατῶντι μῦθοι.

---

4 Since there is no evidence for a specifically Dorian lyre and since the meter of the ode is Aeolic, the reference may apply to the Dorian character of Syracuse (cf. *Pyth.* 1.61–65) and, perhaps, to the presence of the Doric dialect in Pindar's choral lyric.

5 The district around Olympia.

6 Hieron's horse "Victory-Bringer," also victorious at Delphi (cf. *Pyth.* 3.74).

in the finest songs,   15
such as those we men often perform in play
about the friendly table. Come, take
    the Dorian lyre[4] from its peg,
if the splendor of Pisa[5] and of Pherenicus[6] has indeed
enthralled your mind with sweetest considerations,
when he sped beside the Alpheus,[7]   20
giving his limbs ungoaded in the race,
and joined to victorious power his master,

Syracuse's horse-loving   Ep. 1
    king. Fame shines for him
in the colony of brave men founded by Lydian Pelops,[8]
with whom mighty Earthholder Poseidon   25
fell in love, after Clotho[9] pulled him
    from the pure cauldron,
distinguished by his shoulder[10] gleaming with ivory.
Yes, wonders are many, but then too, I think, in men's
    talk
stories are embellished beyond the true account   28b
and deceive by means of
    elaborate lies.

[7] The river that runs through Olympia.

[8] Pelops came from Lydia to colonize the Peloponnesus
("Pelops' Island"), later settled by Dorians, renowned for bravery.

[9] One of the three Fates, associated with births. Pindar here
implies that Pelops was not boiled in a cauldron nor was his shoul-
der replaced with ivory (as in the rejected version of the story), but
he was bathed in one (hence "pure") and was born with an ivory
shoulder.

[10] Or *furnished with a shoulder.*

PINDAR

Β΄ Χάρις δ᾽, ἅπερ ἅπαντα τεύχει τὰ μείλιχα θνατοῖς,
31 ἐπιφέροισα τιμὰν καὶ ἄπιστον ἐμήσατο πιστὸν
ἔμμεναι τὸ πολλάκις·
ἁμέραι δ᾽ ἐπίλοιποι
μάρτυρες σοφώτατοι.
35 ἔστι δ᾽ ἀνδρὶ φάμεν ἐοικὸς ἀμφὶ δαι-
μόνων καλά· μείων γὰρ αἰτία.
υἱὲ Ταντάλου, σὲ δ᾽ ἀντία προτέρων φθέγξομαι,
ὁπότ᾽ ἐκάλεσε πατὴρ τὸν εὐνομώτατον
ἐς ἔρανον φίλαν τε Σίπυλον,
ἀμοιβαῖα θεοῖσι δεῖπνα παρέχων,
40 τότ᾽ Ἀγλαοτρίαιναν ἁρπάσαι,

δαμέντα φρένας ἱμέρῳ, χρυσέαισί τ᾽ ἀν᾽ ἵπποις
ὕπατον εὐρυτίμου ποτὶ δῶμα Διὸς μεταβᾶσαι·
ἔνθα δευτέρῳ χρόνῳ
ἦλθε καὶ Γανυμήδης
45 Ζηνὶ τωὔτ᾽ ἐπὶ χρέος.
ὡς δ᾽ ἄφαντος ἔπελες, οὐδὲ ματρὶ πολ-
λὰ μαιόμενοι φῶτες ἄγαγον,
ἔννεπε κρυφᾷ τις αὐτίκα φθονερῶν γειτόνων,
ὕδατος ὅτι τε πυρὶ ζέοισαν εἰς ἀκμάν

41 χρυσέαισί τ᾽ ἀν᾽ E. Schmid: χρυσέαισιν ἀν᾽ AN^{ac}v: χρυ-
σέαις κἀν C: χρυσέαισιν κ᾽ ἀν᾽ N^{pc}

11 Here personified. One of Pindar's favorite words, the mean-
ings of χάρις range from "beauty/grace/charm," to "splendor/

50

For Charis,[11] who fashions all things pleasant for   Str. 2
    mortals,
by bestowing honor makes even what is unbelievable   31
often believed;
yet days to come
are the wisest witnesses.
It is proper for a man to speak   35
    well of the gods, for less is the blame.
Son of Tantalus, of you I shall say, contrary to my
    predecessors,
that when your father invited the gods
to his most orderly feast and to his friendly Sipylus,[12]
giving them a banquet in return for theirs,
then it was that the Lord of the Splendid Trident seized   40
    you,

his mind overcome by desire, and with golden steeds   Ant. 2
conveyed you to the highest home of widely honored
    Zeus,
where at a later time
Ganymede came as well
for the same service to Zeus.[13]   45
But when you disappeared, and despite much searching
    no men returned you to your mother,
one of the envious neighbors immediately said in secret
that into water boiling rapidly on the fire

glory"(cf. 18), to "favor/gratitude" (cf. 75). *Olympian* 14 contains a
hymn to the three Charites (Graces).

    [12] A Lydian city near Smyrna. The adjective "most orderly"
corrects the older version, which told of a cannibal feast.

    [13] As cupbearer and adolescent lover.

μαχαίρᾳ τάμον κατὰ μέλη,
50 τραπέζαισί τ᾽ ἀμφὶ δεύτατα κρεῶν
σέθεν διεδάσαντο καὶ φάγον.

ἐμοὶ δ᾽ ἄπορα γαστρίμαρ-
γον μακάρων τιν᾽ εἰπεῖν· ἀφίσταμαι·
ἀκέρδεια λέλογχεν θαμινὰ κακαγόρους.
εἰ δὲ δή τιν᾽ ἄνδρα θνατὸν Ὀλύμπου σκοποί
55 ἐτίμασαν, ἦν Τάνταλος οὗτος· ἀλ-
λὰ γὰρ καταπέψαι
μέγαν ὄλβον οὐκ ἐδυνάσθη, κόρῳ δ᾽ ἕλεν
ἄταν ὑπέροπλον, ἄν τοι πατὴρ ὕπερ
57b κρέμασε καρτερὸν αὐτῷ λίθον,
τὸν αἰεὶ μενοινῶν κεφαλᾶς βαλεῖν
εὐφροσύνας ἀλᾶται.

Γ´ ἔχει δ᾽ ἀπάλαμον βίον τοῦτον ἐμπεδόμοχθον
60 μετὰ τριῶν τέταρτον πόνον, ἀθανάτους ὅτι κλέψαις
ἁλίκεσσι συμπόταις
νέκταρ ἀμβροσίαν τε
δῶκεν, οἷσιν ἄφθιτον
θέν νιν. εἰ δὲ θεὸν ἀνήρ τις ἔλπεταί
⟨τι⟩ λαθέμεν ἔρδων, ἁμαρτάνει.
65 τοὔνεκα προῆκαν υἱὸν ἀθάνατοί οἱ πάλιν

57 ἄν τοι Fennell: ἄν οἱ Hermann: τάν οἱ codd.
64 θέν νιν Mommsen: θέσαν αὐτὸν codd. | ⟨τι⟩ suppl. Byz.
65 οἱ transp. Triclinius: τοὔνεκά οἱ vett.

they cut up your limbs with a knife,
and for the final course distributed your flesh   50
around the tables and ate it.

But for my part, I cannot call any of the blessed gods   Ep. 2
    a glutton[14]—I stand back:
impoverishment is often the lot of slanderers.
If in fact the wardens of Olympus honored any mortal
man, Tantalus was that one. He, however,   55
    could not digest
his great good fortune, and because of his greed he won
an overwhelming punishment in the form of a massive
rock which the Father[15] suspended above him;   57b
in his constant eagerness to cast it away from his head
    he is banished from joy.[16]

He has this helpless existence of constant weariness,   Str. 3
the fourth toil along with three others,[17] because he   60
    stole
from the deathless gods the nectar and ambrosia
with which they had made him immortal,
and gave them to the companions who drank
with him. But if any man hopes to hide any deed
    from a god, he is mistaken.
And so, the immortals cast his son back   65

[14] Perhaps a euphemism for cannibal.   [15] Zeus.
[16] In Homer's account (*Od.* 11.582–592) Tantalus stands in
the midst of food and water that elude his grasp.
[17] I.e., the punishments of Tityus, Sisyphus, and Ixion, the
other three arch-sinners. Alternatively, the expression may be
proverbial, meaning toil upon toil.

μετὰ τὸ ταχύποτμον αὖτις ἀνέρων ἔθνος.
πρὸς εὐάνθεμον δ' ὅτε φυάν
λάχναι νιν μέλαν γένειον ἔρεφον,
ἑτοῖμον ἀνεφρόντισεν γάμον

70   Πισάτα παρὰ πατρὸς εὔδοξον Ἱπποδάμειαν
σχεθέμεν. ἐγγὺς ἐλθὼν πολιᾶς ἁλὸς οἶος ἐν ὄρφνᾳ
ἄπυεν βαρύκτυπον
Εὐτρίαιναν· ὁ δ' αὐτῷ
πὰρ ποδὶ σχεδὸν φάνη.
75   τῷ μὲν εἶπε· "Φίλια δῶρα Κυπρίας
ἄγ' εἴ τι, Ποσείδαον, ἐς χάριν
τέλλεται, πέδασον ἔγχος Οἰνομάου χάλκεον,
ἐμὲ δ' ἐπὶ ταχυτάτων πόρευσον ἁρμάτων
ἐς Ἆλιν, κράτει δὲ πέλασον.
ἐπεὶ τρεῖς τε καὶ δέκ' ἄνδρας ὀλέσαις
80   μναστῆρας ἀναβάλλεται γάμον

θυγατρός. ὁ μέγας δὲ κίν-
   δυνος ἄναλκιν οὐ φῶτα λαμβάνει.
θανεῖν δ' οἷσιν ἀνάγκα, τά κέ τις ἀνώνυμον
γῆρας ἐν σκότῳ καθήμενος ἕψοι μάταν,
ἁπάντων καλῶν ἄμμορος; ἀλλ' ἐμοὶ
   μὲν οὗτος ἄεθλος
85   ὑποκείσεται· τὺ δὲ πρᾶξιν φίλαν δίδοι."
ὣς ἔννεπεν· οὐδ' ἀκράντοις ἐφάψατο
86b ἔπεσι. τὸν μὲν ἀγάλλων θεός

71 ἐγγὺς Bergk: ἐγγὺς δ' codd.

54

once again among the shortlived race of men.
And toward the age of youthful bloom,
when downy hair began covering his darkened chin,
he took thought of the marriage that was open to all,

to winning famous Hippodameia from her father,   Ant. 3
the Pisan. He approached the gray sea alone at night   71
and called upon the deep-thundering
Lord of the Fine Trident, who appeared
right by his feet.
He said to him, "If the loving gifts of Cypris[18]   75
    count at all for gratitude, Poseidon,
come! hold back the bronze spear of Oenomaus
and speed me in the swiftest of chariots
to Elis[19] and bring me to victorious power,
for having killed thirteen suitors
he puts off the marriage   80

of his daughter. Great risk   Ep. 3
    does not take hold of a cowardly man.
But since men must die, why would anyone sit
in darkness and coddle a nameless old age to no use,
deprived of all noble deeds? No!
    that contest shall be mine
to undertake; you grant the success I desire."   85
Thus he spoke, and wielded no unfulfilled
words. The god honored him   86b

[18] Aphrodite.
[19] The region in which Olympia and Pisa are located.

ἔδωκεν δίφρον τε χρύσεον πτεροῖ-
σίν τ᾿ ἀκάμαντας ἵππους.

Δ´ ἕλεν δ᾿ Οἰνομάου βίαν παρθένον τε σύνευνον·
ἔτεκε λαγέτας ἓξ ἀρεταῖσι μεμαότας υἱούς.
90 νῦν δ᾿ ἐν αἱμακουρίαις
ἀγλααῖσι μέμικται,
Ἀλφεοῦ πόρῳ κλιθείς,
τύμβον ἀμφίπολον ἔχων πολυξενω-
τάτῳ παρὰ βωμῷ· τὸ δὲ κλέος
τηλόθεν δέδορκε τᾶν Ὀλυμπιάδων ἐν δρόμοις
95 Πέλοπος, ἵνα ταχυτὰς ποδῶν ἐρίζεται
ἀκμαί τ᾿ ἰσχύος θρασύπονοι·
ὁ νικῶν δὲ λοιπὸν ἀμφὶ βίοτον
ἔχει μελιτόεσσαν εὐδίαν

ἀέθλων γ᾿ ἕνεκεν· τὸ δ᾿ αἰεὶ παράμερον ἐσλόν
100 ὕπατον ἔρχεται παντὶ βροτῶν. ἐμὲ δὲ στεφανῶσαι
κεῖνον ἱππίῳ νόμῳ
Αἰοληΐδι μολπᾷ
χρή· πέποιθα δὲ ξένον
μή τιν᾿ ἀμφότερα καλῶν τε ἴδριν †ἅ-
μα καὶ δύναμιν κυριώτερον
105 τῶν γε νῦν κλυταῖσι δαιδαλωσέμεν ὕμνων πτυχαῖς.

89 ἔτεκε Boehmer: τέκε τε Byz.: ἃ τέκε vett.
104 ἅμα vett.: ἄλλον Byz.: ἀλλὰ Hermann

---

[20] The altar of Zeus.

with the gift of a golden chariot
    and winged horses that never tire.

He defeated mighty Oenomaus and won the maiden as   Str. 4
    his wife.
He fathered six sons, leaders eager for achievements.
And now he partakes   90
of splendid blood sacrifices
as he reclines by the course of the Alpheus,
having his much-attended tomb beside the altar
    thronged by visiting strangers.[20] And far shines that
fame of the Olympic festivals gained in the racecourses
of Pelops, where competition is held for swiftness of feet   95
and boldly laboring feats of strength.
And for the rest of his life the victor
enjoys a honey-sweet calm,

so much as games can provide it. But the good that   Ant. 4
    comes each day
is greatest for every mortal.[21] My duty is to crown   100
that man with an equestrian tune
in Aeolic song.[22]
For I am confident that there is no other host
both more expert in noble pursuits and
    more lordly in power
alive today to embellish in famous folds of hymns.   105

[21] Although satisfaction for great achievement may last a life-
time, humans must live each day and not rest on laurels.

[22] The equestrian tune, also called the Castor Song (cf. *Pyth.*
2.69 and *Isth.* 1.16), was sung to honor horsemen. "Aeolic" may
refer to the meter or possibly to the musical mode.

θεὸς ἐπίτροπος ἐὼν τεαῖσι μήδεται
ἔχων τοῦτο κᾶδος, Ἱέρων,
μερίμναισιν· εἰ δὲ μὴ ταχὺ λίποι,
ἔτι γλυκυτέραν κεν ἔλπομαι

110   σὺν ἅρματι θοῷ κλεί-
        ξειν ἐπίκουρον εὑρὼν ὁδὸν λόγων
παρ᾿ εὐδείελον ἐλθὼν Κρόνιον. ἐμοὶ μὲν ὦν
Μοῖσα καρτερώτατον βέλος ἀλκᾷ τρέφει·
ἐν ἄλλοισι δ᾿ ἄλλοι μεγάλοι· τὸ δ᾿ ἔ-
        σχατον κορυφοῦται
βασιλεῦσι. μηκέτι πάπταινε πόρσιον.
115   εἴη σέ τε τοῦτον ὑψοῦ χρόνον πατεῖν,
115b   ἐμέ τε τοσσάδε νικαφόροις
ὁμιλεῖν πρόφαντον σοφίᾳ καθ᾿ Ἑλ-
        λανας ἐόντα παντᾷ.

107 κᾶδος Boeckh: κῦδος CE^{γρ}L: κῆδος rell.
113 ἐν V: om. rell.: ἐπ᾿ Byz.

58

A god acting as guardian makes this his concern:
to devise means, Hieron, for your
aspirations, and unless he should suddenly depart,
I hope to celebrate an even sweeter success

with a speeding chariot,[23] having found   Ep. 4
    a helpful road of words[24]
when coming to Cronus' sunny hill.[25] And now for me   111
the Muse tends the strongest weapon in defense:
others are great in various ways, but
    the summit is crowned
by kings. Look no further.[26]
May you walk on high for the time that is yours,   115
and may I join victors whenever they win   115b
and be foremost in wisdom
    among Hellenes everywhere.

[23] Hieron won the chariot race two Olympiads later (468), but
Bacchylides (in Ode 3), not Pindar, celebrated it.
[24] The road to Olympia will be helpful to the poet by provid-
ing ample material for praise.
[25] The hill of Cronus was adjacent to the precinct of Zeus at
Olympia.
[26] Regardless of whether Hieron furthers his athletic success,
he has reached the pinnacle of political power by being king.

OLYMPIAN 2

Olympians 2 and 3 celebrate the victory of Theron of
Acragas with the *tethrippon* in 476. The city of Acragas
(modern Agrigento), a colony of Gela, flourished under
Theron and his brother Xenocrates (also celebrated in
Pyth. 6 and *Isth.* 2), who belonged to the clan of the Em-
menidae and claimed a Theban hero Thersandrus as an
ancestor. Theron became tyrant of Acragas around 488
and conquered Himera in 482. In 480 he and Gelon of
Syracuse defeated the Carthaginians at the battle of Hi-
mera, spoils from which helped make Acragas one of the
most splendid cities in Western Greece.

The ode opens with a priamel (imitated by Horace,
Odes 1.12), which culminates in Theron's Olympic victory
(1–6). He is praised for his hospitality to foreigners and
for his civic-mindedness, as the most recent in a distin-
guished family of benefactors who have labored on behalf
of Acragas. The poet seals his praise with a prayer to Zeus
as god of Olympia that their progeny may inherit the land
(6–15).

Gnomic reflections follow: time cannot change what
has happened in the past, but good fortune can bring for-
getfulness and quell the pain (15–22). Two Theban exam-
ples are cited: Semele, who, slain by Zeus' thunderbolt, is
beloved on Olympus and Ino, who enjoys immortality in

the sea among the Nereids (22–30). Humans, however, do not know when they will die, or if a day will end well, because they are subject to alternations of happiness and suffering (30–34). So it was with Theron's ancestors: Oedipus slew his father Laius and the Fury of vengeance (Erinys) caused his sons to kill each other, but Polyneices' son Thersandrus survived to win glory in athletics and war and to continue the line of Adrastus, king of Argos (35–45).

As a descendant of Thersandrus, Theron deserves to be celebrated, because he has won an Olympic victory, as his brother has won chariot victories at Delphi and at the Isthmus (46–51). Several gnomic reflections follow on the proper use of wealth for virtuous ends and on the punishment that awaits the spirits of evildoers after death (51–58), in the midst of which Pindar gives an account of the afterlife, the most extensive in his extant poetry, which envisions the transmigration of souls and their reward and punishment. The passage culminates in a description of the Isle of the Blessed, inhabited by those who have lived just lives through three cycles: Peleus, Cadmus, and Achilles (58–83).

Appearing in the guise of an archer, the poet declares that he has many things to say, but declines to do so, further comparing himself to an eagle who is wise by nature in contrast to mere learners who are like crows (83–88). Taking aim with his arrows at Acragas, he declares that no city in a century has produced a man more generous and kind than Theron. He then stops short of enumerating Theron's benefactions because, like grains of sand, they cannot be counted (89–100).

2. ΘΗΡΩΝΙ ΑΚΡΑΓΑΝΤΙΝΩΙ

ΑΡΜΑΤΙ

Α΄ Ἀναξιφόρμιγγες ὕμνοι,
   τίνα θεόν, τίν᾽ ἥρωα, τίνα δ᾽ ἄνδρα κελαδήσομεν;
   ἤτοι Πίσα μὲν Διός· Ὀλυμπιάδα
      δ᾽ ἔστασεν Ἡρακλέης
   ἀκρόθινα πολέμου·
5 Θήρωνα δὲ τετραορίας ἕνεκα νικαφόρου
   γεγωνητέον, ὄπι δίκαιον ξένων,
      ἔρεισμ᾽ Ἀκράγαντος,
   εὐωνύμων τε πατέρων ἄωτον ὀρθόπολιν·

   καμόντες οἳ πολλὰ θυμῷ
   ἱερὸν ἔσχον οἴκημα ποταμοῦ, Σικελίας τ᾽ ἔσαν
10 ὀφθαλμός, αἰὼν δ᾽ ἔφεπε μόρσιμος,
      πλοῦτόν τε καὶ χάριν ἄγων
   γνησίαις ἐπ᾽ ἀρεταῖς.
   ἀλλ᾽ ὦ Κρόνιε παῖ Ῥέας, ἕδος Ὀλύμπου νέμων

6 ξένων Hermann: ξένον codd.

62

2. FOR THERON OF ACRAGAS

WINNER, CHARIOT RACE, 476 B.C.

Hymns that rule the lyre,   Str. 1
what god, what hero, and what man shall we celebrate?
Indeed, Pisa belongs to Zeus, while Heracles
    established the Olympic festival
as the firstfruits of war;[1]
but Theron, because of his victorious four-horse chariot,   5
must be proclaimed—a man just in his regard for guests,
    bulwark of Acragas,
and foremost upholder of his city from a line of famous
        ancestors,

who suffered much in their hearts   Ant. 1
to win a holy dwelling place on the river,[2] and they were
the eye[3] of Sicily, while their allotted time drew on,   10
    adding wealth and glory
to their native virtues.
O son of Cronus and Rhea,[4] ruling over your abode on
        Olympus,

[1] For an account of Heracles' founding of the Olympic games
with the spoils from defeating Augeas, see *Ol.* 10.24–59.

[2] Acragas was located on a river of the same name.

[3] I.e. pride, most precious part (cf. *Ol.* 6.16).   [4] Zeus.

ἀέθλων τε κορυφὰν πόρον τ' Ἀλφεοῦ,
  ἰανθεὶς ἀοιδαῖς
εὔφρων ἄρουραν ἔτι πατρίαν σφίσιν κόμισον

15 λοιπῷ γένει. τῶν δὲ πεπραγμένων
ἐν δίκᾳ τε καὶ παρὰ δίκαν ἀποίητον οὐδ' ἂν
Χρόνος ὁ πάντων πατὴρ
  δύναιτο θέμεν ἔργων τέλος·
λάθα δὲ πότμῳ σὺν εὐδαίμονι γένοιτ' ἄν.
ἐσλῶν γὰρ ὑπὸ χαρμάτων πῆμα θνᾴσκει
20 παλίγκοτον δαμασθέν,

Β' ὅταν θεοῦ Μοῖρα πέμπῃ
ἀνεκὰς ὄλβον ὑψηλόν. ἕπεται δὲ λόγος εὐθρόνοις
Κάδμοιο κούραις, ἔπαθον αἳ μεγάλα·
  πένθος δὲ πίτνει βαρὺ
κρεσσόνων πρὸς ἀγαθῶν.
25 ζώει μὲν ἐν Ὀλυμπίοις ἀποθανοῖσα βρόμῳ
κεραυνοῦ ταννέθειρα Σεμέλα, φιλεῖ
  δέ νιν Παλλὰς αἰεί
καὶ Ζεὺς πατήρ, μάλα φιλεῖ δὲ παῖς ὁ κισσοφόρος·

λέγοντι δ' ἐν καὶ θαλάσσᾳ
μετὰ κόραισι Νηρῆος ἁλίαις βίοτον ἄφθιτον

  26 φιλέοντι δὲ Μοῖσαι post αἰεί secl. Aristophanes metri
causa

over the pinnacle of contests, and over Alpheus' course,
    cheered by my songs
graciously preserve their ancestral land

for their children still to come. Once deeds are done,   Ep. 1
whether in justice or contrary to it, not even   16
Time, the father of all,
    could undo their outcome.
But with a fortunate destiny forgetfulness may result,
for under the force of noble joys the pain dies
and its malignancy is suppressed,   20

whenever divine Fate sends   Str. 2
happiness towering upwards. This saying befits
Cadmus' fair-throned daughters,[5] who suffered greatly;
    but grievous sorrow subsides
in the face of greater blessings.
Long-haired Semele lives among the Olympians   25
after dying in the roar of a thunderbolt;
    Pallas loves her ever
and father Zeus; and her ivy-bearing son loves her very
    much.

They say, too, that in the sea   Ant. 2
Ino has been granted an immortal life

[5] Of Cadmus' four daughters (cf. *Pyth.* 3.96–99), Pindar here
singles out Semele and Ino. Semele was killed by lightning when
she requested to see her lover Zeus in his full splendor; Zeus
rescued Dionysus (her "ivy-bearing son," 27) from the ashes. Ino
leapt into the sea to escape her mad husband Athamas and be-
came a Nereid, also called Leucothea (cf. *Od.* 5.333–335).

PINDAR

30 Ἰνοῖ τετάχθαι τὸν ὅλον ἀμφὶ χρόνον.
    ἤτοι βροτῶν γε κέκριται
πεῖρας οὔ τι θανάτου,
οὐδ᾽ ἡσύχιμον ἀμέραν ὁπότε παῖδ᾽ ἀελίου
ἀτειρεῖ σὺν ἀγαθῷ τελευτάσομεν·
    ῥοαὶ δ᾽ ἄλλοτ᾽ ἄλλαι
εὐθυμιᾶν τε μέτα καὶ πόνων ἐς ἄνδρας ἔβαν.

35 οὕτω δὲ Μοῖρ᾽, ἅ τε πατρώιον
τῶνδ᾽ ἔχει τὸν εὔφρονα πότμον, θεόρτῳ σὺν ὄλβῳ
ἐπί τι καὶ πῆμ᾽ ἄγει,
    παλιντράπελον ἄλλῳ χρόνῳ·
ἐξ οὗπερ ἔκτεινε Λᾷον μόριμος υἱός
συναντόμενος, ἐν δὲ Πυθῶνι χρησθέν
40 παλαίφατον τέλεσσεν.

Γ΄ ἰδοῖσα δ᾽ ὀξεῖ᾽ Ἐρινύς
ἔπεφνέ οἱ σὺν ἀλλαλοφονίᾳ γένος ἀρήιον·
λείφθη δὲ Θέρσανδρος ἐριπέντι Πολυ-
    νείκει, νέοις ἐν ἀέθλοις
ἐν μάχαις τε πολέμου
45 τιμώμενος, Ἀδραστιδᾶν θάλος ἀρωγὸν δόμοις·
ὅθεν σπέρματος ἔχοντα ῥίζαν πρέπει
    τὸν Αἰνησιδάμου
ἐγκωμίων τε μελέων λυρᾶν τε τυγχανέμεν.

66

among the sea-dwelling daughters of Nereus for all time. 30
    Truly, in the case of mortals
death's end is not at all determined,
nor when we shall complete the day, the child of the
        sun,
in peace with our blessings unimpaired.
    For various streams bearing
pleasures and pains come at various times upon men.

Thus it is that Fate, who controls the kindly destiny Ep. 2
that is the patrimony of this family, adds to their 36
heaven-sent happiness some misery as well,
    to be reversed at another time—
from that day when his fated son[6] met and killed Laius
and fulfilled the oracle
declared long before at Pytho. 40

When the sharp-eyed Fury saw it, Str. 3
she killed his warrior progeny[7] in mutual slaughter;
but Thersandrus, who survived the fallen Polyneices,
    gained honor in youthful contests
and in the battles of war,
to be a savior son to the house of Adrastus' line.[8] 45
It is fitting that the son of Aenesidamus,[9]
    whose roots spring from that seed,
should meet with victory songs and lyres.

[6] Oedipus.   [7] Eteocles and Polyneices.
[8] He was the son of Polyneices and of Adrastus' daughter, Argeia. He saved the line because Adrastus' own son was killed in the attack of the Epigoni against Thebes (cf. *Pyth.* 8.48–55).
[9] Theron.

Ὀλυμπίᾳ μὲν γὰρ αὐτός
γέρας ἔδεκτο, Πυθῶνι δ' ὁμόκλαρον ἐς ἀδελφεόν
50 Ἰσθμοῖ τε κοιναὶ Χάριτες ἄνθεα τε-
θρίππων δυωδεκαδρόμων
ἄγαγον· τὸ δὲ τυχεῖν
πειρώμενον ἀγωνίας δυσφρονᾶν παραλύει.
ὁ μὰν πλοῦτος ἀρεταῖς δεδαιδαλμένος
φέρει τῶν τε καὶ τῶν
καιρὸν βαθεῖαν ὑπέχων μέριμναν ἀγροτέραν,

55 ἀστὴρ ἀρίζηλος, ἐτυμώτατον
ἀνδρὶ φέγγος· εἰ δέ νιν ἔχων τις οἶδεν τὸ μέλλον,
ὅτι θανόντων μὲν ἐν-
θάδ' αὐτίκ' ἀπάλαμνοι φρένες
ποινὰς ἔτεισαν—τὰ δ' ἐν τᾷδε Διὸς ἀρχᾷ
ἀλιτρὰ κατὰ γᾶς δικάζει τις ἐχθρᾷ
60 λόγον φράσαις ἀνάγκᾳ·

Δ′ ἴσαις δὲ νύκτεσσιν αἰεί,
ἴσαις δ' ἀμέραις ἄλιον ἔχοντες, ἀπονέστερον

52 δυσφρονᾶν Dindorf, Schroeder: δυσφροσυναν Aa: δυ-
σφροσύνας Cᵖᶜ: ἀφροσυν[Π²: ἀφροσυνᾶν Mommsen e schol.:
ἀφροσύνας Bowra
62 ἴσαις δ' Mommsen: ἴσαις δ' ἐν vett.Π²: ἴσα δ' ἐν Byz.

For at Olympia he himself   Ant. 3
received the prize, while at Pytho and the Isthmus
Graces shared by both bestowed upon his equally   50
    fortunate brother[10] crowns for his team of four
horses that traverse twelve laps. Winning
releases from anxieties[11] one who engages in
        competition.
Truly, wealth embellished with virtues
    provides fit occasion for various achievements
by supporting a profound and questing ambition;

it[12] is a conspicuous lodestar, the truest   Ep. 3
light for a man. If one has it and knows the future,   56
that the helpless spirits
    of those who have died on earth immediately
pay the penalty—and upon sins committed here
in Zeus' realm, a judge beneath the earth
pronounces sentence with hateful necessity;   60

but forever having sunshine in equal nights   Str. 4
and in equal days,[13] good men

---

[10] Xenocrates, celebrated in *Pyth.* 6 and *Isth.* 2.

[11] If δυσφρονᾶν is read, the gnome repeats a major theme of
the ode (cf. 18–22). A scholiast read ἀφροσυνᾶν ("from folly")
and P. Oxy. 2092 gives ἀφροσυν[. The thought can be paralleled
(cf. *Ol.* 5.16, Solon 13.70, Theogn. 590, and Thuc. 6.16.3), but it
seems less germane here.

[12] I.e. wealth used in accordance with ἀρετά in quest of noble
achievements (cf. lines 10–11).

[13] *Fr.* 129 (from a dirge) says that the sun shines in Hades
during nighttime on earth, but this passage seems to envision a
continual equinox.

69

ἐσλοὶ δέκονται βίοτον, οὐ χθόνα τα-
    ράσσοντες ἐν χερὸς ἀκμᾷ
οὐδὲ πόντιον ὕδωρ
65 κεινὰν παρὰ δίαιταν, ἀλλὰ παρὰ μὲν τιμίοις
θεῶν οἵτινες ἔχαιρον εὐορκίαις
    ἄδακρυν νέμονται
αἰῶνα, τοὶ δ᾽ ἀπροσόρατον ὀκχέοντι πόνον.

ὅσοι δ᾽ ἐτόλμασαν ἐστρὶς
ἑκατέρωθι μείναντες ἀπὸ πάμπαν ἀδίκων ἔχειν
70 ψυχάν, ἔτειλαν Διὸς ὁδὸν παρὰ Κρό-
    νου τύρσιν· ἔνθα μακάρων
νᾶσον ὠκεανίδες
αὖραι περιπνέοισιν· ἄνθεμα δὲ χρυσοῦ φλέγει,
τὰ μὲν χερσόθεν ἀπ᾽ ἀγλαῶν δενδρέων,
    ὕδωρ δ᾽ ἄλλα φέρβει,
ὅρμοισι τῶν χέρας ἀναπλέκοντι καὶ στεφάνους

75 βουλαῖς ἐν ὀρθαῖσι Ῥαδαμάνθυος,
ὃν πατὴρ ἔχει μέγας ἑτοῖμον αὐτῷ πάρεδρον,
πόσις ὁ πάντων Ῥέας
    ὑπέρτατον ἐχοίσας θρόνον.
Πηλεύς τε καὶ Κάδμος ἐν τοῖσιν ἀλέγονται·

76 μέγας Π²: γᾶς codd.

receive a life of less toil,
    for they do not vex the earth
or the water of the sea with the strength of their hands
to earn a paltry living. No, in company with the honored   65
gods, those who joyfully kept their oaths
    spend a tearless
existence, whereas the others endure pain too terrible to
    behold.

But those with the courage to have lived   Ant. 4
three times in either realm,[14] while keeping their souls
free from all unjust deeds, travel the road of Zeus   70
    to the tower of Cronus,[15] where ocean breezes
blow round
the Isle of the Blessed, and flowers of gold are ablaze,
some from radiant trees on land, while the water
    nurtures others; with these they weave
garlands for their hands and crowns for their heads,

in obedience to the just counsels of Rhadamanthys,   Ep. 4
whom the great father[16] keeps ever seated at his side,   76
the husband of Rhea, she who has
    the highest throne of all.
Peleus and Cadmus are numbered among them,

[14] Or *in both realms* (on earth and in Hades) for a total of six times.

[15] The road of Zeus and tower of Cronus are not otherwise known. For other accounts of an afterlife in the Isle(s) of the Blessed, see *Od.* 4.563–569, Hes. *Op.* 169–173, and Plato, *Gorg.* 523AE.

[16] Cronus, husband of Rhea.

Ἀχιλλέα τ᾽ ἔνεικ᾽, ἐπεὶ Ζηνὸς ἦτορ
80 λιταῖς ἔπεισε, μάτηρ·

Ε΄ ὃς Ἕκτορα σφᾶλε, Τροίας
ἄμαχον ἀστραβῆ κίονα, Κύκνον τε θανάτῳ πόρεν,
Ἀοῦς τε παῖδ᾽ Αἰθίοπα. πολλά μοι ὑπ᾽
    ἀγκῶνος ὠκέα βέλη
ἔνδον ἐντὶ φαρέτρας

85 φωνάεντα συνετοῖσιν· ἐς δὲ τὸ πᾶν ἑρμανέων
χατίζει. σοφὸς ὁ πολλὰ εἰδὼς φυᾷ·
    μαθόντες δὲ λάβροι
παγγλωσσίᾳ κόρακες ὣς ἄκραντα γαρύετον

Διὸς πρὸς ὄρνιχα θεῖον·
ἔπεχε νῦν σκοπῷ τόξον, ἄγε θυμέ· τίνα βάλλομεν
90 ἐκ μαλθακᾶς αὖτε φρενὸς εὐκλέας ὀ-
    ιστοὺς ἱέντες; ἐπί τοι
Ἀκράγαντι τανύσαις
αὐδάσομαι ἐνόρκιον λόγον ἀλαθεῖ νόῳ,

87 γαρύετων Bergk
92 αὐδάσομεν B(schol. D)

---

17 Cycnus was Poseidon's son, Memnon the son of Eos and
Tithonus; for a similar catalog of Achilles' victims, see *Isth.* 5.39.
18 Or *but in general.* The translation of τὸ πάν as "crowd"
adopted by many editors cannot be paralleled. I interpret verses
83–88 to express Pindar's intention of dispensing with further de-
tails about the afterlife (as much as "those who understand" might

OLYMPIAN 2

and Achilles too, whom his mother brought,
after she persuaded the heart of Zeus with her   80
    entreaties.

He laid low Hector, Troy's   Str. 5
invincible pillar of strength, and gave to death Cycnus
and Dawn's Ethiopian son.[17] I have many swift arrows
    under my arm
in their quiver
that speak to those who understand, but for the whole   85
    subject,[18] they need
interpreters. Wise is he who knows many things
    by nature, whereas learners who are boisterous
and long-winded are like a pair of crows[19] that cry in
    vain

against the divine bird of Zeus.[20]   Ant. 5
Now aim the bow at the mark, come, my heart. At whom
do we shoot, and this time launch from a kindly spirit   90
    our arrows of fame? Yes,
bending the bow at Acragas,
I will proclaim a statement on oath with a truthful mind,

appreciate them), in order to provide a categorical evaluation of
Theron's generosity.
   [19] The scholia claim that the two crows (or ravens) represent
Bacchylides and Simonides, but the dual may reflect traditional
stories of pairs of crows.
   [20] The eagle. For a similar contrast (with jackdaws), see *Nem.*
3.80–82.

τεκεῖν μή τιν' ἑκατόν γε ἐτέων πόλιν
    φίλοις ἄνδρα μᾶλλον
εὐεργέταν πραπίσιν ἀφθονέστερόν τε χέρα

95 Θήρωνος. ἀλλ' αἶνον ἐπέβα κόρος
    οὐ δίκᾳ συναντόμενος, ἀλλὰ μάργων ὑπ' ἀνδρῶν,
    τὸ λαλαγῆσαι θέλων
        κρυφόν τε θέμεν ἐσλῶν καλοῖς
    ἔργοις· ἐπεὶ ψάμμος ἀριθμὸν περιπέφευγεν,
    καὶ κεῖνος ὅσα χάρματ' ἄλλοις ἔθηκεν,
100 τίς ἂν φράσαι δύναιτο;

    97 θέλων codd.: θέλον Coppola: θέλει Wilamowitz | κρύφον
    (vel κρυφόν) Aristarchus: κρύφιόν codd. | τε θέμεν codd.: τιθέ-
    μεν Hermann | ἐσλῶν καλοῖς Aristarchus: ἐσ(θ)λὸν (ἑλὼν A)
    κακοῖς codd.

that no city within a century has produced
  a man more beneficent to his friends
in spirit and more generous of hand than

Theron. But enough: upon praise comes tedious   Ep. 5
      excess,[21]
which does not keep to just limits, but at the instigation   96
of greedy men is eager to prattle on
  and obscure noble men's good
deeds; for grains of sand escape counting,
and all the joys which that man has wrought for others,
who could declare them?   100

[21] Κόρος is excess in praise that becomes tedious to the audience and obstructs a just assessment of achievements (cf. *Pyth.* 1.82, 8.32, and *Nem.* 10.20).

OLYMPIAN 3

This ode celebrates the same victory as *Ol.* 2. The scholia report that it was performed for the Theoxenia (feast of welcome for gods) honoring the children of Tyndareus, but the evidence for this theory is derived from the poem itself and has no compelling authority. The centerpiece of the poem is the etiological narrative, structured in ring composition, that tells how Heracles brought the olive tree from the land of the Hyperboreans to grace the Olympic festival that he had just founded.

The poet hopes to please the Tyndaridae and their sister Helen as he honors Acragas in celebration of Theron's Olympic victory (1–4). The Muse has assisted him in his endeavor to compose this new ode in Doric meter for a victor crowned by the Olympic judges with a wreath of olive, which Heracles brought from the region of the Danube (4–15). The narrative relates how, after arranging the games, Heracles realized that the precinct lacked trees to provide either shade or victory crowns. During a previous trip to the Hyperboreans in search of Artemis' golden-horned doe, he had admired their olive trees, and upon returning there, he obtained their permission to take some to plant at Olympia (16–34). After his apotheosis on Olympus, Heracles entrusted supervision of the games to the Tyndaridae, and it is because of Theron's and his family's devoted entertainment of these heroes that they have won such honor in the games (34–41). He concludes the poem with a priamel that echoes the opening of *Ol.* 1, declaring that Theron has reached the limits of human achievement, the Pillars of Heracles, beyond which only fools would attempt to travel (42–45).

3. ΘΗΡΩΝΙ ΑΚΡΑΓΑΝΤΙΝΩΙ

ΑΡΜΑΤΙ

Αʹ Τυνδαρίδαις τε φιλοξείνοις ἁδεῖν
   καλλιπλοκάμῳ θ᾽ Ἑλένᾳ
   κλεινὰν Ἀκράγαντα γεραίρων εὔχομαι,
   Θήρωνος Ὀλυμπιονίκαν
      ὕμνον ὀρθώσαις, ἀκαμαντοπόδων
   ἵππων ἄωτον. Μοῖσα δ᾽ οὕτω ποι παρέ-
      στα μοι νεοσίγαλον εὑρόντι τρόπον
5 Δωρίῳ φωνὰν ἐναρμόξαι πεδίλῳ

   ἀγλαόκωμον· ἐπεὶ χαίταισι μὲν
      ζευχθέντες ἔπι στέφανοι
   πράσσοντί με τοῦτο θεόδματον χρέος,
   φόρμιγγά τε ποικιλόγαρυν
      καὶ βοὰν αὐλῶν ἐπέων τε θέσιν
   Αἰνησιδάμου παιδὶ συμμεῖξαι πρεπόν-
      τως, ἅ τε Πίσα με γεγωνεῖν· τᾶς ἄπο
10 θεόμοροι νίσοντ᾽ ἐπ᾽ ἀνθρώπους ἀοιδαί,

3. FOR THERON OF ACRAGAS

WINNER, CHARIOT RACE, 476 B.C.

I pray that I may please the hospitable Tyndaridae[1]
    and Helen of the beautiful locks,
as I honor famous Acragas,
when, for Theron, I raise up an Olympic
    victory hymn, the finest reward for horses
with untiring feet. And for that reason, I believe, the
    Muse stood beside me as I found a newly shining way
to join to Dorian measure[2] a voice

        Str. 1

        5

of splendid celebration, because crowns
    bound upon his hair
exact from me this divinely inspired debt
to mix in due measure the varied strains of the lyre,
    the sound of pipes, and the setting of words
for Aenesidamus' son;[3] and Pisa too
    bids me lift up my voice, for from there
come divinely allotted songs to men,

        Ant. 1

        10

[1] Castor and Polydeuces (Latinized as Pollux); Helen is their sister.

[2] Perhaps a reference to the ode's Doric meter, dactylo-epitritic.

[3] Theron.

PINDAR

ᾧ τινι κραίνων ἐφετμὰς Ἡρακλέος προτέρας
ἀτρεκὴς Ἑλλανοδίκας γλεφάρων Αἰ-
τωλὸς ἀνὴρ ὑψόθεν
ἀμφὶ κόμαισι βάλῃ
    γλαυκόχροα κόσμον ἐλαίας, τάν ποτε
Ἴστρου ἀπὸ σκιαρᾶν
    παγᾶν ἔνεικεν Ἀμφιτρυωνιάδας,
15 μνᾶμα τῶν Οὐλυμπίᾳ κάλλιστον ἀέθλων,

Β΄ δᾶμον Ὑπερβορέων πείσαις Ἀπόλ-
    λωνος θεράποντα λόγῳ·
πιστὰ φρονέων Διὸς αἴτει πανδόκῳ
ἄλσει σκιαρόν τε φύτευμα
    ξυνὸν ἀνθρώποις στέφανόν τ᾽ ἀρετᾶν.
ἤδη γὰρ αὐτῷ, πατρὶ μὲν βωμῶν ἁγι-
    σθέντων, διχόμηνις ὅλον χρυσάρματος
20 ἑσπέρας ὀφθαλμὸν ἀντέφλεξε Μήνα,

καὶ μεγάλων ἀέθλων ἁγνὰν κρίσιν
    καὶ πενταετηρίδ᾽ ἁμᾶ
θῆκε ζαθέοις ἐπὶ κρημνοῖς Ἀλφεοῦ·
ἀλλ᾽ οὐ καλὰ δένδρε᾽ ἔθαλλεν
    χῶρος ἐν βάσσαις Κρονίου Πέλοπος.

---

4 The Hellanodicae, who claimed descent from Aetolians,
were the judges of the Olympic games, famous for their strictness.

whenever for one of them, in fulfillment of Heracles'   Ep. 1
ancient mandates, the strict Aetolian judge[4]
    places above his brows
about his hair
    the gray-colored adornment of olive, which once
Amphitryon's son[5] brought
    from the shady springs of Ister[6]
to be the fairest memorial of the contests at Olympia,   15

after he persuaded the Hyperborean people,   Str. 2
    Apollo's servants, with his speech;
with trustworthy intention he requested for Zeus'
all-welcoming precinct[7] a plant to provide shade
    for men to share and a crown for deeds of excellence.
Already the altars had been dedicated to his father,[8]
    and the Moon in her golden chariot at mid-month
had shown back to him her full eye at evening,[9]   20

and he had established the holy judging of the great   Ant. 2
    games together with their four-year festival
on the sacred banks of the Alpheus.
But as yet the land of Pelops in the vales of Cronus' hill
    was not flourishing with beautiful trees.

[5] Heracles.

[6] The upper Danube, region of the fabled Hyperboreans ("those beyond the North Wind").

[7] The Altis, the sacred precinct at Olympia, was a Panhellenic ("all-welcoming") site.

[8] Zeus.

[9] The Olympic festival was held after the second or third full moon following the summer solstice.

τούτων ἔδοξεν γυμνὸς αὐτῷ κᾶπος ὀ-
ξείαις ὑπακουέμεν αὐγαῖς ἀελίου.
25 δὴ τότ' ἐς γαῖαν πορεύεν θυμὸς ὥρμα

'Ιστρίαν νιν· ἔνθα Λατοῦς ἱπποσόα θυγάτηρ
δέξατ' ἐλθόντ' 'Αρκαδίας ἀπὸ δειρᾶν
    καὶ πολυγνάμπτων μυχῶν,
εὖτέ νιν ἀγγελίαις
    Εὐρυσθέος ἔντυ' ἀνάγκα πατρόθεν
χρυσόκερων ἔλαφον
    θήλειαν ἄξονθ', ἄν ποτε Ταϋγέτα
30 ἀντιθεῖσ' 'Ορθωσίᾳ ἔγραψεν ἱεράν.

Γ΄ τὰν μεθέπων ἴδε καὶ κείναν χθόνα
    πνοιαῖς ὄπιθεν Βορέα
ψυχροῦ· τόθι δένδρεα θάμβαινε σταθείς.
    τῶν νιν γλυκὺς ἵμερος ἔσχεν
        δωδεκάγναμπτον περὶ τέρμα δρόμου
    ἵππων φυτεῦσαι. καὶ νυν ἐς ταύταν ἑορ-
        τὰν ἵλαος ἀντιθέοισιν νίσεται
35 σὺν βαθυζώνοιο διδύμοις παισὶ Λήδας.

30 'Ορθωσίας Ahrens

Without them, the enclosure seemed naked to him
    and subject to the piercing rays of the sun.
Then it was that his heart urged him to go   25

to the Istrian land, where Leto's horse-driving   Ep. 2
    daughter[10]
had welcomed him on his arrival from Arcadia's ridges
    and much-winding valleys,
when through the commands of Eurystheus
    his father's[11] compulsion
impelled him to bring back
    the golden-horned doe, which formerly Taygeta
had inscribed as a holy offering to Orthosia.[12]   30

In pursuit of her he saw, among other places, that land   Str. 3
    beyond the blasts of the cold
North Wind, where he stood and wondered at the trees.
A sweet desire seized him
    to plant some of them around the twelve-lap turn
of the hippodrome. And now he gladly attends
    that festival[13] with the godlike twins,
the sons of deep-girdled Leda,[14]   35

[10] Artemis.   [11] Zeus'.
[12] Artemis. When Taygeta, one of the Pleiades, was pursued
by Zeus, Artemis helped her escape by changing her into a doe;
on returning to her human form, she consecrated a doe to the
goddess. This is the only account to associate this episode with
the land of the Hyperboreans.
[13] The Olympic festival.
[14] Castor and Polydeuces.

PINDAR

τοῖς γὰρ ἐπέτραπεν Οὔλυμπόνδ' ἰὼν
  θαητὸν ἀγῶνα νέμειν
ἀνδρῶν τ' ἀρετᾶς πέρι καὶ ῥιμφαρμάτου
διφρηλασίας. ἐμὲ δ' ὦν πᾳ
  θυμὸς ὀτρύνει φάμεν Ἐμμενίδαις
  Θήρωνί τ' ἐλθεῖν κῦδος εὐίππων διδόν-
  των Τυνδαριδᾶν, ὅτι πλείσταισι βροτῶν
40 ξεινίαις αὐτοὺς ἐποίχονται τραπέζαις,

εὐσεβεῖ γνώμᾳ φυλάσσοντες μακάρων τελετάς.
εἰ δ' ἀριστεύει μὲν ὕδωρ, κτεάνων δὲ
  χρυσὸς αἰδοιέστατος,
νῦν δὲ πρὸς ἐσχατιὰν
  Θήρων ἀρεταῖσιν ἱκάνων ἅπτεται
οἴκοθεν Ἡρακλέος
  σταλᾶν. τὸ πόρσω δ' ἐστὶ σοφοῖς ἄβατον
45 κἀσόφοις. οὔ νιν διώξω· κεινὸς εἴην.

42 αἰδοιέστατος A: αἰδοιέστατον Cv
43 δὲ A(schol. B): γε a
45 νιν ζ: μιν β: μην AB | κενεὸς Schroeder

84

for to them, as he went to Olympus, he entrusted   Ant. 3
     supervision of the splendid contest[15]
involving the excellence of men and the driving
of swift chariots. And so, I believe, my heart
     bids me affirm that to the Emmenidae[16]
and Theron glory has come as a gift
     from Tyndareus' horsemen sons, because of all
         mortals
they attend them with the most numerous feasts of   40
     welcome

as with pious minds they preserve the rites of the   Ep. 3
     blessed gods.
If water is best, while gold is
     the most revered of possessions,
then truly has Theron now reached the furthest point
     with his achievements and
from his home[17] grasps the pillars
     of Heracles. What lies beyond neither wise men
nor fools can tread. I will not pursue it; I would be   45
     foolish.

[15] This supervision of the Olympic games is mentioned only here.

[16] Theron's clan.

[17] I.e. through his native virtues (schol.).

OLYMPIAN 4

Olympians 4 and 5 celebrate victories of Psaumis of Camarina, a city on the south shore of Sicily between Acragas and Syracuse. The scholia give the occasion of *Ol.* 4 as a chariot victory in the 82nd Olympiad (452 B.C.), confirmed by the entry in P. Oxy. 222: σαμιου καμ[αριναιου τεθριππον, where σαμιου is undoubtedly a mistake for Ψαυμι(δ)ος, and by P. Oxy. 2438. The words Ἐλατήρ (1), ὀχέων (11), and ἵππων (14) point to a victory with the *tethrippon*, but some argue that the ode celebrates a different victory entirely—that for the mule car commemorated in *Ol.* 5.

What we know of Psaumis must be inferred from these two odes. He appears to have been a wealthy private citizen who helped rebuild Camarina in 461/460 after its destruction by Gelon of Syracuse in the 480's.

The poem opens with an invocation of Zeus as charioteer of the storm cloud, occasioned because his daughters the Horae (Seasons) have sent the poet as a witness of the greatest games (1–3). After a gnomic reflection on the joy occasioned by news of a friend's success, Pindar reinvokes Zeus as subduer of Typhos and lord of Mt. Aetna, and requests that he receive favorably this Olympic victory ode for Psaumis, who comes in his chariot, crowned with an olive wreath (4–12). The victor is praised for his horse-breeding, his hospitality to many guests, and for his devotion to Hesychia (Peace, Concord) in his city (14–16).

The poet claims that his praise is truthful and justifies it by citing the example of Erginus, one of the Argonauts, who, in spite of appearing too old, won the race in armor during the games held by Hypsipyle on Lemnos (17–27).

4. ΨΑΥΜΙΔΙ ΚΑΜΑΡΙΝΑΙΩΙ

ΑΡΜΑΤΙ

Ἐλατὴρ ὑπέρτατε βροντᾶς ἀκαμαντόποδος
    Ζεῦ· τεαὶ γὰρ Ὧραι
ὑπὸ ποικιλοφόρμιγγος ἀοιδᾶς ἑλισσόμεναί μ'
    ἔπεμψαν
ὑψηλοτάτων μάρτυρ' ἀέθλων·
ξείνων δ' εὖ πρασσόντων
5   ἔσαναν αὐτίκ' ἀγγελίαν ποτὶ γλυκεῖαν ἐσλοί·
ἀλλὰ Κρόνου παῖ, ὃς Αἴτναν ἔχεις
ἶπον ἀνεμόεσσαν ἑκατογκεφάλα Τυφῶνος ὀβρίμου,
    Οὐλυμπιονίκαν
δέξαι Χαρίτων θ' ἕκατι τόνδε κῶμον,

10 χρονιώτατον φάος εὐρυσθενέων ἀρετᾶν.
    Ψαύμιος γὰρ ἵκει
ὀχέων, ὃς ἐλαίᾳ στεφανωθεὶς Πισάτιδι κῦδος ὄρσαι

    6 ἀλλ' ὦ ζ: ἀλλὰ rell.
    7 ἶπον ΒΕ: ἵππον Αζ
    10 ἥκει Α: ἵκει rell.

88

4. FOR PSAUMIS OF CAMARINA

WINNER, CHARIOT RACE, 452 B.C.

Driver most high of thunder with untiring feet,   Str.
    Zeus; on you I call because your Horae[1]
in their circling round have sent me, accompanied by
        song with the lyre's varied tones,
as a witness of the loftiest games;
and when guest-friends are successful,
good men are immediately cheered at the sweet news.   5
But, son of Cronus, you who rule Mt. Aetna,
windy burden for hundred-headed Typhos the mighty,[2]
receive an Olympic victor,
and, with the aid of the Graces, this celebratory revel,

longest-lasting light for achievements of great strength.   Ant.
    For it[3] comes in honor of the chariot of Psaumis,
who, crowned with Pisan olive, is eager to arouse   11

---

[1] The Horae were the goddesses of seasons and of civic order
(cf. Hes. *Th.* 901–903 and *Ol.* 13.17).

[2] Typhos (elsewhere called Typhoeus or Typhon) was pinned
under Mt. Aetna (cf. *Pyth.* 1.15–28).

[3] The revel ($\kappa\hat{\omega}\mu o\varsigma$).

σπεύδει Καμαρίνᾳ. θεὸς εὔφρων
εἴη λοιπαῖς εὐχαῖς·
ἐπεί νιν αἰνέω, μάλα μὲν τροφαῖς ἑτοῖμον ἵππων,
15 χαίροντά τε ξενίαις πανδόκοις,
καὶ πρὸς Ἡσυχίαν φιλόπολιν καθαρᾷ γνώμᾳ
τετραμμένον.
οὐ ψεύδεϊ τέγξω
λόγον· διάπειρά τοι βροτῶν ἔλεγχος·

ἅπερ Κλυμένοιο παῖδα
20 Λαμνιάδων γυναικῶν
ἔλυσεν ἐξ ἀτιμίας.
χαλκέοισι δ᾽ ἐν ἔντεσι νικῶν δρόμον
ἔειπεν Ὑψιπυλείᾳ μετὰ στέφανον ἰών·
"οὗτος ἐγὼ ταχυτᾶτι·
25 χεῖρες δὲ καὶ ἦτορ ἴσον. φύονται δὲ καὶ νέοις
ἐν ἀνδράσιν πολιαί
θαμάκι παρὰ τὸν ἁλικίας ἐοικότα χρόνον."

27 θαμάκι Α: θαμὰ καὶ α

90

glory for Camarina. May the god[4] look favorably
on his future prayers,
for I praise him, a most zealous raiser of horses,
delighting in acts of all-welcoming hospitality,   15
and devoted to city-loving Hesychia[5] with a sincere
    mind.
I will not taint my account
with a lie; trial is truly the test of mortals,

and this very thing rescued Clymenus' son[6]   Ep.
from the scorn   20
of the Lemnian women.
When he won the race in bronze armor,
he said to Hypsipyle as he stepped forward for his
    crown,
"Such am I for speed;
my hands and heart are just as good. Even on young   25
    men
gray hairs often grow
before the fitting time of their life."

  [4] Either Zeus or the gods in general. Pindar often uses θεός
or δαίμων without a specific reference.
  [5] The personification of civic Peace and daughter of Justice,
one of the Horae (cf. *Pyth.* 8.1–18).
  [6] Erginus, one of the Argonauts, won the race in armor at
the games held on Lemnos during their sojourn there (cf. *Pyth.*
4.252–254).

OLYMPIAN 5

This is the only victory ode in our MSS whose Pindaric authorship has been questioned. A heading in the Ambrosian MS (1.138.21 Dr.) states, "this poem was not among the texts, but in the commentaries of Didymus [1st cent. B.C.] it was said to be Pindar's." Although this information has occasioned much discussion of the poem's status, no compelling arguments for its exclusion from Pindar's works have been advanced. It celebrates Psaumis' victory in the mule car (*apene*), at some time between the resettlement of the city of Camarina in 461/460 and the elimination of the event from the Olympic games in 444. The most probable date is 448.

Each of its three triads (the shortest in the victory odes) addresses a different deity. In the first, Camarina is asked to welcome Psaumis, who exalted the city that bears her name at the Olympic games by providing feasts of oxen and furnishing entries in the races with chariots, mules, and single horses. His victory has brought glory to his newly built city and to his father Acron (1–8).

Upon his return from Olympia, Psaumis sings the praises of Pallas Athena, the Oanus River, the lake of Camarina, and the Hipparis River, which sustains the citizens through its canals. Psaumis apparently aided his people by building houses for them (9–14). Hard work and expenses are required to compete for a victory whose achievement is risky and uncertain, but when a man succeeds, even his townsmen credit him with wisdom (15–16).

Finally, the poet invokes Zeus the Savior to grant the city more deeds of valor and wishes Psaumis a happy old age with his sons at his side (17–23). He concludes with the observation that a man who possesses adequate wealth and uses it to acquire fame has reached a mortal's limits (23–24).

5. ΨΑΥΜΙΔΙ ΚΑΜΑΡΙΝΑΙΩΙ

ΑΠΗΝΗΙ

Α΄ Ὑψηλᾶν ἀρετᾶν καὶ στεφάνων ἄωτον γλυκύν
     τῶν Οὐλυμπίᾳ, Ὠκεανοῦ θύγατερ, καρδίᾳ γελανεῖ
     ἀκαμαντόποδός τ' ἀπήνας δέκευ Ψαύμιός τε δῶρα·

     ὃς τὰν σὰν πόλιν αὔξων, Καμάρινα, λαοτρόφον,
5   βωμοὺς ἓξ διδύμους ἐγέραρεν ἑορταῖς θεῶν
          μεγίσταις
     ὑπὸ βουθυσίαις ἀέθλων τε πεμπαμέροις ἁμίλλαις,

     ἵπποις ἡμιόνοις τε μοναμπυκίᾳ τε. τὶν δὲ κῦδος
          ἁβρόν
     νικάσας ἀνέθηκε, καὶ ὃν πατέρ' Ἄ-
     κρων' ἐκάρυξε καὶ τὰν νέοικον ἕδραν.

6 πεμπαμέροις Π³⁹, Triclinius: πεμπταμέροις Aa

---

¹ Camarina, nymph of the nearby lake for which the city was named.   ² According to Herodorus (quoted by the schol.), Heracles dedicated six double altars to Zeus-Poseidon, Hera-Athena, Hermes-Apollo, Charites-Dionysus, Artemis-Alpheus, and Cronus-Rhea.

5. FOR PSAUMIS OF CAMARINA

WINNER, MULE RACE, 448 B.C.

Daughter of Ocean,[1] with a glad heart receive this finest   Str. 1
sweet reward for lofty deeds and crowns won at
     Olympia,
gifts of the tirelessly running mule car and of Psaumis,

who, exalting your people-nourishing city, Camarina,   Ant. 1
honored the six double altars[2] at the gods' greatest   5
     festival
with sacrifices of oxen and in the five days[3] of athletic
     contests

with chariots, mules, and single-horse racing. By   Ep. 1
     winning,[4]
he has dedicated luxurious glory to you and proclaimed
     his father Acron and your[5] newly founded home.

[3] The reading πεμπταμέροις "on the fifth day" in most MSS
does not make sense because the equestrian events were held
early in the Olympic program (Paus. 5.9.3). Evidently Psaumis
was conspicuous throughout the festival for his large sacrifices.

[4] Presumably only in the mule race (cf. ἀπήνας, 3).

[5] Or *his*. The herald at the games announced the victor's father
and city.

Β΄ ἵκων δ' Οἰνομάου καὶ Πέλοπος παρ' εὐηράτων
10 σταθμῶν, ὦ πολιάοχε Παλλάς, ἀείδει μὲν ἄλσος
  ἁγνόν
  τὸ τεὸν ποταμόν τε Ὤανον ἐγχωρίαν τε λίμναν

  καὶ σεμνοὺς ὀχετούς, Ἵππαρις οἷσιν ἄρδει στρατόν,
  κολλᾷ τε σταδίων θαλάμων ταχέως ὑψίγυιον ἄλσος,
  ὑπ' ἀμαχανίας ἄγων ἐς φάος τόνδε δᾶμον ἀστῶν·

15 αἰεὶ δ' ἀμφ' ἀρεταῖσι πόνος δαπάνα τε μάρναται
  πρὸς ἔργον
  κινδύνῳ κεκαλυμμένον· εὖ δὲ τυχόν-
  τες σοφοὶ καὶ πολίταις ἔδοξαν ἔμμεν.

Γ΄ Σωτὴρ ὑψινεφὲς Ζεῦ, Κρόνιόν τε ναίων λόφον
  τιμῶν τ' Ἀλφεὸν εὐρὺ ῥέοντα Ἰδαῖόν τε σεμνὸν
  ἄντρον,
  ἱκέτας σέθεν ἔρχομαι Λυδίοις ἀπύων ἐν αὐλοῖς,

14 ὑπ' vett.: ἀπ' Byz.
16 εὖ δὲ τυχόντες Boeckh: εὖ δ(ὲ) ἔχοντες codd.

---

6 Olympia; the names recall the equestrian events (cf. *Ol.* 1.86–96).

7 Camarina.

8 Or *it*, the Hipparis River, implying that wood for building was transported on its canals.

Coming from the lovely abodes of Oenomaus and   Str. 2
     Pelops,[6]
O city-guarding Pallas, he sings of your holy sanctuary,   10
the river Oanus and the lake nearby,[7]

and the sacred canals, through which the Hipparis   Ant. 2
     waters the people,
and he[8] quickly welds a towering grove of sturdy
     dwellings,
bringing this community of townsmen from helplessness
     to light.

Always do toil and expense strive for achievements   Ep. 2
     toward
an accomplishment hidden in danger, but those who   16
     succeed
   are considered wise even by their fellow citizens.

Savior Zeus in the clouds on high, you who inhabit   Str. 3
     Cronus' hill,
and honor the broad-flowing Alpheus and the sacred
     cave of Ida,[9]
as your suppliant I come, calling to the sound of Lydian
     pipes,

[9] The scholia report a cave of Ida near Olympia, but the most famous was on Mt. Ida in Crete.

20 αἰτήσων πόλιν εὐανορίαισι τάνδε κλυταῖς
     δαιδάλλειν, σέ τ’, Ὀλυμπιόνικε, Ποσειδανίοισιν
          ἵπποις
     ἐπιτερπόμενον φέρειν γῆρας εὔθυμον ἐς τελευτάν

     υἱῶν, Ψαῦμι, παρισταμένων. ὑγίεντα δ’ εἴ τις ὄλβον
          ἄρδει,
     ἐξαρκέων κτεάτεσσι καὶ εὐλογίαν
          προστιθείς, μὴ ματεύσῃ θεὸς γενέσθαι.

to ask that you embellish this city with famous feats of courage,   Ant. 3

and that you, Olympic victor, while delighting in Poseidon's horses   21

may carry to the end a cheerful old age,

Psaumis, with your sons about you. If a man fosters a sound prosperity   Ep. 3

by having sufficient possessions and adding
    praise thereto, let him not seek to become a god.

OLYMPIAN 6

Hagesias, son of Sostratus, was apparently a close associate of Hieron and a prominent Syracusan, but his family lived in Stymphalus in Arcadia, and it was evidently there that this ode was first performed. From his father's side Hagesias inherited the prophetic gifts of the family of the Iamidae and the position of custodial priest of the prophetic altar of Zeus at Olympia. In one of his most celebrated narratives, Pindar tells of the birth of the family's founder, Iamus, whose father was Apollo. From his mother's side, Hagesias inherited Arcadian martial and athletic prowess. Pindar hopes that Hagesias will enjoy a warm welcome from Hieron (who is highly praised) when he arrives in Syracuse. The most probable dates for the victory are 472 or 468, during the latter years of Hieron's reign. Unfortunately, P. Oxy. 222 provides no confirmation since it does not list victors in the mule race.

Pindar opens by comparing his poem to a splendid palace and his introduction to a porch with golden columns (1–4). He sketches Hagesias' achievements: Olympic victor, steward of Zeus' altar at Olympia, and a founder of Syracuse (4–9). The gnomic observation that only deeds achieved through risk and toil are memorable leads to Adrastus' praise of the dead Amphiaraus as a good seer and fighter (9–21).

Pindar orders Phintis (presumably Hagesias' driver) to yoke the victorious mules to his chariot of song so that they can drive to Laconian Pitana to celebrate Hagesias' ancestry (22–28). The nymph Pitana secretly bore Poseidon's child Euadne and sent her to Aepytus of Elis to raise. When she was grown, Euadne had intercourse with Apollo, and while the angry Aepytus was in Delphi inquiring about her pregnancy, she bore a boy in a thicket, where he was fed by snakes (29–47). After Aepytus' return, the boy remained hidden in the wilds among violets (ἴα), for which his mother named him Iamus (48–57).

When Iamus became a young man, he went at night into the Alpheus River and prayed to his grandfather Poseidon and father Apollo that he might gain honor as a leader (57–61). Apollo's voice led him to Olympia, where he granted him the gift of prophecy and made his family (the Iamidae) custodians of Zeus' altar there. Since that time they have been celebrated throughout Hellas (61–74). After stating that victory in equestrian competitions is especially subject to envy (74–76), the poet observes that Hagesias' athletic success stems from the men in Arcadia on his mother's side, who have gained the favor of Hermes and Zeus through their piety (77–81).

Pindar claims personal ties with the city of Stymphalus, since Metope, the mother of Thebe (the eponymous nymph of Thebes), came from there (82–87). He orders Aeneas, probably the chorus trainer, to celebrate Hera and to show how sophisticated they are (in spite of being Boeotians) by praising Syracuse and its king Hieron. Pindar prays that Hieron's happiness may continue and that he may welcome this celebratory revel when it arrives from Arcadia (87–100). A concluding prayer expresses the hope that both Stymphalians and Syracusans may enjoy a glorious destiny and that Poseidon will provide a safe voyage for the poem (101–105).

6. ΑΓΗΣΙΑΙ ΣΤΡΑΚΟΣΙΩΙ

ΑΠΗΝΗΙ

Α΄   Χρυσέας ὑποστάσαντες εὐ-
      τειχεῖ προθύρῳ θαλάμου
   κίονας ὡς ὅτε θαητὸν μέγαρον
   πάξομεν· ἀρχομένου δ᾽ ἔργου πρόσωπον
   χρὴ θέμεν τηλαυγές. εἰ δ᾽ εἴ-
      η μὲν Ὀλυμπιονίκας,
5 βωμῷ τε μαντείῳ ταμίας Διὸς ἐν Πίσᾳ,
   συνοικιστήρ τε τᾶν κλεινᾶν Συρακοσ-
      σᾶν, τίνα κεν φύγοι ὕμνον
   κεῖνος ἀνήρ, ἐπικύρσαις
      ἀφθόνων ἀστῶν ἐν ἱμερταῖς ἀοιδαῖς;

   ἴστω γὰρ ἐν τούτῳ πεδί-
      λῳ δαιμόνιον πόδ᾽ ἔχων
   Σωστράτου υἱός. ἀκίνδυνοι δ᾽ ἀρεταί
10 οὔτε παρ᾽ ἀνδράσιν οὔτ᾽ ἐν ναυσὶ κοίλαις

102

6. FOR HAGESIAS OF SYRACUSE

WINNER, MULE RACE, 472/468 B.C.

Let us set up golden columns to support   Str. 1
   the strong-walled porch of our abode
and construct, as it were, a splendid
palace; for when a work is begun, it is necessary to make
its front shine from afar. If someone should be
   an Olympic victor,
and steward of the prophetic altar of Zeus at Pisa,   5
and fellow-founder[1] of famous Syracuse,
   what hymn of praise could he escape,
a man such as that, if he finds his townsmen
   ungrudging in the midst of delightful songs?

Let the son of Sostratus[2] be assured   Ant. 1
   that he has his blessed foot
in such a sandal. Achievements without risk
win no honor among men or on hollow ships,   10

---

[1] "Fellow-founder" is a poetic exaggeration. According to the scholia Hagesias' Iamid ancestors settled Syracuse with Archias (cf. Thuc. 6.3.2).

[2] Hagesias.

τίμιαι· πολλοὶ δὲ μέμναν-
   ται, καλὸν εἴ τι ποναθῇ.
Ἀγησία, τὶν δ' αἶνος ἑτοῖμος, ὃν ἐν δίκᾳ
ἀπὸ γλώσσας Ἄδραστος μάντιν Οἰκλεί-
   δαν ποτ' ἐς Ἀμφιάρηον
φθέγξατ', ἐπεὶ κατὰ γαῖ' αὐ-
   τόν τέ νιν καὶ φαιδίμας ἵππους ἔμαρψεν.

15   ἑπτὰ δ' ἔπειτα πυρᾶν νε-
   κρῶν τελεσθέντων Ταλαϊονίδας
εἶπεν ἐν Θήβαισι τοιοῦτόν τι ἔπος·
   "Ποθέω στρατιᾶς ὀφθαλμὸν ἐμᾶς
ἀμφότερον μάντιν τ' ἀγαθὸν καὶ
   δουρὶ μάρνασθαι." τὸ καί
ἀνδρὶ κώμου δεσπότᾳ πάρεστι Συρακοσίῳ.
οὔτε δύσηρις ἐὼν οὔτ' ὦν φιλόνικος ἄγαν,
20   καὶ μέγαν ὅρκον ὀμόσσαις τοῦτό γέ οἱ σαφέως
μαρτυρήσω· μελίφθογγοι δ' ἐπιτρέψοντι Μοῖσαι.

Β΄   ὦ Φίντις, ἀλλὰ ζεῦξον ἤ-
   δη μοι σθένος ἡμιόνων,
ᾇ τάχος, ὄφρα κελεύθῳ τ' ἐν καθαρᾷ
βάσομεν ὄκχον, ἵκωμαί τε πρὸς ἀνδρῶν
25   καὶ γένος· κεῖναι γὰρ ἐξ ἀλ-
   λᾶν ὁδὸν ἁγεμονεῦσαι

15 νεκροῖς Wilamowitz | τελεσθεισᾶν Pauw
19 φιλόνικος Cobet: φιλόνεικος codd.

104

but many remember
    if a noble deed is accomplished with toil.
Hagesias, the praise stands ready for you
that Adrastus once justly proclaimed aloud
    about the seer Amphiaraus, son of Oecles,
when the earth had swallowed up the man himself
    and his shining steeds.

Afterwards, when the corpses of the seven funeral pyres   Ep. 1
    had been consumed,[3] Talaus' son[4]
spoke a word such as this at Thebes: 16
    "I dearly miss the eye of my army,
good both as a seer and at fighting
    with the spear." This is true as well
for the man from Syracuse who is master of the revel.
Though not quarrelsome nor one too fond of victory, yet
I shall swear a great oath and bear clear witness for him   20
that this at least is so; and the honey-voiced Muses will
        assist.

O Phintis,[5] come yoke at once   Str. 2
    the strong mules for me,
as quickly as possible, so that we may drive our chariot
on a clear path and I may come to his family's
very lineage, because those mules beyond all others   25
    know how to lead the way

[3] These are apparently pyres for each of the seven contingents
led by Adrastus against Thebes.
[4] Adrastus.
[5] The driver of the mule team (schol.).

ταύταν ἐπίστανται, στεφάνους ἐν Ὀλυμπίᾳ
ἐπεὶ δέξαντο· χρὴ τοίνυν πύλας ὕ-
μνων ἀναπιτνάμεν αὐταῖς·
πρὸς Πιτάναν δὲ παρ' Εὐρώ-
τα πόρον δεῖ σάμερον ἐλθεῖν ἐν ὥρᾳ·

ἅ τοι Ποσειδάωνι μι-
χθεῖσα Κρονίῳ λέγεται
30   παῖδα ἰόπλοκον Εὐάδναν τεκέμεν.
κρύψε δὲ παρθενίαν ὠδῖνα κόλποις·
κυρίῳ δ' ἐν μηνὶ πέμποισ'
ἀμφιπόλους ἐκέλευσεν
ἥρωι πορσαίνειν δόμεν Εἰλατίδᾳ βρέφος,
ὃς ἀνδρῶν Ἀρκάδων ἄνασσε Φαισά-
να, λάχε τ' Ἀλφεὸν οἰκεῖν·
35   ἔνθα τραφεῖσ' ὑπ' Ἀπόλλω-
νι γλυκείας πρῶτον ἔψαυσ' Ἀφροδίτας.

οὐδ' ἔλαθ' Αἴπυτον ἐν παν-
τὶ χρόνῳ κλέπτοισα θεοῖο γόνον.
ἀλλ' ὁ μὲν Πυθῶνάδ', ἐν θυμῷ πιέσαις
χόλον οὐ φατὸν ὀξείᾳ μελέτᾳ,
ᾤχετ' ἰὼν μαντευσόμενος ταύ-
τας περ' ἀτλάτου πάθας.
ἁ δὲ φοινικόκροκον ζώναν καταθηκαμένα
40   κάλπιδά τ' ἀργυρέαν λόχμας ὑπὸ κυανέας

on that road, for they won crowns
at Olympia. Therefore we must throw open
    for them the gates of song,
for today it is necessary to go to Pitana
    by the course of the Eurotas in good time;

she,[6] they say,	Ant. 2

    lay with Cronus' son Poseidon
and bore a daughter, Euadne of the violet hair.   30
But she hid her maidenly birth pain in the folds of her
      robe,
and, when the appointed month came, sent her servants
    with instructions
to give the child to the care of the hero, Elatus' son,[7]
who ruled over the men of Arcadia at Phaesana
    and had his allotted home on the Alpheus.
She was brought up there and in submission to Apollo   35
    first experienced sweet Aphrodite.

She could not conceal from Aepytus forever	Ep. 2

    that she was hiding the god's offspring.
But he went to Pytho, suppressing the unspeakable anger
    in his heart with stern discipline,
to obtain an oracle concerning
    that unbearable calamity.
She, though, laid down her crimson girdle
and silver pitcher under a dark thicket and began to bear   40

[6] Pitana, the city's eponymous nymph.
[7] Aepytus.

τίκτε θεόφρονα κοῦρον. τᾷ μὲν ὁ χρυσοκόμας
πραΰμητίν τ᾽ Ἐλείθυιαν παρέστασέν τε Μοίρας·

Γ' ἦλθεν δ᾽ ὑπὸ σπλάγχνων ὑπ᾽ ὠ-
δῖνός τ᾽ ἐρατᾶς Ἴαμος
ἐς φάος αὐτίκα. τὸν μὲν κνιζομένα
45 λεῖπε χαμαί· δύο δὲ γλαυκῶπες αὐτόν
δαιμόνων βουλαῖσιν ἐθρέ-
ψαντο δράκοντες ἀμεμφεῖ
ἰῷ μελισσᾶν καδόμενοι. βασιλεὺς δ᾽ ἐπεί
πετραέσσας ἐλαύνων ἵκετ᾽ ἐκ Πυ-
θῶνος, ἅπαντας ἐν οἴκῳ
εἴρετο παῖδα, τὸν Εὐά-
δνα τέκοι· Φοίβου γὰρ αὐτὸν φᾶ γεγάκειν

50 πατρός, περὶ θνατῶν δ᾽ ἔσεσθαι μάντιν ἐπιχθονίοις
ἔξοχον, οὐδέ ποτ᾽ ἐκλείψειν γενεάν.
ὣς ἄρα μάννε. τοὶ δ᾽ οὔτ᾽ ὦν ἀκοῦσαι
οὔτ᾽ ἰδεῖν εὔχοντο πεμπται-
ον γεγενημένον. ἀλλ᾽ ἐν
κέκρυπτο γὰρ σχοίνῳ βατιᾷ τ᾽ ἐν ἀπειρίτῳ,
55 ἴων ξανθαῖσι καὶ παμπορφύροις ἀ-
κτῖσι βεβρεγμένος ἁβρόν

42 παρέστασέν codd.: παρέστασ᾽ ἔν Peek
43 ὠδῖνός τ᾽ ἐρατᾶς (τ᾽ om. A) codd.: ὠδίνεσσ᾽ ἐραταῖς
Wilamowitz
54 βατιᾷ Wilamowitz: βατείᾳ vett.: βατίᾳ recc.

a divinely inspired boy. To aid her, the golden-haired
god[8] sent gentle-counseling Eleithyia[9] and the Fates,

and from her womb amid the welcome   Str. 3
   birth pains Iamus
came immediately into the light. In her distress
she had to leave him on the ground, but two gray-eyed   45
serpents tended him through the gods' designs
   and nourished him with the blameless
venom of bees.[10] But when the king
arrived after driving from rocky Pytho,
   he questioned everyone in the house
about the child whom Euadne
   bore, for Phoebus, he said, was his

father, and he would become foremost of mortals   Ant. 3
as a seer for mankind, and his lineage would never fail.   51
Such did he declare to them, but they vowed
not to have seen or heard of him,
   although it was the fifth day since his birth. But in fact,
he had been hidden in a bed of reeds within a vast
      thicket,
while his tender body was bathed   55
   by the golden and purple rays

[8] Apollo.
[9] The goddess of childbirth (cf. *Nem.* 7.1–6).
[10] A kenning for "honey" (cf. *Pyth.* 6.54).

109

PINDAR

σῶμα· τὸ καὶ κατεφάμι-
ξεν καλεῖσθαί νιν χρόνῳ σύμπαντι μάτηρ

τοῦτ' ὄνυμ' ἀθάνατον. τερ-
πνᾶς δ' ἐπεὶ χρυσοστεφάνοιο λάβεν
καρπὸν Ἥβας, Ἀλφεῷ μέσσῳ καταβαὶς
ἐκάλεσσε Ποσειδᾶν' εὐρυβίαν,
ὃν πρόγονον, καὶ τοξοφόρον Δά-
λου θεοδμάτας σκοπόν,
60 αἰτέων λαοτρόφον τιμάν τιν' ἑᾷ κεφαλᾷ,
νυκτὸς ὑπαίθριος. ἀντεφθέγξατο δ' ἀρτιεπὴς
πατρία ὄσσα, μετάλλασέν τέ νιν. "Ὄρσο, τέκνον,
δεῦρο πάγκοινον ἐς χώραν ἴμεν φάμας ὄπισθεν."

Δ´ ἵκοντο δ' ὑψηλοῖο πέ-
τραν ἀλίβατον Κρονίου
65 ἔνθα οἱ ὤπασε θησαυρὸν δίδυμον
μαντοσύνας, τόκα μὲν φωνὰν ἀκούειν
ψευδέων ἄγνωτον, εὖτ' ἂν
δὲ θρασυμάχανος ἐλθὼν
Ἡρακλέης, σεμνὸν θάλος Ἀλκαϊδᾶν, πατρί
ἑορτάν τε κτίσῃ πλειστόμβροτον τε-
θμόν τε μέγιστον ἀέθλων,
70 Ζηνὸς ἐπ' ἀκροτάτῳ βω-
μῷ τότ' αὖ χρηστήριον θέσθαι κέλευσεν.

---

11 A play on ἴα (violets) and Ἴαμος. The word ἰός (47)
"venom" also plays on the name Iamus.

of violets. That was why his mother declared
  that for all time he would be called

by that immortal name.[11] And when he had plucked   Ep. 3
  the fruit of delightful golden-crowned
Hebe,[12] he went down into the middle of the Alpheus
  and called upon widely ruling Poseidon,
his grandfather, and upon the bow-wielding watcher
  over god-built Delos,
and under the nighttime sky asked for himself some   60
    office
that would serve his people. The clear-speaking voice
of his father responded and sought him out: "Arise, my
    son,
and follow my voice here to a land shared by all."

And so they came to the steep rock   Str. 4
  of Cronus' lofty hill,
where he gave him a twofold treasury   65
of prophecy, first to hear the voice
that knows no falsehood, and later, when bold
  and resourceful Heracles,
the honored offspring of the Alcaïdae,[13] should come
to found for his father[14] a festival thronged by people
  and the greatest institution of games,
then it was that he ordered him to establish his oracle   70
  on the summit of Zeus' altar.

[12] Hebe is "Youth"; i.e. when he grew into a young man.
[13] Amphitryon, Heracles' titular father, was the son of
Alcaeus.   [14] Zeus.

ἐξ οὗ πολύκλειτον καθ᾽ Ἑλ-
λανας γένος Ἰαμιδᾶν·
ὄλβος ἅμ᾽ ἕσπετο· τιμῶντες δ᾽ ἀρετάς
ἐς φανερὰν ὁδὸν ἔρχονται· τεκμαίρει
χρῆμ᾽ ἕκαστον· μῶμος ἐξ ἄλ-
λων κρέμαται φθονεόντων
75 τοῖς, οἷς ποτε πρώτοις περὶ δωδέκατον δρόμον
ἐλαυνόντεσσιν αἰδοία ποτιστά-
ξῃ Χάρις εὐκλέα μορφάν.
εἰ δ᾽ ἐτύμως ὑπὸ Κυλλά-
νας ὄρος, Ἁγησία, μάτρωες ἄνδρες

ναιετάοντες ἐδώρη-
σαν θεῶν κάρυκα λιταῖς θυσίαις
πολλὰ δὴ πολλαῖσιν Ἑρμᾶν εὐσεβέως,
ὃς ἀγῶνας ἔχει μοῖράν τ᾽ ἀέθλων,
80 Ἀρκαδίαν τ᾽ εὐάνορα τιμᾷ·
κεῖνος, ὦ παῖ Σωστράτου,
σὺν βαρυγδούπῳ πατρὶ κραίνει σέθεν εὐτυχίαν.
δόξαν ἔχω τιν᾽ ἐπὶ γλώσσᾳ λιγυρᾶς ἀκόνας,
ἅ μ᾽ ἐθέλοντα προσέρπει καλλιρόαισι πνοαῖς.

74 μῶμος ἐξ Boeckh: μῶμος δ᾽ ἐξ codd.
77 ὄρος Π¹: ὄροις codd.
82 λιγυρᾶς ἀκόνας Bergk: ἀκόνας λιγυρᾶς codd.
83 προσέρπει vett.: προσέλκοι Ε^{γρ}: προσέλκει G^{γρ}Η^{γρ},
Triclinius

112

Since then has the race of the Iamidae been   Ant. 4
    much renowned among Hellenes.
Prosperity attended them, and by esteeming virtuous deeds
they travel along a conspicuous road;[15] everything they do
confirms this. But blame coming from
    others who are envious hangs over
those who ever drive first around the twelve-lap course   75
and on whom revered Charis sheds
    a glorious appearance.
If truly the men on your mother's side, Hagesias,
    who dwell beneath Mt. Cyllene,[16]

have regaled the herald of the gods   Ep. 4
    with prayerful sacrifices
again and again in pious fashion, Hermes,
    who has charge of contests and the awarding of prizes
and who honors Arcadia's land of brave men,   80
    he it is, O son of Sostratus, who
with his loudly thundering father[17] fulfills your success.
Upon my tongue I have the sensation of a clear-sounding
       whetstone,
which I welcome as it comes over me with lovely
       streams of breath.[18]

[15] Cf. *Ol.* 2.53–56 for wealth adorned with virtues as a light for man.

[16] In Arcadia (cf. *Il.* 2.603: ὑπὸ Κυλλήνης ὄρος).

[17] Zeus.

[18] Pindar's tongue is sharpened to sing further, a bold metaphor for poetic inspiration. In what follows, he discovers a personal connection with his subject.

ματρομάτωρ ἐμὰ Στυμφαλίς, εὐανθὴς Μετώπα,

Ε΄ πλάξιππον ἃ Θήβαν ἔτι-
    κτεν, τᾶς ἐρατεινὸν ὕδωρ
86 πίομαι, ἀνδράσιν αἰχματαῖσι πλέκων
  ποικίλον ὕμνον. ὄτρυνον νῦν ἑταίρους,
  Αἰνέα, πρῶτον μὲν Ἥραν
    Παρθενίαν κελαδῆσαι,
  γνῶναί τ᾽ ἔπειτ᾽, ἀρχαῖον ὄνειδος ἀλαθέσιν
90 λόγοις εἰ φεύγομεν, Βοιωτίαν ὗν.
    ἐσσὶ γὰρ ἄγγελος ὀρθός,
  ἠυκόμων σκυτάλα Μοι-
    σᾶν, γλυκὺς κρατὴρ ἀγαφθέγκτων ἀοιδᾶν·

  εἶπον δὲ μεμνᾶσθαι Συρα-
    κοσσᾶν τε καὶ Ὀρτυγίας·
  τὰν Ἱέρων καθαρῷ σκάπτῳ διέπων,
  ἄρτια μηδόμενος, φοινικόπεζαν
95 ἀμφέπει Δάματρα λευκίπ-
    που τε θυγατρὸς ἑορτάν

---

19 The eponymous nymph of Lake Metope near Stymphalus. She married the Boeotian river Asopus and bore Thebe, the eponymous nymph of Thebes.

20 The trainer of the chorus (schol.).

21 For the worship of Hera as Maiden in Stymphalus, see Paus. 8.22.2.

22 The Boeotians were considered dull and rustic (cf. *fr*. 83),

My grandmother was Stymphalian, blooming Metope,[19]

who bore horse-driving Thebe,	Str. 5
whose lovely water	
I shall drink, as I weave for spearmen	86
my varied hymn. Now, Aeneas,[20] urge your companions	
first to celebrate	
Hera the Maiden,[21]	
and then to know if by our truthful words	
we escape the age-old taunt of "Boeotian pig,"[22]	90
for you are a true messenger,	
a message stick[23] of the fair-haired Muses,	
a sweet mixing bowl of loudly ringing songs.	

Tell them to remember Syracuse	Ant. 5
and Ortygia,[24]	
which Hieron administers with an unsullied scepter,	
as he devises fitting counsels, and is devoted to	
red-footed Demeter and the festival	95
of her daughter with the white horses,[25]	

especially by the Athenians (cf. Plato *Symp.* 182B and Plut. *de esu carnium* 1.6).

[23] The σκυτάλα was a Spartan message stick around which writing material was wound, inscribed, and cut into a strip. Only with a duplicate stick could the strip be correctly wound to reveal the message.

[24] Ortygia, a small island off the mainland, was the first part of Syracuse to be settled and remained its oldest quarter.

[25] The worship of Demeter and Core (Persephone) was prominent in Syracuse. It is not known why Demeter should be said to have a red foot; Hecate has the same epithet at *Pae.* 2.77, while at *Pyth.* 9.9 Aphrodite is silver-footed.

PINDAR

καὶ Ζηνὸς Αἰτναίου κράτος. ἀδύλογοι δέ νιν
λύραι μολπαί τε γινώσκοντι. μὴ θράσ-
   σοι χρόνος ὄλβον ἐφέρπων,
σὺν δὲ φιλοφροσύναις εὐ-
   ηράτοις Ἁγησία δέξαιτο κῶμον

οἴκοθεν οἴκαδ' ἀπὸ Στυμ-
   φαλίων τειχέων ποτινισόμενον,
100 ματέρ' εὐμήλοιο λείποντ' Ἀρκαδίας.
   ἀγαθαὶ δὲ πέλοντ' ἐν χειμερίᾳ
νυκτὶ θοᾶς ἐκ ναὸς ἀπεσκίμ-
   φθαι δύ' ἄγκυραι. θεός
τῶνδε κείνων τε κλυτὰν αἶσαν παρέχοι φιλέων.
δέσποτα ποντόμεδον, εὐθὺν δὲ πλόον καμάτων
ἐκτὸς ἐόντα δίδοι, χρυσαλακάτοιο πόσις
105 Ἀμφιτρίτας, ἐμῶν δ' ὕμνων ἄεξ' εὐτερπὲς ἄνθος.

97 θράσσοι Boeckh, Schneidewin: θραύσοι codd.

116

and to powerful Zeus of Aetna.[26] Sweetly speaking
lyres and songs know him. May approaching time
   not disrupt his happiness,
but with acts of loving friendship
   may he welcome Hagesias' revel band

as it proceeds from one home to another,   Ep. 5
   leaving the walls of Stymphalus,
the mother city of flock-rich Arcadia.   100
   On a stormy night it is good
for two anchors to have been cast
   from a swift ship. May the god
lovingly grant a glorious destiny for these and for them.[27]
Lordly ruler of the sea, vouchsafe a direct voyage
that is free from hardship, and, husband of golden-
      spindled
Amphitrite, cause my hymns' pleasing flower to burgeon.   105

[26] Worship of Aetnaean Zeus was especially significant for
Hieron because he had established the city of Aetna in 476/5. See
Pyth. 1, Introduction.
   [27] Stymphalians and Syracusans.

OLYMPIAN 7

Diagoras of Rhodes was probably the most famous boxer in antiquity. He himself was a *periodonikēs* (winner at all four major games), while three of his sons and two of his grandsons were Olympic victors. Their statues stood in Olympia (Paus. 6.7.1–2). Pindar provides extensive praise of the Rhodian traditions in a narrative triptych in ring composition that proceeds in reverse chronological order, beginning with the colonization by Tlapolemus, moving back to the institution of a fireless sacrifice to honor the newly born Athena, and concluding with the birth of the island itself from the depths of the sea as the favored land of Helius, the Sun god. These three episodes are linked by the fact that in each case a mistake resulted in benefits for the island and its people.

In an elaborate simile, Pindar compares his epinician poetry to the wine in a golden bowl with which a father toasts his new son-in-law (1–10). After observing that Charis (Grace, Charm) favors many men with celebratory song, Pindar announces that he has come to praise Rhodes (the island's eponymous nymph), Diagoras for his Olympic and Pythian boxing victories, and his father Damagetus (11–19), and states that he will give a true account of the Rhodians' ancestry from Heracles and Amyntor (20–24).

The poet introduces the narrative panels with a gnome:

the minds of men are beset by countless mistakes and one cannot know what will turn out best in the end (24–26). Tlapolemus slew his great-uncle Licymnius in anger and was told by Apollo to sail to the island of Rhodes where Zeus had sent down a snow of gold when Athena was born from his head (27–38). Helius enjoined his children to set up a ritual sacrifice to win the new goddess' favor, but they forgot to bring fire with them and so had to make a fireless sacrifice. As a result of their devotion, however, Zeus rained gold upon them, and Athena gave them unsurpassed artistic skill to produce lifelike sculptures (39–53).

Ancient tales relate that before Rhodes had appeared from the sea, Helius was absent while the gods were being allotted their lands and thus received no portion. Zeus proposed recasting the lots, but Helius requested Rhodes for his own when it should rise from the sea (54–69). When it did, Helius lay with the nymph Rhodes and fathered seven wise sons, one of whom begot three sons bearing the names of prominent Rhodian cities, Camirus, Ialysus, and Lindus (69–76).

The Rhodians continue to celebrate their founder Tlapolemus with festivities and athletic contests, in which Diagoras was twice victorious (77–81). An impressive catalog of his victories follows, culminating in the present one at Olympia (81–90). The poet praises the victor for his upright conduct, and mentions his clan, the Eratidae, and an ancestor Callianax (90–94). The poem concludes with a gnomic reminder of life's vicissitudes (94–95).

7. ΔΙΑΓΟΡΑΙ ΡΟΔΙΩΙ

ΠΥΚΤΗΙ

Α΄ Φιάλαν ὡς εἴ τις ἀφνειᾶς ἀπὸ χειρὸς ἑλὼν
   ἔνδον ἀμπέλου καχλάζοισαν δρόσῳ
   δωρήσεται
   νεανίᾳ γαμβρῷ προπίνων
      οἴκοθεν οἴκαδε, πάγχρυσον, κορυφὰν κτεάνων,
5 συμποσίου τε χάριν κᾶ-
      δός τε τιμάσαις ἑόν, ἐν δὲ φίλων
   παρεόντων θῆκέ νιν ζαλωτὸν ὁμόφρονος εὐνᾶς·

   καὶ ἐγὼ νέκταρ χυτόν, Μοισᾶν δόσιν, ἀεθλοφόροις
   ἀνδράσιν πέμπων, γλυκὺν καρπὸν φρενός,
   ἱλάσκομαι,
10 Ὀλυμπίᾳ Πυθοῖ τε νικών-
      τεσσιν· ὁ δ᾽ ὄλβιος, ὃν φᾶμαι κατέχοντ᾽ ἀγαθαί·
   ἄλλοτε δ᾽ ἄλλον ἐποπτεύ-
      ει Χάρις ζωθάλμιος ἁδυμελεῖ
   θαμὰ μὲν φόρμιγγι παμφώνοισί τ᾽ ἐν ἔντεσιν
      αὐλῶν.

5 ἑόν codd.: νέον Bergk   10 κατεχωντ Π²²

120

7. FOR DIAGORAS OF RHODES

WINNER, BOXING, 464 B.C.

As when a man takes from his rich hand a bowl[1]   Str. 1
foaming inside with dew of the vine
and presents it
to his young son-in-law with a toast from one home
    to another—an all-golden bowl, crown of
        possessions—
as he honors the joy of the symposium   5
    and his own alliance, and thereby with his friends
present makes him envied for his harmonious marriage,

so I too, by sending the poured nectar, gift of the Muses   Ant. 1
and sweet fruit of the mind, to men who win prizes,
gain the favor
of victors at Olympia and Pytho.   10
    Fortunate is the man who is held in good repute.
Charis, who makes life blossom, looks with favor
    now upon one man, now another, often with sweetly
singing lyre and pipes, instruments of every voice.

[1] A *phiale* was a shallow bowl used for drinking and for pouring libations.

PINDAR

καί νυν ὑπ' ἀμφοτέρων σὺν
  Διαγόρᾳ κατέβαν, τὰν ποντίαν
ὑμνέων παῖδ' Ἀφροδίτας
  Ἀελίοιό τε νύμφαν, Ῥόδον,
15 εὐθυμάχαν ὄφρα πελώριον ἄνδρα παρ' Ἀλ-
  φειῷ στεφανωσάμενον
αἰνέσω πυγμᾶς ἄποινα
  καὶ παρὰ Κασταλίᾳ, πα-
τέρα τε Δαμάγητον ἁδόντα Δίκᾳ,
Ἀσίας εὐρυχόρου τρίπολιν νᾶσον πέλας
ἐμβόλῳ ναίοντας Ἀργείᾳ σὺν αἰχμᾷ.

Β΄ ἐθελήσω τοῖσιν ἐξ ἀρχᾶς ἀπὸ Τλαπολέμου
21 ξυνὸν ἀγγέλλων διορθῶσαι λόγον,
  Ἡρακλέος
εὐρυσθενεῖ γέννᾳ. τὸ μὲν γὰρ
  πατρόθεν ἐκ Διὸς εὔχονται· τὸ δ' Ἀμυντορίδαι
ματρόθεν Ἀστυδαμείας.
  ἀμφὶ δ' ἀνθρώπων φρασὶν ἀμπλακίαι
25 ἀναρίθμητοι κρέμανται· τοῦτο δ' ἀμάχανον εὑρεῖν,

ὅ τι νῦν ἐν καὶ τελευτᾷ φέρτατον ἀνδρὶ τυχεῖν.
καὶ γὰρ Ἀλκμήνας κασίγνητον νόθον
σκάπτῳ θενών

122

And now, to the accompaniment of both,   Ep. 1
    I have disembarked with Diagoras, singing a hymn
to Rhodes of the sea, the child of Aphrodite
    and bride of Helius,
so that I may praise, in recompense for his boxing,   15
    that straight-fighting man of prodigious power,
who won a crown by the Alpheus
and at Castalia,[2] and may praise his father,
    Damagetus, who is favored by Justice;
they dwell on the island with its three cities near
to the jutting coast of broad Asia among Argive
        spearmen.

I intend, in proclaiming my message, to set forth truly   Str. 2
for them from its origin, beginning with Tlapolemus,   21
the history they share as members of Heracles'
mighty race, for they claim descent from Zeus
    on their father's side, while on their mother's
they are Amyntor's descendants through Astydameia.[3]
    But about the minds of humans hang
numberless errors, and it is impossible to discover   25

what now and also in the end is best to happen to a man.   Ant. 2
Thus it is that the founder of this land[4]
once struck

  [2] The spring at Delphi.
  [3] They trace their lineage to the marriage of Tlapolemus
(Heracles' son and Zeus' grandson) and Astydameia (Amyntor's
daughter). See genealogy of Tlapolemus in Appendix.
  [4] Tlapolemus (cf. *Il.* 2.653–670).

σκληρᾶς ἐλαίας ἔκτανεν Τί-
ρυνθι Λικύμνιον ἐλθόντ᾽ ἐκ θαλάμων Μιδέας
30 τᾶσδέ ποτε χθονὸς οἰκι-
στὴρ χολωθείς. αἱ δὲ φρενῶν ταραχαί
παρέπλαγξαν καὶ σοφόν. μαντεύσατο δ᾽ ἐς θεὸν
ἐλθών.

τῷ μὲν ὁ χρυσοκόμας εὐ-
ώδεος ἐξ ἀδύτου ναῶν πλόον
εἶπε Λερναίας ἀπ᾽ ἀκτᾶς
εὐθὺν ἐς ἀμφιθάλασσον νομόν,
ἔνθα ποτὲ βρέχε θεῶν βασιλεὺς ὁ μέγας
χρυσέαις νιφάδεσσι πόλιν,
35 ἁνίχ᾽ Ἁφαίστου τέχναισιν
χαλκελάτῳ πελέκει πα-
τέρος Ἀθαναία κορυφὰν κατ᾽ ἄκραν
ἀνορούσαισ᾽ ἀλάλαξεν ὑπερμάκει βοᾷ.
Οὐρανὸς δ᾽ ἔφριξέ νιν καὶ Γαῖα μάτηρ.

Γ´ τότε καὶ φαυσίμβροτος δαίμων Ὑπεριονίδας
40 μέλλον ἔντειλεν φυλάξασθαι χρέος
παισὶν φίλοις,

33 εὐθὺν Εγρ, Boeckh: εὔθυν᾽ ACE: εὐθῦν᾽ B: εὐθὺν et
εὐθῦν(αι) vel εὔθυν(ε) schol.

---

5 Son of Alcmene's father Electryon and his concubine Midea
(from a town in Argos of the same name). See Appendix.

Alcmene's bastard brother Licymnius[5]
    with a staff of hard olive in Tiryns
when he came from Midea's[6] chambers and killed him   30
    in a fit of anger. Disturbances of the mind
lead astray even a wise man. He went to the god[7] for an
        oracle,

and from the fragrant inner sanctum of his temple   Ep. 2
    the golden-haired god
told him to sail from the shore of Lerna
    straight to the seagirt pasture,
where once the great king of the gods[8] showered
    the city with snows of gold,
when, by the skills of Hephaestus   35
with the stroke of a bronze-forged axe,[9]
    Athena sprang forth on the top of her father's head
and shouted a prodigious battle cry,
and Heaven shuddered at her, and mother Earth.

At that time Hyperion's son,[10] divine bringer of light   Str. 3
to mortals, charged his dear children[11]   40
    to observe the obligation that was to come,

[6] Either Licymnius' mother or the city near Tiryns, where
Electryon was king (cf. *Ol.* 10.66). Homer (*Il.* 2.661–663) gives no
reason for the killing; Diod. Sic. 4.58.7 reports that they were
quarreling; Apollod. 2.8.2 says that it was an accident.
    [7] Apollo.   [8] Zeus.
    [9] To allow Athena to emerge, Hephaestus struck Zeus' head
with an axe.
    [10] Helius.
    [11] The Heliadae, his children on Rhodes (cf. 71–76).

ὡς ἂν θεᾷ πρῶτοι κτίσαιεν
βωμὸν ἐναργέα, καὶ σεμνὰν θυσίαν θέμενοι
πατρί τε θυμὸν ἰάναι-
εν κόρᾳ τ᾽ ἐγχειβρόμῳ. ἐν δ᾽ ἀρετάν
ἔβαλεν καὶ χάρματ᾽ ἀνθρώποισι προμαθέος αἰδώς·

45 ἐπὶ μὰν βαίνει τι καὶ λάθας ἀτέκμαρτα νέφος,
καὶ παρέλκει πραγμάτων ὀρθὰν ὁδόν
ἔξω φρενῶν.
καὶ τοὶ γὰρ αἰθοίσας ἔχοντες
σπέρμ᾽ ἀνέβαν φλογὸς οὔ· τεῦξαν δ᾽ ἀπύροις
ἱεροῖς
ἄλσος ἐν ἀκροπόλει. κεί-
νοις ὁ μὲν ξανθὰν ἀγαγὼν νεφέλαν
50 πολὺν ὗσε χρυσόν· αὐτὰ δέ σφισιν ὤπασε τέχναν

πᾶσαν ἐπιχθονίων Γλαυκ-
ῶπις ἀριστοπόνοις χερσὶ κρατεῖν.
ἔργα δὲ ζωοῖσιν ἑρπόν-
τεσσί θ᾽ ὁμοῖα κέλευθοι φέρον·

49 κείνοις ὁ μὲν Mingarelli: κείνοισι μὲν codd. | νεφέλαν
Byz.: νεφέλαν Ζεύς vett.

126

that they might be the first to build for the goddess
  an altar in full view, and by making
a sacred sacrifice might cheer the hearts of the father
  and his daughter of the thundering spear. Reverence[12]
for one who has foresight plants excellence and its joys
    in humans,

but without warning some cloud of forgetfulness comes   Ant. 3
    upon them
and wrests the straight path of affairs   46
from their minds.
Thus it was that they made their ascent without taking
  the seed of blazing flame, and with fireless sacrifices
they made a sanctuary on the acropolis.[13]
  He[14] brought a yellow cloud and upon them
rained gold in abundance; but the Gray-eyed Goddess   50

herself gave them every kind of skill to surpass mortals   Ep. 3
  with their superlative handiwork.
Their streets bore works of art in the likeness of beings
  that lived and moved,

[12] Some editors personify the terms: *Reverence, daughter of
Foresight*.
[13] Of Lindus, where a temple to Athena stood, and in which,
according to a schol., this ode, written in gold letters, was dedi-
cated.
[14] Zeus.

PINDAR

ἦν δὲ κλέος βαθύ. δαέντι δὲ καὶ σοφία
    μείζων ἄδολος τελέθει.
φαντὶ δ᾽ ἀνθρώπων παλαιαὶ
55 ῥήσιες, οὔπω, ὅτε χθό-
    να δατέοντο Ζεύς τε καὶ ἀθάνατοι,
φανερὰν ἐν πελάγει Ῥόδον ἔμμεν ποντίῳ,
ἁλμυροῖς δ᾽ ἐν βένθεσιν νᾶσον κεκρύφθαι.

Δ΄ ἀπεόντος δ᾽ οὔτις ἔνδειξεν λάχος Ἀελίου·
    καί ῥά νιν χώρας ἀκλάρωτον λίπον,
60 ἁγνὸν θεόν.
    μνασθέντι δὲ Ζεὺς ἄμπαλον μέλ-
    λεν θέμεν. ἀλλά νιν οὐκ εἴασεν· ἐπεὶ πολιᾶς
εἶπέ τιν᾽ αὐτὸς ὁρᾶν ἔν-
    δον θαλάσσας αὐξομέναν πεδόθεν
πολύβοσκον γαῖαν ἀνθρώποισι καὶ εὔφρονα μήλοις.

ἐκέλευσεν δ᾽ αὐτίκα χρυσάμπυκα μὲν Λάχεσιν
65 χεῖρας ἀντεῖναι, θεῶν δ᾽ ὅρκον μέγαν
    μὴ παρφάμεν,
    ἀλλὰ Κρόνου σὺν παιδὶ νεῦσαι,
    φαεννὸν ἐς αἰθέρα νιν πεμφθεῖσαν ἑᾷ κεφαλᾷ

---

15 I interpret this controversial sentence to mean that Athena added skill (τέχναν, 50) to their native talent, so that they combined natural wisdom (σοφία ἄδολος) and expertise (δαέντι); cf.

and great was their fame. When one is expert,
    even native talent becomes greater.[15]
The ancient reports of men
tell that when Zeus and the immortals   55
    were apportioning the earth,
Rhodes had not yet appeared in the expanse of the sea,
but the island lay hidden in the salty depths.

Since he was absent, no one designated a lot for Helius,   Str. 4
and thus they left him with no portion of land,
although he was a holy god.   60
And when he spoke of it, Zeus was about to recast
    the lots for him, but he would not allow it, because
he said that he himself could see a land
    rising from the floor of the gray sea
that would be bountiful for men and favorable for flocks.

He immediately ordered Lachesis of the golden   Ant. 4
        headband
to raise her hands and not to forswear   65
the mighty oath of the gods,
but to consent with Cronus' son
    that once it had arisen into the bright air

D. C. Young, *American Journal of Philology* 108 (1987) 152–157,
who aptly quotes Horace, *Odes* 4.4.33: *doctrina sed vim promovet
insitam*. Others translate it as "to the expert even greater skill is
free from guile" and see here a defense of the Telchines, mythical
inhabitants of Rhodes skilled in metal working (cf. Diod. Sic. 5.55
and Strabo 14.2.7), against charges of wizardry.

ἐξοπίσω γέρας ἔσσε-
σθαι. τελεύταθεν δὲ λόγων κορυφαί
ἐν ἀλαθείᾳ πετοῖσαι· βλάστε μὲν ἐξ ἁλὸς ὑγρᾶς

70 νᾶσος, ἔχει τέ νιν ὀξει-
αν ὁ γενέθλιος ἀκτίνων πατήρ,
πῦρ πνεόντων ἀρχὸς ἵππων·
ἔνθα Ῥόδῳ ποτὲ μιχθεὶς τέκεν
ἑπτὰ σοφώτατα νοήματ' ἐπὶ προτέρων
ἀνδρῶν παραδεξαμένους
παῖδας, ὧν εἷς μὲν Κάμιρον
πρεσβύτατόν τε Ἰάλυ-
σον ἔτεκεν Λίνδον τ'· ἀπάτερθε δ' ἔχον,

75 διὰ γαῖαν τρίχα δασσάμενοι πατρωίαν,
ἀστέων μοῖραν, κέκληνται δέ σφιν ἕδραι.

Ε´ τόθι λύτρον συμφορᾶς οἰκτρᾶς γλυκὺ Τλαπολέμῳ
ἵσταται Τιρυνθίων ἀρχαγέτᾳ,
ὥσπερ θεῷ,

80 μήλων τε κνισάεσσα πομπὰ
καὶ κρίσις ἀμφ' ἀέθλοις. τῶν ἄνθεσι Διαγόρας
ἐστεφανώσατο δίς, κλει-
νᾷ τ' ἐν Ἰσθμῷ τετράκις εὐτυχέων,
Νεμέᾳ τ' ἄλλαν ἐπ' ἄλλᾳ, καὶ κρανααῖς ἐν Ἀθάναις.

68 τελεύταθεν Β^{γρ}Β^{l}C^{l}E^{l}: τελεύτασαν codd.
74 ἔχον A: ἔχοντι ζβ: ἔχοντα B
76 μοίρας Meineke

130

it would henceforth remain a possession of honor
    for himself. The essential points of these words
fell in with truth and were fulfilled. The island grew

from the watery sea and belongs to the father   Ep. 4
    who engenders the piercing sunbeams,
the master of the fire-breathing horses.   71
    There at a later time he lay with Rhodes and fathered
seven sons who inherited the wisest thoughts
    among men of old,
one of whom sired Camirus,
and Ialysus the eldest,
    and Lindus. They divided
their inherited land into three parts and separately held   75
their allotment of cities, places that still bear their
        names.[16]

There, in sweet recompense for the lamentable mishap,   Str. 5
is established for Tlapolemus, the Tirynthians' colony-
        founder,
as if for a god,
a procession of rich sacrificial flocks and the judging   80
    of athletic contests, with whose flowers Diagoras
has twice crowned himself. Four times did he succeed
    at the famous Isthmus,
and time after time at Nemea and in rocky Athens.

[16] The three main cities on Rhodes (cf. τρίπολιν, 18).

ὅ τ᾽ ἐν Ἄργει χαλκὸς ἔγνω νιν, τά τ᾽ ἐν Ἀρκαδίᾳ
ἔργα καὶ Θήβαις, ἀγῶνές τ᾽ ἔννομοι
85 Βοιωτίων,
Πελλανά τ᾽ Αἴγινά τε νικῶνθ᾽
   ἑξάκις· ἐν Μεγάροισίν τ᾽ οὐχ ἕτερον λιθίνα
ψᾶφος ἔχει λόγον. ἀλλ᾽ ὦ
   Ζεῦ πάτερ, νώτοισιν Ἀταβυρίου
μεδέων, τίμα μὲν ὕμνου τεθμὸν Ὀλυμπιονίκαν,

ἄνδρα τε πὺξ ἀρετὰν εὑ-
   ρόντα, δίδοι τέ οἱ αἰδοίαν χάριν
90 καὶ ποτ᾽ ἀστῶν καὶ ποτὶ ξεί-
   νων· ἐπεὶ ὕβριος ἐχθρὰν ὁδὸν
εὐθυπορεῖ, σάφα δαεὶς ἅ τε οἱ πατέρων
   ὀρθαὶ φρένες ἐξ ἀγαθῶν
ἔχρεον. μὴ κρύπτε κοινόν
   σπέρμ᾽ ἀπὸ Καλλιάνακτος·
Ἐρατιδᾶν τοι σὺν χαρίτεσσιν ἔχει
θαλίας καὶ πόλις· ἐν δὲ μιᾷ μοίρᾳ χρόνου
95 ἄλλοτ᾽ ἀλλοῖαι διαιθύσσοισιν αὖραι.

86 πελλάνα τ᾽ αἴγινά τε A(C)OLH: πελλάνᾳ τ᾽ αἰγίνᾳ τε
(N)BEG: Πέλλανά τ᾽· Αἰγίνᾳ τε Boeckh
92 ἔχρεον A: ἔχραον a

The bronze[17] in Argos came to know him, as did the   Ant. 5
    works
of art[18] in Arcadia and Thebes, and the duly ordered
    games
of the Boeotians   85
and Pellana; and Aegina knew him victorious
    six times, while in Megara the record in stone
tells no other tale. But, O
    father Zeus, you who rule Atabyrion's[19]
slopes, honor the hymn ordained for an Olympic victory

and the man who has won success at boxing,   Ep. 5
    and grant him respectful favor
from both townsmen and foreigners,   90
    for he travels straight down a road
that abhors insolence, having clearly learned
    what an upright mind inherited from noble forebears
declared to him. Keep not in obscurity the lineage
they share from the time of Callianax,[20]
    for at the celebrations of the Eratidae
the city too holds festivals. But in a single portion of time
the winds shift rapidly now here, now there.   95

[17] A shield given as prize.
[18] Probably tripods.
[19] The highest mountain on Rhodes, on which was a temple
of Zeus (cf. Strabo 10.454 and 14.655).
[20] A forebear of Diagoras (schol.).

OLYMPIAN 8

This is the one Olympian ode to a victor from Aegina, the island city for which Pindar composed more odes than for any other place. Alcimedon, a member of the Blepsiad clan, won the boys' wrestling, probably in 460. Aegina boasted a rich mythological tradition associated with Aeacus and his sons (see genealogy of Aeacus in Appendix), four generations of whom were involved with Troy. Aeacus helped build its wall, Telamon was the first to sack it, Achilles and Ajax attacked it a second time, and Neoptolemus ultimately destroyed it. Pindar perhaps intends us to see a similar pattern in Alcimedon's family that culminates in his Olympic victory.

Zeus, the patron god of the clan, figures prominently in the ode (3, 16, 21, 43, and 83). Because of the invocation of Olympia, many commentators have supposed that the ode was composed immediately after the victory and performed at Olympia, but the words "this island" (25) and "here" (51) indicate that it was performed on Aegina. The praise of Melesias is the most extensive tribute to a trainer in the odes.

Pindar invokes Olympia as the site of divination for aspiring athletes and requests that she welcome the present victory celebration (1–11). A summary priamel sketches the variety of human successes and singles out

134

Timosthenes (presumably the victor's brother) for his victory at Nemea and Alcimedon for his Olympic victory (12–20). Aegina is then praised for its worship of Zeus Xenius, its fair dealing, and its hospitality to foreigners since the time of Aeacus (21–30). Poseidon and Apollo summoned Aeacus to help build Troy's wall because the city was destined to fall at the place where a mortal had constructed the defense. When the wall was finished, two snakes failed to scale it, but a third succeeded. Apollo interpreted the omen to mean that Troy would be taken by the first and fourth generations of Aeacus' children (31–46). Thereupon, Apollo went to the land of the Hyperboreans and Poseidon brought Aeacus to Aegina on his way to his Corinthian festival (46–52).

After observing that no one thing can please everyone, Pindar nonetheless expects that his forthcoming praise of Melesias will give no offense, because the trainer himself had won a Nemean victory as a boy and another as a man in the pancratium (53–59). He praises Melesias for his experience and skill as a teacher and declares that Alcimedon has gained for him his thirtieth victory in the major games; moreover, Alcimedon won the hard way, having to defeat four successive opponents (59–69). In so doing, he has cheered his aged grandfather and brought the Blepsiadae their sixth major victory (70–76). The boy's achievement also brings joy to his dead father, Iphion, who, although in Hades, hears his name proclaimed and informs his relative Callimachus (77–84). The poem ends with prayers for Zeus to continue his bounty to the family and their city (84–88).

8. ΑΛΚΙΜΕΔΟΝΤΙ ΑΙΓΙΝΗΤΗΙ
ΠΑΙΔΙ ΠΑΛΑΙΣΤΗΙ

Α′ Μᾶτερ ὦ χρυσοστεφάνων ἀέθλων, Οὐλυμπία,
    δέσποιν᾽ ἀλαθείας, ἵνα μάντιες ἄνδρες
    ἐμπύροις τεκμαιρόμενοι παραπειρῶν-
        ται Διὸς ἀργικεραύνου,
    εἴ τιν᾽ ἔχει λόγον ἀνθρώπων πέρι
5 μαιομένων μεγάλαν
    ἀρετὰν θυμῷ λαβεῖν,
    τῶν δὲ μόχθων ἀμπνοάν·

    ἄνεται δὲ πρὸς χάριν εὐσεβίας ἀνδρῶν λιταῖς·
    ἀλλ᾽ ὦ Πίσας εὔδενδρον ἐπ᾽ Ἀλφεῷ ἄλσος,
10 τόνδε κῶμον καὶ στεφαναφορίαν δέ-
        ξαι· μέγα τοι κλέος αἰεί,
    ᾧτινι σὸν γέρας ἕσπετ᾽ ἀγλαόν.
    ἄλλα δ᾽ ἐπ᾽ ἄλλον ἔβαν
    ἀγαθῶν, πολλαὶ δ᾽ ὁδοί
    σὺν θεοῖς εὐπραγίας.

15 Τιμόσθενες, ὔμμε δ᾽ ἐκλάρωσεν πότμος

136

8. FOR ALCIMEDON OF AEGINA

WINNER, BOYS' WRESTLING, 460 B.C.

O mother of the golden-crowned games, Olympia,   Str. 1
mistress of truth, where men who are seers
examine burnt offerings and test
    Zeus of the bright thunderbolt,
to see if he has any word concerning mortals
who are striving in their hearts   5
to gain a great success
and respite from their toils;

but men's prayers are fulfilled in return for piety.   Ant. 1
O sanctuary of Pisa with beautiful trees on the Alpheus,
receive this revel band and its wearing of crowns;   10
    for great fame is always his
whom your illustrious prize attends.
To different men come different
blessings, and many are the paths
to god-given success.

Timosthenes,[1] destiny allotted your family   Ep. 1

[1] Alcimedon's brother (schol.). Zeus is patron of both the
Olympic and Nemean games.

Ζηνὶ γενεθλίῳ· ὃς σὲ μὲν Νεμέᾳ πρόφατον,
Ἀλκιμέδοντα δὲ πὰρ Κρόνου λόφῳ
θῆκεν Ὀλυμπιονίκαν.
ἦν δ' ἐσορᾶν καλός, ἔργῳ τ' οὐ κατὰ εἶδος ἐλέγχων
20 ἐξένεπε κρατέων
    πάλᾳ δολιχήρετμον Αἴγιναν πάτραν·
ἔνθα σώτειρα Διὸς ξενίου
πάρεδρος ἀσκεῖται Θέμις

B' ἔξοχ' ἀνθρώπων. ὅ τι γὰρ πολὺ καὶ πολλᾷ ῥέπῃ,
ὀρθᾷ διακρίνειν φρενὶ μὴ παρὰ καιρόν
25 δυσπαλές· τεθμὸς δέ τις ἀθανάτων καὶ
    τάνδ' ἁλιερκέα χώραν
παντοδαποῖσιν ὑπέστασε ξένοις
κίονα δαιμονίαν—
ὁ δ' ἐπαντέλλων χρόνος
τοῦτο πράσσων μὴ κάμοι—

30 Δωριεῖ λαῷ ταμιευομέναν ἐξ Αἰακοῦ·
τὸν παῖς ὁ Λατοῦς εὐρυμέδων τε Ποσειδάν,

16 ὃς σὲ μὲν Νεμέᾳ Boeckh: ὃς (om. A^a cum schol., BG^{ac})
σὲ μὲν ἐν Νεμέᾳ codd.
23 ῥέπῃ Bergk: ῥέποι codd.
24 διακρίνειν a: διακρῖναι A

---

[2] Themis, the goddess of universal right and mother of the
Horae, is honored so highly because as a great commercial state

to Zeus, its progenitor, who made you famous at Nemea,   16
but by the hill of Cronus made Alcimedon
an Olympic victor.
He was beautiful to behold, in action he did not discredit
his looks, and by winning in the wrestling match   20
   he proclaimed long-oared Aegina as his fatherland,
where Themis, the saving goddess
enthroned beside Zeus, respecter of strangers, is
     venerated

most among men,[2] for when much hangs in the balance   Str. 2
     with many ways to go,
deciding with correct judgment while avoiding
     impropriety
is a difficult problem to wrestle with.[3] But some   25
     ordinance
   of the immortal gods has set up this seagirt land
for foreigners from all places
as a divine pillar—
and may time to come not tire
of accomplishing this—

a land governed by[4] Dorian people from the time of   Ant. 2
     Aeacus,
whom Leto's son[5] and wide-ruling Poseidon,   31

Aegina must rely on fair dealing with many foreigners (παντο-
δαποῖσιν ξένοις, 26; cf. Διὸς ξενίου, 21).

   [3] The word δυσπαλές puns on the victor's event (πάλᾳ, 20);
cf. also ἀντίπαλον at 71.

   [4] Or *held in trust for*.

   [5] Apollo.

Ἰλίῳ μέλλοντες ἐπὶ στέφανον τεῦ-
  ξαι, καλέσαντο συνεργόν
τείχεος, ἦν ὅτι νιν πεπρωμένον
ὀρνυμένων πολέμων
35 πτολιπόρθοις ἐν μάχαις
λάβρον ἀμπνεῦσαι καπνόν.

γλαυκοὶ δὲ δράκοντες, ἐπεὶ κτίσθη νέον,
πύργον ἐσαλλόμενοι τρεῖς, οἱ δύο μὲν κάπετον,
αὖθι δ' ἀτυζόμενοι ψυχὰς βάλον,
40 εἷς δ' ἐνόρουσε βοάσαις.
ἔννεπε δ' ἀντίον ὁρμαίνων τέρας εὐθὺς Ἀπόλλων·
"Πέργαμος ἀμφὶ τεαῖς,
  ἥρως, χερὸς ἐργασίαις ἁλίσκεται·
ὡς ἐμοὶ φάσμα λέγει Κρονίδα
πεμφθὲν βαρυγδούπου Διός·

Γ΄ οὐκ ἄτερ παίδων σέθεν, ἀλλ' ἅμα πρώτοις ἄρξεται
46 καὶ τετράτοις." ὡς ἦρα θεὸς σάφα εἴπαις
Ξάνθον ἤπειγεν καὶ Ἀμαζόνας εὐίπ-
  πους καὶ ἐς Ἴστρον ἐλαύνων.
Ὀρσοτρίαινα δ' ἐπ' Ἰσθμῷ ποντία

39 ἀτιζομένῳ C, v.l. in v
40 ἐνόρουσε Christ: ἀνόρουσε B(schol.): ὄρουσε A: ἐπόρου-
σε O: ἐσόρουσε rell.
45 ἄρξεται codd.: ῥάξεται Gildersleeve, Wilamowitz
46 τετράτοις (τετάρτοις E) codd.: τερτάτοις Ahrens | ἦρα
Schroeder: ἄρα codd.

140

as they were preparing to crown Ilion with battlements,
    summoned to help build
the wall, because the city was destined
at the outbreak of wars
in city-sacking battles   35
to breathe forth ravening smoke.

And when the wall was freshly built, three blue-gray   Ep. 2
    snakes tried to jump upon the rampart: two fell down
and, stricken by terror, gave up their lives on the spot,
but one leapt in with a shout of triumph.   40
Apollo considered the adverse omen and immediately
    said:
"Pergamus is to be captured,
    hero, at the site of your handiwork—
thus does the vision sent by the son of Cronus,
loudly thundering Zeus, inform me—

not without your children; but it will begin with the first   Str. 3
    ones
and also with the fourth."[6] Upon speaking these clear   46
    words,
the god sped his team to Xanthus, to the Amazons
    of the fine horses, and to the Ister.
But the Wielder of the Trident drove his swift chariot

[6] Aeacus' son Telamon took Troy in the first generation (after
Aeacus), while Neoptolemus and Epeius (who devised the Trojan
horse) destroyed it in the fourth (now counting Aeacus as the
first). Cf. *Isth.* 5.35–38. Ahrens' emendation to τερτάτοις (an un-
attested Aeolic form for τριτάτοις "third") has no support from
the scholia.

ἅρμα θοὸν τάννεν,
50 ἀποπέμπων Αἰακόν
δεῦρ' ἀν' ἵπποις χρυσέαις

καὶ Κορίνθου δειράδ' ἐποψόμενος δαιτικλυτάν.
τερπνὸν δ' ἐν ἀνθρώποις ἴσον ἔσσεται οὐδέν.
εἰ δ' ἐγὼ Μελησία ἐξ ἀγενείων
κῦδος ἀνέδραμον ὕμνῳ,
55 μὴ βαλέτω με λίθῳ τραχεῖ φθόνος·
καὶ Νεμέᾳ γὰρ ὁμῶς
ἐρέω ταύταν χάριν,
τὰν δ' ἔπειτ' ἀνδρῶν μάχας

ἐκ παγκρατίου. τὸ διδάξασθαι δέ τοι
60 εἰδότι ῥᾴτερον· ἄγνωμον δὲ τὸ μὴ προμαθεῖν·
κουφότεραι γὰρ ἀπειράτων φρένες.
κεῖνα δὲ κεῖνος ἂν εἴποι
ἔργα περαίτερον ἄλλων, τίς τρόπος ἄνδρα προβάσει
ἐξ ἱερῶν ἀέθλων
μέλλοντα ποθεινοτάταν δόξαν φέρειν.
65 νῦν μὲν αὐτῷ γέρας Ἀλκιμέδων
νίκαν τριακοστὰν ἑλών·

Δ΄ ὃς τύχᾳ μὲν δαίμονος, ἀνορέας δ' οὐκ ἀμπλακών
ἐν τέτρασιν παίδων ἀπεθήκατο γυίοις

52 δαιτικλυτάν Bergk: δαῖτα κλυτάν codd.
54 μελησίᾳ A(sed non A¹)B(et schol.): μελησία rell.

142

to the Isthmus on the sea,
as he escorted Aeacus   50
here with his golden horses

on his way to visit the ridge of Corinth famed for festivals.   Ant. 3
Nothing will be equally pleasing among men.
But if I have recounted in my hymn Melesias' glory
    gained from beardless youths,
let no ill will cast a rough stone at me,   55
because I will likewise declare
a glory of this sort[7] at Nemea too,
and the one gained thereafter in the men's bouts

of the pancratium. Truly teaching is easier for one   Ep. 3
who knows, and it is foolish not to have learned in   60
        advance,
for less weighty are the minds of men without experience.
But he, beyond all others, could tell
of such feats and what maneuver will advance a man
who from the sacred games
    is bent upon winning the fame he most desires.
At this point his prize is Alcimedon,   65
who has won for him his thirtieth victory—

who, with divine favor, but also by not failing his   Str. 4
        manhood,
put away from himself onto four boys' bodies

[7] Like that of Alcimedon in boys' wrestling.

---

58 μάχας Schroeder: μάχαν codd.

PINDAR

νόστον ἔχθιστον καὶ ἀτιμοτέραν γλῶσ-
σαν καὶ ἐπίκρυφον οἶμον,
70 πατρὶ δὲ πατρὸς ἐνέπνευσεν μένος
γήραος ἀντίπαλον·
Ἀίδα τοι λάθεται
ἄρμενα πράξαις ἀνήρ.

ἀλλ᾽ ἐμὲ χρὴ μναμοσύναν ἀνεγείροντα φράσαι
75 χειρῶν ἄωτον Βλεψιάδαις ἐπίνικον,
ἕκτος οἷς ἤδη στέφανος περίκειται
φυλλοφόρων ἀπ᾽ ἀγώνων.
ἔστι δὲ καί τι θανόντεσσιν μέρος
κὰν νόμον ἐρδομένων·
κατακρύπτει δ᾽ οὐ κόνις
80 συγγόνων κεδνὰν χάριν.

Ἑρμᾶ δὲ θυγατρὸς ἀκούσαις Ἰφίων
Ἀγγελίας, ἐνέποι κεν Καλλιμάχῳ λιπαρόν
κόσμον Ὀλυμπίᾳ, ὅν σφι Ζεὺς γένει
ὤπασεν. ἐσλὰ δ᾽ ἐπ᾽ ἐσλοῖς
85 ἔργα θέλοι δόμεν, ὀξείας δὲ νόσους ἀπαλάλκοι.

78 ἐρδομένων E. Schmid: ἐρδόμενον codd.

144

a most hateful homecoming, words less respectful,
    and a hidden path,[8]
but into his father's father he breathed courage   70
to wrestle against old age.
Truly, a man forgets about Hades
when he has done fitting things.

But I must awaken memory to announce   Ant. 4
the foremost victories won by the hands of the   75
      Blepsiadae,
whose sixth garland now wreathes them,
    won from the games that award crowns of leaves.[9]
And for those who have died there is also some share
in ritual observances,
nor does the dust bury
the cherished glory of kinsmen.   80

When Iphion[10] hears the report from Hermes' daughter   Ep. 4
Angelia,[11] he could tell Callimachus of the shining
adornment at Olympia that Zeus granted
to their family. May he[12] willingly provide
success upon success and ward off painful diseases.   85

---

[8] For another example of a wrestler defeating four successive opponents with similar details of the losers' inglorious return home, see *Pyth.* 8.81–87.

[9] The four crown games.

[10] Iphion is probably the father, Callimachus the uncle, of Alcimedon (most schol.).

[11] The personification of Report. Hermes is the god of heralds and messengers.

[12] Zeus.

εὔχομαι ἀμφὶ καλῶν
   μοίρᾳ νέμεσιν διχόβουλον μὴ θέμεν·
ἀλλ' ἀπήμαντον ἄγων βίοτον
αὐτούς τ' ἀέξοι καὶ πόλιν.

I pray that in their allotment of blessings
    he not make the apportionment dubious,[13]
but rather grant them a lifetime free from pain,
and exalt them and their city.

[13] The scholia interpret νέμεσιν διχόβουλον to mean "hostile resentment"; many editors capitalize: "Nemesis of divided mind."

OLYMPIAN 9

Opus was a city of the Eastern Locrians, located north of Boeotia, whose early history Pindar briefly sketches in the poem. By winning this Olympic victory in 468 (confirmed by P. Oxy. 222), Epharmostus became a *periodonikēs* (victor in all four crown games).

The ode opens with a contrast between the spontaneous chant of Archilochus (a sort of "Hail to the Conquering Hero"), sung by Epharmostus' friends at Olympia, and the more studied composition of the present ode, inspired by the Muses, with its extensive praise of the victor and of his city Opus for its orderly life and its athletic successes at Delphi and Olympia (1–20). The poet hopes to proclaim the Opuntians' achievement with the aid of the Graces (20–27). The maxim that bravery and wisdom are divinely granted is illustrated by the example of Heracles, who held his own while fighting against three gods (28–35). But suddenly the poet rejects that story as boastfully disparaging of the gods and proposes as his theme the city of Protogeneia (Opus), first settled by Pyrrha and Deucalion, who came down from Mt. Parnassus and created a race of people from stones (35–46).

Implying that he is treating an old theme in a new song (47–49), Pindar begins with an account of the great flood and the establishment of a dynasty of native kings, which

148

continued until Zeus impregnated the daughter of Opus of Elis and gave her as a bride to Locrus, the childless king of the Locrian city (49–62), who named his adopted son Opus for the child's maternal grandfather and handed the city over to him. His outstanding qualities attracted many immigrants, foremost of whom was Menoetius, whose son, Patroclus, stood by Achilles against the onslaught of Telephus (63–79).

After a brief prayer for inspiration (80–83), Pindar catalogs Epharmostus' earlier victories, singling out his remarkable triumph in the games at Marathon, when he was taken from the class for youths ("beardless") and made to compete against grown men. To the delight of the crowd, he won without losing a fall (83–99). Pindar concludes that natural abilities are better and more praiseworthy than learned ones that lack a divine component (100–107). Accordingly, he rejects the long and arduous ways of art in favor of a simple vaunt, declaring that Epharmostus has been favored by divine help and natural talent. The poem ends with an address to Ajax, son of Ileus, a local hero, on whose altar the victor is placing his crown (107–112).

9. ΕΦΑΡΜΟΣΤΩΙ ΟΠΟΥΝΤΙΩΙ

ΠΑΛΑΙΣΤΗΙ

Α΄ Τὸ μὲν Ἀρχιλόχου μέλος
φωνᾶεν Ὀλυμπίᾳ,
   καλλίνικος ὁ τριπλόος κεχλαδώς,
ἄρκεσε Κρόνιον παρ᾽ ὄχθον ἀγεμονεῦσαι
κωμάζοντι φίλοις Ἐφαρμόστῳ σὺν ἑταίροις·
5 ἀλλὰ νῦν ἑκαταβόλων Μοισᾶν ἀπὸ τόξων
Δία τε φοινικοστερόπαν σεμνόν τ᾽ ἐπίνειμαι
ἀκρωτήριον Ἄλιδος
τοιοῖσδε βέλεσσιν,
τὸ δή ποτε Λυδὸς ἥρως Πέλοψ
10 ἐξάρατο κάλλιστον ἕδνον Ἱπποδαμείας·

πτερόεντα δ᾽ ἵει γλυκύν
Πυθῶνάδ᾽ ὀιστόν· οὔ-
   τοι χαμαιπετέων λόγων ἐφάψεαι,

8 βέλεσ(σ)ι v.l. in ν: μέλεσ(σ)ι(ν) rell.

---

[1] The victory chant attributed to Archilochus (*fr.* 324 West) contained a refrain addressed to the victor, probably repeated three times, of τήνελλα καλλίνικε, in which the first word imi-

9. FOR EPHARMOSTUS OF OPUS

WINNER, WRESTLING, 468 B.C.

The song of Archilochus	Str. 1
resounding at Olympia,	
that triumphal hymn swelling with three refrains,[1]	
sufficed for Epharmostus to lead the way by Cronus' hill	
as he celebrated with his close companions,	
but now, from the far-shooting bows of the Muses	5
shoot a volley of arrows such as these	
at Zeus of the red lightning	
and at the sacred hilltop of Elis,[2]	
which Pelops, the Lydian hero, once won	
as the fairest dowry of Hippodameia;[3]	10

and cast a sweet winged	Ant. 1
arrow at Pytho.[4]	
You will surely take up no words that fall to the	
ground,	

tated the sound of a lyre string. The song continued with χαῖρε
ἄναξ Ἡράκλεις, | αὐτός τε καὶόλαος, αἰχμητὰ δύο, "Hail, lord
Heracles, you and Iolaus, a pair of warriors."   [2] The hill of
Cronus at Olympia in the district of Elis.   [3] Cf. *Ol.* 1.67–88.

    [4] This indicates that Epharmostus had previously won at the
Pythian games in Delphi, where the Castalian spring was located.

ἀνδρὸς ἀμφὶ παλαίσμασιν φόρμιγγ᾽ ἐλελίζων
κλεινᾶς ἐξ Ὀπόεντος· αἰνήσαις ἓ καὶ υἱόν,
15 ἃν Θέμις θυγάτηρ τέ οἱ σώτειρα λέλογχεν
μεγαλόδοξος Εὐνομία. θάλλει δ᾽ ἀρεταῖσιν
σόν τε, Κασταλία, πάρα
Ἀλφεοῦ τε ῥέεθρον·
ὅθεν στεφάνων ἄωτοι κλυτάν
20 Λοκρῶν ἐπαείροντι ματέρ᾽ ἀγλαόδενδρον.

ἐγὼ δέ τοι φίλαν πόλιν
μαλεραῖς ἐπιφλέγων ἀοιδαῖς,
καὶ ἀγάνορος ἵππου
θᾶσσον καὶ ναὸς ὑποπτέρου παντᾷ
25 ἀγγελίαν πέμψω ταύταν,
εἰ σύν τινι μοιριδίῳ παλάμᾳ
ἐξαίρετον Χαρίτων νέμομαι κᾶπον·
κεῖναι γὰρ ὤπασαν τὰ τέρπν᾽· ἀγαθοὶ
δὲ καὶ σοφοὶ κατὰ δαίμον᾽ ἄνδρες

Β΄ ἐγένοντ᾽· ἐπεὶ ἀντίον
30 πῶς ἂν τριόδοντος Ἡ-
ρακλέης σκύταλον τίναξε χερσίν,
ἁνίκ᾽ ἀμφὶ Πύλον σταθεὶς ἤρειδε Ποσειδάν,

16–17 ἀρεταῖσιν σόν τε Bergk: ἀρεταῖσι σόν τε (ἴσόν τε)
Aˢa: ἀρεταῖσιν ἔν τε A (παρά τε τὸ σὸν schol.)

5 Epharmostus.   6 Eunomia, one of the Horae, the
daughters of Themis (cf. Ol. 13.6–8).

while making the lyre vibrate in honor of the wrestling
of a man from famous Opus. Praise the son[5] and his city,
which Themis and her glorious daughter, saving Order,[6]   15
have as their allotment. It flourishes with achievements
by your stream, Castalia,
and that of Alpheus;
the choicest of crowns won there exalt
the Locrians' famous mother city with its splendid trees.   20

But as for me, while I light up that dear city   Ep. 1
with my blazing songs,
more swiftly than either a high-spirited horse
or a winged ship
I shall send this announcement everywhere,   25
if with the help of some skill granted by destiny
I cultivate the choice garden of the Graces,
for it is they who bestow what is delightful. But men
    become brave and wise as divinity

determines: for how else   Str. 2
could Heracles have brandished   30
    his club in his hands against the trident,
when Poseidon stood before Pylos and pressed him
    hard[7]

[7] According to the scholia Heracles fought Poseidon at Pylos
because Poseidon's son Neleus would not purge him of blood
guilt; he fought against Apollo after stealing a tripod from Delphi.
The third encounter appears to be based on *Il.* 5.395–397, which
alludes to Heracles' wounding of Hades with an arrow at Pylos.

ἤρειδεν δέ νιν ἀργυρέῳ τόξῳ πολεμίζων
Φοῖβος, οὐδ' Ἀίδας ἀκινήταν ἔχε ῥάβδον,
βρότεα σώμαθ' ᾇ κατάγει κοίλαν πρὸς ἄγυιαν
35 θνασκόντων; ἀπό μοι λόγον
τοῦτον, στόμα, ῥῖψον·
ἐπεὶ τό γε λοιδορῆσαι θεούς
ἐχθρὰ σοφία, καὶ τὸ καυχᾶσθαι παρὰ καιρόν

μανίαισιν ὑποκρέκει.
40 μὴ νῦν λαλάγει τὰ τοι-
    αῦτ'· ἔα πόλεμον μάχαν τε πᾶσαν
χωρὶς ἀθανάτων· φέροις δὲ Πρωτογενείας
ἄστει γλῶσσαν, ἵν' αἰολοβρόντα Διὸς αἴσᾳ
Πύρρα Δευκαλίων τε Παρνασσοῦ καταβάντε
δόμον ἔθεντο πρῶτον, ἄτερ δ' εὐνᾶς ὁμόδαμον
45 κτισσάσθαν λίθινον γόνον·
λαοὶ δ' ὀνύμασθεν.
ἔγειρ' ἐπέων σφιν οἶμον λιγύν,
αἴνει δὲ παλαιὸν μὲν οἶνον, ἄνθεα δ' ὕμνων

νεωτέρων. λέγοντι μάν
50 χθόνα μὲν κατακλύσαι μέλαιναν
ὕδατος σθένος, ἀλλά
Ζηνὸς τέχναις ἀνάπωτιν ἐξαίφνας

32 δέ Hermann: τέ codd.
42 αἰολοβρέντα coni. Snell e Pae. 12.9

154

and Phoebus pressed him while battling with his
silver bow, nor did Hades keep still his staff, with which
he leads down to his hollow abode the mortal bodies
of those who die? But cast that story   35
away from me, my mouth!
for reviling the gods
is a hateful skill, and boasting inappropriately

sounds a note of madness.   Ant. 2
Stop babbling of such things now!   40
    Keep war and all fighting
clear of the immortals; apply your speech to
        Protogeneia's
city,[8] where, by decree of Zeus of the bright
        thunderbolt,
Pyrrha and Deucalion came down from Parnassus
and first established their home, and, without coupling,
founded one folk, an offspring of stone: 45
and they were called people.[9]
Awaken for them a clear-sounding path of words;
praise wine that is old, but the blooms of hymns

that are newer. Indeed they tell that   Ep. 2
mighty waters had flooded over   50
the dark earth, but,
through Zeus' contriving, an ebb tide suddenly

[8] Opus.

[9] A play on λᾶες (stones) and λαοί (people); cf. Hes. *fr.* 234
M-W. After the flood, Pyrrha and Deucalion brought a new race
into being by throwing stones behind them.

ἄντλον ἑλεῖν. κείνων δ' ἔσαν
χαλκάσπιδες ὑμέτεροι πρόγονοι
55 ἀρχᾶθεν, Ἰαπετιονίδος φύτλας
κοῦροι κορᾶν καὶ φερτάτων Κρονιδᾶν,
ἐγχώριοι βασιλῆες αἰεί,

Γ'   πρὶν Ὀλύμπιος ἁγεμών
θύγατρ' ἀπὸ γᾶς Ἐπει-
ῶν Ὀπόεντος ἀναρπάσαις, ἕκαλος
μίχθη Μαιναλίαισιν ἐν δειραῖς, καὶ ἔνεικεν
60 Λοκρῷ, μὴ καθέλοι νιν αἰὼν πότμον ἐφάψαις
ὀρφανὸν γενεᾶς. ἔχεν δὲ σπέρμα μέγιστον
ἄλοχος, εὐφράνθη τε ἰδὼν ἥρως θετὸν υἱόν,
μάτρωος δ' ἐκάλεσσέ νιν
ἰσώνυμον ἔμμεν,
65 ὑπέρφατον ἄνδρα μορφᾷ τε καί
ἔργοισι. πόλιν δ' ὤπασεν λαόν τε διαιτᾶν.

ἀφίκοντο δέ οἱ ξένοι
ἔκ τ' Ἄργεος ἔκ τε Θη-
βᾶν, οἱ δ' Ἀρκάδες, οἱ δὲ καὶ Πισᾶται·
υἱὸν δ' Ἄκτορος ἐξόχως τίμασεν ἐποίκων
70 Αἰγίνας τε Μενοίτιον· τοῦ παῖς ἅμ' Ἀτρείδαις
Τεύθραντος πεδίον μολὼν ἔστα σὺν Ἀχιλλεῖ

---

10 Pyrrha and Deucalion; perhaps also the Locrian ancestors.

11 Iapetus the Titan was Deucalion's grandfather. See geneal-
ogy of Protogeneia.

12 The original inhabitants of Elis (cf. *Od.* 13.275).

drained the floodwater. From them[10] came
your ancestors of the bronze shields
in the beginning, sons from the daughters of Iapetus'   55
race[11] and from the mightiest sons of Cronus,
    being always a native line of kings,

until the lord of Olympus   Str. 3
carried off the daughter of Opus
    from the land of the Epeians[12] and quietly
lay with her in the Maenalian glens,[13] and brought her
to Locrus, lest time destroy him and impose a destiny   60
with no children. But his spouse was bearing the
        greatest
seed, and the hero rejoiced to see his adopted son;
he called him by the same name
as the mother's father,[14]
and he became a man beyond description for his beauty   65
and deeds. And he gave him his city and people to
        govern.

Foreigners came to him   Ant. 3
from Argos and from Thebes;
    others were Arcadians and still others Pisans;
but of the settlers he honored most the son of Actor
and Aegina, Menoetius, whose child[15] went with the   70
        Atreidae
to the plain of Teuthras[16] and stood by Achilles

---

[13] In Arcadia.   [14] Opus.   [15] Patroclus.
[16] King of Mysia, whose successor Telephus, a son of Heracles, opposed the Greeks when they landed in his country on their way to Troy.

μόνος, ὅτ᾽ ἀλκάεντας Δαναοὺς τρέψαις ἁλίαισιν
πρύμναις Τήλεφος ἔμβαλεν·
ὥστ᾽ ἔμφρονι δεῖξαι
75 μαθεῖν Πατρόκλου βιατὰν νόον·
ἐξ οὗ Θέτιος †γόνος οὐλίῳ νιν ἐν Ἄρει

παραγορεῖτο μή ποτε
σφετέρας ἄτερθε ταξιοῦσθαι
δαμασιμβρότου αἰχμᾶς.
80 εἴην εὑρησιεπὴς ἀναγεῖσθαι
πρόσφορος ἐν Μοισᾶν δίφρῳ·
τόλμα δὲ καὶ ἀμφιλαφὴς δύναμις
ἔσποιτο. προξενίᾳ δ᾽ ἀρετᾷ τ᾽ ἦλθον
τιμάορος Ἰσθμίαισι Λαμπρομάχου
μίτραις, ὅτ᾽ ἀμφότεροι κράτησαν

Δ´   μίαν ἔργον ἂν᾽ ἀμέραν.
86 ἄλλαι δὲ δύ᾽ ἐν Κορίν-
θου πύλαις ἐγένοντ᾽ ἔπειτα χάρμαι,
ταὶ δὲ καὶ Νεμέας Ἐφαρμόστῳ κατὰ κόλπον·
Ἄργει τ᾽ ἔσχεθε κῦδος ἀνδρῶν, παῖς δ᾽ ἐν Ἀθάναις,
οἷον δ᾽ ἐν Μαραθῶνι συλαθεὶς ἀγενείων

76 γόνος codd.: γ᾽ ἶνις Bothe: γ᾽ ἔρνος Turyn: πῶλος Post:
ἐξ οὔτε γόνος Θέτιος Theiler
83 ἔσποιτο codd. plerique: ἔποιτο HN: ἔσποιτ᾽ αἰεὶ ACᵖᶜ

all alone, when Telephus routed the valiant Danaans
and attacked their seaworthy sterns,
so as to show a man of understanding how to discern
Patroclus' mighty spirit.   75
From then on the offspring of Thetis[17] exhorted

him never to post himself   Ep. 3
in deadly combat far
from his man-subduing spear.[18]
May I find the right words and fittingly   80
drive forward in the chariot of the Muses,
and may boldness and ample power
attend me. Because of guest friendship and achievement
I have come to honor the Isthmian fillets
    of Lampromachus,[19] when both[20] won

their victories in one day.   Str. 4
There were two more occasions for joy afterwards   86
    at the gates of Corinth,[21]
and others for Epharmostus in the valley of Nemea;
at Argos he won glory among men and as a boy at Ath-
    ens.
And what a contest he endured at Marathon against
    older men

[17] Achilles.   [18] Achilles' spear of Pelian ash, which only
he could wield (cf. *Il.* 16.140–144); it figured prominently in this
episode, for it both wounded and healed Telephus.

[19] A relative of Epharmostus (schol). Ribbons of wool were
tied around the victors' heads and limbs.

[20] He and Epharmostus.

[21] At the Isthmian games.

90   μένεν ἀγῶνα πρεσβυτέρων ἀμφ᾽ ἀργυρίδεσσιν·
     φῶτας δ᾽ ὀξυρεπεῖ δόλῳ
     ἀπτωτὶ δαμάσσαις
     διήρχετο κύκλον ὅσσᾳ βοᾷ,
     ὡραῖος ἐὼν καὶ καλὸς κάλλιστά τε ῥέξαις.

95   τὰ δὲ Παρρασίῳ στρατῷ
     θαυμαστὸς ἐὼν φάνη
       Ζηνὸς ἀμφὶ πανάγυριν Λυκαίου,
     καὶ ψυχρᾶν ὁπότ᾽ εὐδιανὸν φάρμακον αὐρᾶν
     Πελλάνᾳ φέρε· σύνδικος δ᾽ αὐτῷ Ἰολάου
     τύμβος ἐνναλία τ᾽ Ἐλευσὶς ἀγλαΐαισιν.
100τὸ δὲ φυᾷ κράτιστον ἅπαν· πολλοὶ δὲ διδακταῖς
     ἀνθρώπων ἀρεταῖς κλέος
     ὤρουσαν ἀρέσθαι·
     ἄνευ δὲ θεοῦ, σεσιγαμένον
     οὐ σκαιότερον χρῆμ᾽ ἕκαστον· ἐντὶ γὰρ ἄλλαι

105 ὁδῶν ὁδοὶ περαίτεραι,
     μία δ᾽ οὐχ ἅπαντας ἄμμε θρέψει
     μελέτα· σοφίαι μέν
     αἰπειναί· τοῦτο δὲ προσφέρων ἄεθλον,
     ὄρθιον ὤρυσαι θαρσέων,
110 τόνδ᾽ ἀνέρα δαιμονίᾳ γεγάμεν

for the silver cups, when wrested from the beardless   90
    class:
with deftly shifting feints
he subdued the men without falling once,
and passed through the ring of spectators to such great
    shouting,
being young and fair and performing the fairest deeds.

Then too he made a marvelous appearance   Ant. 4
among the Parrhasian host   96
    at the festival of Lycaean Zeus,[22]
and at Pellana, when he carried off the warming remedy
for chill winds.[23] Witnesses to his splendid successes
are Iolaus' tomb[24] and Eleusis by the sea.
What comes by nature is altogether best. Many men   100
strive to win fame
with abilities that are taught,
but when god takes no part, each deed is no worse
for being left in silence; for some paths

are longer than others,   Ep. 4
and no single training will develop   106
us all. The ways of wisdom
are steep, but when you present this prize
boldly shout straight out
that with divine help this man was born with   110

[22] In Arcadia.
[23] In Achaea; the prize was a woolen cloak.
[24] At the Iolaea at Thebes.

εὔχειρα, δεξιόγυιον, ὁρῶντ᾽ ἀλκάν,
Αἶαν, τεόν τ᾽ ἐν δαιτί, Ἰλιάδα,
νικῶν ἐπεστεφάνωσε βωμόν.

112 Αἶαν, τεόν Hermann: αἰάντειόν codd.

quick hands, nimble legs, determination in his look;
and at your feast, Ajax, son of Ileus,[25]

    the victor has placed a crown upon your altar.

[25] Known as the "lesser Ajax," his father's name is usually
spelled Oïleus (cf. *Il.* 2.527–535).

OLYMPIAN 10

Western (or Epizephyrian) Locri was located on the toe of Italy. The poet opens by asserting that he has forgotten his agreement to compose the ode. Since the victory (confirmed by P. Oxy. 222) was in 476, the same year that *Ol.* 1, 2, and 3 were composed for Hieron and Theron, it is likely that the more imposing commissions took precedence over this one for a boy victor. Pindar, however, promises interest (τόκος) on his overdue debt and atones with an especially rich ode that tells in loving detail of Heracles' founding of the Olympic games, the first contests held there, and the celebrations that followed. Indeed, its lateness makes it all the more appreciated for the immortality it confers on the victor.

Acknowledging that the ode is late, the poet invokes the Muse and Truth to help absolve him from blame (1–6). In recompense, he will pay interest on his debt by praising the Western Locrians, who appreciate strict dealing, poetry, and martial prowess (7–15). After a reference to Heracles' difficulties in defeating Cycnus, he advises Hagesidamus to be grateful to his trainer Ilas, who sharpened his natural talents (15–21). Yet effort is also required for victory (22–23).

The poet is inspired by the ordinances of Zeus (probably those governing the festival in his honor) to tell of the

164

founding of the Olympic games by Heracles, established
with the spoils he had taken when he destroyed the city
of Augeas, who refused to pay Heracles for cleansing his
stables (24–51). He recounts that the Fates and Time at-
tended the initial festival, catalogs the winners of the six
events, and concludes with the festivities and victory songs
that followed in the evening (52–77). Accordingly, the
poet offers the present ode, which, although late, is all the
more welcome—like a son finally born to an old man with
no heirs (78–93). Pindar assures Hagesidamus that this
ode will preserve his fame, reiterates his praise of the
Western Locrians, and implies that through his verses
Hagesidamus, like another Ganymede, will become im-
mortal (93–105).

10. ΑΓΗΣΙΔΑΜΩΙ ΛΟΚΡΩΙ
ΕΠΙΖΕΦΥΡΙΩΙ

ΠΑΙΔΙ ΠΥΚΤΗΙ

Α΄ Τὸν Ὀλυμπιονίκαν ἀνάγνωτέ μοι
Ἀρχεστράτου παῖδα, πόθι φρενός
ἐμᾶς γέγραπται· γλυκὺ γὰρ αὐτῷ μέλος ὀφείλων
ἐπιλέλαθ'· ὦ Μοῖσ', ἀλλὰ σὺ καὶ θυγάτηρ
Ἀλάθεια Διός, ὀρθᾷ χερί
5   ἐρύκετον ψευδέων
ἐνιπὰν ἀλιτόξενον.

ἔκαθεν γὰρ ἐπελθὼν ὁ μέλλων χρόνος
ἐμὸν καταίσχυνε βαθὺ χρέος.
ὅμως δὲ λῦσαι δυνατὸς ὀξεῖαν ἐπιμομφὰν
τόκος. ὁράτω νῦν ψᾶφον ἑλισσομέναν
10 ὁπᾷ κῦμα κατακλύσσει ῥέον,
ὁπᾷ τε κοινὸν λόγον
φίλαν τείσομεν ἐς χάριν.

8 καταίσχυνε Boeckh: καταισχύνει codd.
9 ὁράτω Fennell: θνατῶν codd.: ὀνάτωρ Hermann: ὁρᾶτ' ὦν
Schneidewin: ἀνάτως (vel ἀνατί) Erbse

10. FOR HAGESIDAMUS OF WESTERN LOCRI

WINNER, BOYS' BOXING, 476 B.C.

Read me the name of the Olympic victor,   Str. 1
the son of Archestratus, where it is written
in my mind, for I owe[1] him a sweet song
    and have forgotten. O Muse, but you and Zeus'
      daughter,
Truth, with a correcting hand
ward off from me the charge of harming a guest friend   5
with broken promises.

For what was then the future has approached from afar   Ant. 1
and shamed my deep indebtedness.
Nevertheless, interest on a debt can absolve one from
    a bitter reproach. Let him see[2] now:
just as a flowing wave washes over a rolling pebble,   10
so shall we pay back a theme of general concern
as a friendly favor.

[1] The opening strophe and antistrophe use the language of
business (record-keeping, debts, interest, repayment) to discuss
the lateness of this ode.
[2] I have accepted Fennell's emendation for the MSS's un-
metrical θνατῶν ("mortals"); "him" is Hagesidamus.

167

νέμει γὰρ Ἀτρέκεια πόλιν Λοκρῶν Ζεφυρίων,
μέλει τέ σφισι Καλλιόπα
15 καὶ χάλκεος Ἄρης. τράπε δὲ Κύ-
κνεια μάχα καὶ ὑπέρβιον
Ἡρακλέα· πύκτας δ᾽ ἐν Ὀλυμπιάδι νικῶν
Ἴλᾳ φερέτω χάριν
Ἀγησίδαμος, ὡς
Ἀχιλεῖ Πάτροκλος.
20 θάξαις δέ κε φύντ᾽ ἀρετᾷ ποτί
πελώριον ὁρμάσαι κλέος ἀ-
νὴρ θεοῦ σὺν παλάμαις·

Β΄ ἄπονον δ᾽ ἔλαβον χάρμα παῦροί τινες,
ἔργων πρὸ πάντων βιότῳ φάος.
ἀγῶνα δ᾽ ἐξαίρετον ἀεῖσαι θέμιτες ὦρσαν
Διός, ὃν ἀρχαίῳ σάματι πὰρ Πέλοπος
25 βωμῶν ἑξάριθμον ἐκτίσσατο,
ἐπεὶ Ποσειδάνιον
πέφνε Κτέατον ἀμύμονα,

21 παλάμαις ACN^{ac}?: παλάμᾳ v
25 βωμῶν AE^{i}: βωμὸν ζ: βωμῶ(ῳ) BF^{i} GH?: πόνων Christ

---

3 Strictness (Ἀτρέκεια) may refer to the severe early lawcode of Zaleucus (schol.), but it also refers to the Locrians' accuracy in business dealings.
4 The scholia say that Pindar is following the account in Stesichorus' *Cycnus* (*fr.* 207 Campbell), which must have differed from the version at [Hes.] *Scutum* 57–423. The particular incident

For Strictness[3] rules the city of the Western Locrians,   Ep. 1
and dear to them are Calliope
and brazen Ares. The battle with Cycnus   15
    turned back even mighty
Heracles,[4] and as a victorious boxer at the Olympic
        games,
let Hagesidamus offer
gratitude to Ilas[5]
as Patroclus did to Achilles.
By honing[6] someone born for excellence   20
a man may, with divine help,
    urge him on to prodigious fame;

and few have won without effort that joy   Str. 2
which is a light for life above all deeds.
But the ordinances of Zeus have prompted me to sing
    of the choice contest, which Heracles founded
with its six altars[7] by the ancient tomb of Pelops,   25
after he killed the son of Poseidon,
goodly Cteatus,

referred to is not known, nor is the following one about Patroclus
and Achilles, which probably derives from the cyclic tradition.

5 Hagesidamus' trainer (schol.).

6 The image is one of a whetstone. In lines 20–22 Pindar ad-
umbrates four elements required for success: natural ability,
training, divine assistance, and effort.

7 I have printed βωμῶν (AE^i) against the meter; the reference
is to the six double altars dedicated to the twelve gods worshiped
at Olympia (cf. 49 and *Ol.* 5.5). Some read Christ's πόνων "with six
toils" as a reference to the six events listed in 64–72.

PINDAR

πέφνε δ᾽ Εὔρυτον, ὡς Αὐγέαν λάτριον
ἀέκονθ᾽ ἑκὼν μισθὸν ὑπέρβιον
30 πράσσοιτο, λόχμαισι δὲ δοκεύσαις ὑπὸ Κλεωνᾶν
    δάμασε καὶ κείνους Ἡρακλέης ἐφ᾽ ὁδῷ,
ὅτι πρόσθε ποτὲ Τιρύνθιον
ἔπερσαν αὐτῷ στρατόν
μυχοῖς ἥμενον Ἄλιδος

Μολίονες ὑπερφίαλοι. καὶ μὰν ξεναπάτας
35 Ἐπειῶν βασιλεὺς ὄπιθεν
οὐ πολλὸν ἴδε πατρίδα πολυ-
    κτέανον ὑπὸ στερεῷ πυρί
πλαγαῖς τε σιδάρου βαθὺν εἰς ὀχετὸν ἄτας
ἴζοισαν ἐὰν πόλιν.
νεῖκος δὲ κρεσσόνων
40 ἀποθέσθ᾽ ἄπορον.
καὶ κεῖνος ἀβουλίᾳ ὕστατος
ἁλώσιος ἀντάσαις θάνατον
    αἰπὺν οὐκ ἐξέφυγεν.

Γ΄ ὁ δ᾽ ἄρ᾽ ἐν Πίσᾳ ἔλσαις ὅλον τε στρατόν
    λᾷάν τε πᾶσαν Διὸς ἄλκιμος
45 υἱὸς σταθμᾶτο ζάθεον ἄλσος πατρὶ μεγίστῳ·
    περὶ δὲ πάξαις Ἄλτιν μὲν ὅγ᾽ ἐν καθαρῷ
διέκρινε, τὸ δὲ κύκλῳ πέδον
ἔθηκε δόρπου λύσιν,
τιμάσαις πόρον Ἀλφεοῦ

170

and killed Eurytus, so that he might exact the wage   Ant. 2
for his menial service from mighty Augeas,[8] who was
unwilling to give it. Hiding in a thicket below Cleonae,   30
    Heracles overcame them in turn on the road,
because before that the overbearing Moliones[9]
had destroyed his army of Tirynthians
when it was encamped

in the valleys of Elis. And indeed, not long afterwards,   Ep. 2
the guest-cheating king of the Epeians[10]   35
saw his wealthy homeland
    sink into the deep trench of ruin
beneath a ruthless fire and strokes of iron—
even his own city.
Strife with those more powerful
one cannot put aside.   40
So that man, through lack of counsel, at last
met with capture
    and did not escape sheer death.

Thereupon, Zeus' valiant son gathered the entire army   Str. 3
and all the booty at Pisa,
and measured out a sacred precinct for his father   45
    most mighty. He fenced in the Altis[11] and set it apart
in the open, and he made the surrounding plain
a resting place for banqueting,
and honored the stream of Alpheus

[8] Heracles cleaned his stables by diverting the Alpheus river.
[9] Cteatus and Eurytus (cf. *Il.* 11.750–752, Paus. 5.2.1, and
Diod. Sic. 4.33.3–4).   [10] Augeas; the Epeians are the inhab-
itants of Elis (cf. *Ol.* 9.58).   [11] The precinct of Zeus.

μετὰ δώδεκ' ἀνάκτων θεῶν· καὶ πάγον
50   Κρόνου προσεφθέγξατο· πρόσθε γὰρ
νώνυμνος, ἃς Οἰνόμαος ἆρχε, βρέχετο πολλᾷ
        νιφάδι. ταύτᾳ δ' ἐν πρωτογόνῳ τελετᾷ
παρέσταν μὲν ἄρα Μοῖραι σχεδόν
ὅ τ' ἐξελέγχων μόνος
ἀλάθειαν ἐτήτυμον

55   Χρόνος. τὸ δὲ σαφανὲς ἰὼν πόρσω κατέφρασεν,
ὁπᾷ τὰν πολέμοιο δόσιν
ἀκρόθινα διελὼν ἔθυε καὶ
        πενταετηρίδ' ὅπως ἄρα
ἔστασεν ἑορτὰν σὺν Ὀλυμπιάδι πρώτᾳ
νικαφορίαισί τε.
60   τίς δὴ ποταίνιον
ἔλαχε στέφανον
χείρεσσι ποσίν τε καὶ ἅρματι,
ἀγώνιον ἐν δόξᾳ θέμενος
        εὖχος, ἔργῳ καθελών;

Δ´   στάδιον μὲν ἀρίστευσεν, εὐθὺν τόνον
65   ποσσὶ τρέχων, παῖς ὁ Λικυμνίου
Οἰωνός· ἷκεν δὲ Μιδέαθεν στρατὸν ἐλαύνων·
        ὁ δὲ πάλᾳ κυδαίνων Ἔχεμος Τεγέαν·
Δόρυκλος δ' ἔφερε πυγμᾶς τέλος,

64 εὐθὺν τόνον Thiersch: εὐθύτονον codd.

along with[12] the twelve ruling gods. And he gave the hill   Ant. 3
of Cronus its name, because before that it had none,   50
when, during Oenomaus' reign, it was drenched
    with much snow. And at that founding ceremony
the Fates stood near at hand,
as did the sole assayer
of genuine truth,

Time, which in its onward march clearly revealed   Ep. 3
how Heracles divided up that gift of war[13]   56
and offered up its best portion,
    and how he then founded
the quadrennial festival with the first Olympiad
and its victories.
Who then won   60
the new crown
with hands or feet or with chariot,
after fixing in his thoughts a triumph
    in the contest and achieving it in deed?

The winner of the stadion, as he ran the straight stretch   Str. 4
with his feet, was Licymnius' son,   65
Oeonus, who came at the head of his army from Midea.
    In the wrestling Echemus gained glory for Tegea.
Doryclus won the prize in boxing,

---

[12] Or *among*. One of the six double altars was dedicated to Alpheus and Artemis (cf. *Ol.* 5.5).

[13] The booty he had taken from destroying Augeas' city (44).

Τίρυνθα ναίων πόλιν·
ἀν᾽ ἵπποισι δὲ τέτρασιν

70 ἀπὸ Μαντινέας Σᾶμος ὁ Ἁλιροθίου·
ἄκοντι Φράστωρ ἔλασε σκοπόν·
μᾶκος δὲ Νικεὺς ἔδικε πέτρῳ χέρα κυκλώσαις
    ὑπὲρ ἁπάντων, καὶ συμμαχία θόρυβον
παραίθυξε μέγαν. ἐν δ᾽ ἕσπερον
ἔφλεξεν εὐώπιδος
75 σελάνας ἐρατὸν φάος.

ἀείδετο δὲ πὰν τέμενος τερπναῖσι θαλίαις
τὸν ἐγκώμιον ἀμφὶ τρόπον.
ἀρχαῖς δὲ προτέραις ἑπόμενοι
    καὶ νυν ἐπωνυμίαν χάριν
νίκας ἀγερώχου κελαδησόμεθα βροντάν
80 καὶ πυρπάλαμον βέλος
ὀρσικτύπου Διός,
ἐν ἅπαντι κράτει
αἴθωνα κεραυνὸν ἀραρότα·
χλιδῶσα δὲ μολπὰ πρὸς κάλαμον
ἀντιάξει μελέων,

E´ τὰ παρ᾽ εὐκλέι Δίρκᾳ χρόνῳ μὲν φάνεν·
86 ἀλλ᾽ ὧτε παῖς ἐξ ἀλόχου πατρί

70 Σᾶμος ὁ Ἁλιροθίου Boeckh: σᾶμ᾽ ἀλιρ(ρ)οθίου (-ους A)
Aa: Σᾶμος (vel Σῆρος) Ἁλιρροθίου Σ^γρ
71 ἄκοντι Moschopulus: ἄκοντι δὲ vett.
86 ὧτε Boeckh: ὥστε codd.

174

who lived in the city of Tiryns,
and in the four-horse chariot race

it was Samus of Mantinea, son of Halirothius.   Ant. 4
Phrastor hit the mark with the javelin,   71
while with a swing of his hand Niceus cast the stone[14]
    a distance beyond all others, and his fellow soldiers
let fly a great cheer. Then the lovely light
of the moon's beautiful face
lit up the evening,[15]   75

and all the sanctuary rang with singing amid festive joy   Ep. 4
in the fashion of victory celebration.
And faithful to those ancient beginnings,
    now too we shall sing a song of glory named
for proud victory[16] to celebrate the thunder
and fire-flung weapon   80
of thunder-rousing Zeus,
the blazing lightning
that befits every triumph,
and the swelling strains of song
    shall answer to the pipe's reed,

songs that have at last appeared by famous Dirce.[17]   Str. 5
But as a son, born from his wife, is longed for   86

[14] The early discuses were made of stone, and accuracy rather
than distance was required in the javelin throw. Eventually these
two events were incorporated into the pentathlon (cf. *Isth.* 1.24–
27).   [15] For the full moon at the time of the Olympic festi-
val, see *Ol.* 3.19–20.
[16] I.e. ὕμνος ἐπινίκιος ("victory hymn").
[17] The spring near Pindar's Thebes.

ποθεινὸς ἵκοντι νεότατος τὸ πάλιν ἤδη,
    μάλα δέ οἱ θερμαίνει φιλότατι νόον·
ἐπεὶ πλοῦτος ὁ λαχὼν ποιμένα
ἐπακτὸν ἀλλότριον
90 θνᾴσκοντι στυγερώτατος·

καὶ ὅταν καλὰ ἔρξαις ἀοιδᾶς ἄτερ,
Ἀγησίδαμ', εἰς Ἀίδα σταθμὸν
ἀνὴρ ἵκηται, κενεὰ πνεύσαις ἔπορε μόχθῳ
    βραχύ τι τερπνόν. τὶν δ' ἀδυεπής τε λύρα
γλυκύς τ' αὐλὸς ἀναπάσσει χάριν·
95 τρέφοντι δ' εὐρὺ κλέος
κόραι Πιερίδες Διός.

ἐγὼ δὲ συνεφαπτόμενος σπουδᾷ, κλυτὸν ἔθνος
Λοκρῶν ἀμφέπεσον, μέλιτι
εὐάνορα πόλιν καταβρέχων·
    παῖδ' ἐρατὸν <δ'> Ἀρχεστράτου
100 αἴνησα, τὸν εἶδον κρατέοντα χερὸς ἀλκᾷ
βωμὸν παρ' Ὀλύμπιον
κεῖνον κατὰ χρόνον
ἰδέᾳ τε καλόν
ὥρᾳ τε κεκραμένον, ἅ ποτε
105 ἀναιδέα Γανυμήδει μόρον ἄ-
    λαλκε σὺν Κυπρογενεῖ.

87 νεότατος Aˢ(schol.)ζ: νεότατι rell.   91 καλὰ Byz:
καλὰ μὲν vett.   99 <δ'> suppl. Moschopulus

by a father already come to the opposite of youth
    and warms his mind with great love
(since wealth that falls to the care
of a stranger from elsewhere
is most hateful to a dying man),   90

so, when a man who has performed noble deeds,   Ant. 5
Hagesidamus, goes without song to Hades'
dwelling, in vain has he striven and gained for his toil
    but brief delight. Upon you, however, the sweetly
speaking lyre and melodious pipe are shedding glory,
and the Pierian daughters of Zeus[18]   95
are fostering your widespread fame.

And I have earnestly joined in and embraced   Ep. 5
the famous race of the Locrians, drenching with honey
their city of brave men.
    I have praised the lovely son of Archestratus,
whom I saw winning with the strength of his hand   100
by the Olympic altar
at that time,
beautiful of form
and imbued with the youthfulness that once averted
ruthless death from Ganymede,   105
    with the aid of the Cyprus-born goddess.[19]

[18] The Muses were born in Pieria, north of Mt. Olympus (cf. Hes. *Th.* 53).
[19] Aphrodite.

---

105 μόρον Mommsen: θάνατον codd.: πότμον Hermann | ἄλαλκε codd.: ἆλκε (vel ἆλξε) Maas

OLYMPIAN 11

This poem commemorates the same event as the previous one, and their relationship has long been debated. The scholia claim that *Ol.* 11 was written to pay the interest on the debt mentioned in *Ol.* 10, while many modern editors (e.g., Dissen, Gildersleeve, Fennell, and Farnell) have followed Boeckh in reversing the order of the two odes on the supposition that *Ol.* 11 was performed immediately at Olympia and that it promises the longer ode (*Ol.* 10). The latter view gains some support from the poet's statement at *Ol.* 10.100 that he saw Hagesidamus win at Olympia, but neither poem makes an explicit reference to the other.

The poem opens with a priamel in which the needs of sailors for winds and of farmers for rain are capped by the need of victors for commemorative songs (1–6). In a brief *praeteritio* (recognized as such by E. L. Bundy), the poet asserts that much can be said in praise of Olympic victors, and that he is eager to praise at length, but declines to do so by saying that with divine help and poetic skill he can succeed just as effectively with a succinct account (7–10). He briefly states Hagesidamus' achievement and offers to grace his Olympic crown by honoring the people of Western Locri (11–15). The poet dispatches the Muses to the celebration there (i.e. in Western Locri) and praises the Locrians for their hospitality, good taste, intelligence, and

178

martial prowess (16–19). He assures the Muses that they will find the Locrians as he has described them, for no more than foxes or lions could they change their nature (19–20).

11. ΑΓΗΣΙΔΑΜΩΙ ΛΟΚΡΩΙ
ΕΠΙΖΕΦΤΡΙΩΙ

ΠΑΙΔΙ ΠΤΚΤΗΙ

Ἔστιν ἀνθρώποις ἀνέμων ὅτε πλεῖστα
χρῆσις· ἔστιν δ' οὐρανίων ὑδάτων,
ὀμβρίων παίδων νεφέλας·
εἰ δὲ σὺν πόνῳ τις εὖ πράσσοι,
  μελιγάρυες ὕμνοι
5 ὑστέρων ἀρχὰ λόγων
τέλλεται καὶ πιστὸν ὅρκιον μεγάλαις ἀρεταῖς.

ἀφθόνητος δ' αἶνος Ὀλυμπιονίκαις
οὗτος ἄγκειται. τὰ μὲν ἁμετέρα
γλῶσσα ποιμαίνειν ἐθέλει,
10 ἐκ θεοῦ δ' ἀνὴρ σοφαῖς ἀνθεῖ
  πραπίδεσσιν ὁμοίως.
ἴσθι νῦν, Ἀρχεστράτου
παῖ, τεᾶς, Ἀγησίδαμε, πυγμαχίας ἕνεκεν

  5 ἀρχὰ A: ἀρχαὶ a
  8 ἄγκειται Byz. (ἀνάκειται schol.): ἔγκειται vett.
  10 ὁμοίως Leutsch e schol.: ὅμως ὦν ζ: om. Av

11. FOR HAGESIDAMUS OF WESTERN LOCRI

WINNER, BOYS' BOXING, 476 B.C.

There is a time when it is for winds that men have   Str.
    greatest
need; there is a time when it is for heavenly waters,
the drenching children of the cloud;
but if through toil someone should succeed,
    honey-sounding hymns
are a beginning for later words of renown,   5
and the faithful pledge of great achievements.

Without stint is that praise dedicated to   Ant.
Olympic victors. My tongue is eager
to shepherd those praises,
but with help from a god a man flourishes   10
    with a wise mind just as well.[1]
Be assured now, son of Archestratus,[2]
that because of your boxing, Hagesidamus,

---

[1] Others, following a scholion (10c), interpret this very difficult sentence to mean that a poet needs a god's help to succeed just as (ὁμοίως) the victor does.

[2] Hagesidamus.

κόσμον ἐπὶ στεφάνῳ χρυσέας ἐλαίας
ἁδυμελῆ κελαδήσω,
15 Ζεφυρίων Λοκρῶν γενεὰν ἀλέγων.
ἔνθα συγκωμάξατ'· ἐγγυάσομαι
μή μιν, ὦ Μοῖσαι, φυγόξεινον στρατόν
μηδ' ἀπείρατον καλῶν
ἀκρόσοφόν τε καὶ αἰχματὰν ἀφίξε-
σθαι. τὸ γὰρ ἐμφυὲς οὔτ' αἴθων ἀλώπηξ
20 οὔτ' ἐρίβρομοι λέοντες διαλλάξαιντο ἦθος.

15 Ζεφυρίων Boehmer: τῶν ἐπιζεφυρίων (ἐπι- om. A¹) codd.
17 μή μιν codd.: ὔμμιν Jongh e paraphr.: μὴ μὲν Hartung:
μή τιν' Thiersch
18 μηδ' codd.: μήτ' Bergk
20 διαλλάξαιντο codd.: διαλλάξαιντ' ἂν Cˢ: μεταλλάξαι-
ντο Choricius: διαλλάξαντο Lehrs: διαλλαξαίατ' Wackernagel

I shall adorn your crown of golden olive   Ep.
with my sweet song of celebration,
as I pay respect to the race of the Epizephyrian Locrians.   15
There join the celebration: I shall promise,
O Muses, that you will come to no people who shun a
        guest
or are inexperienced in beautiful things;
they are supremely wise[3] and spearmen as well.
    Take my word: neither ruddy fox
nor roaring lions could change their inborn character.[4]   20

---

[3] As with "wise" in line 10, the reference is primarily to poetic
skill and appreciation.

[4] The fox (cleverness) and the lions (prowess) point to the na-
tive qualities of intellect (ἀκρόσοφον) and courage (αἰχματάν) in
the Western Locrians (cf. *Ol.* 10.14–15). For the same qualities
in a pancratiast, see *Isth.* 4.45–47.

OLYMPIAN 12

Exiled from Cnossos by political unrest, Ergoteles settled in Himera on the north coast of Sicily and went on to become a double *periodonikēs* in the dolichos (Paus. 6.4.11). The bronze inscription for his statue was discovered at Olympia in 1953, and is dated to 464 or later (Ebert, #20). When this ode was composed (most likely in 466), he was in mid-career and had not yet won his second Olympic victory. The city of Himera had recently been freed from the control of Acragas by Hieron, perhaps occasioning the epithet of Deliverer for Zeus (1).

The poet invokes Tyche (Fortune) as a savior goddess, daughter of Zeus the Deliverer, and asks her to protect Himera (1–2). After describing her powers over sailing, war, and assemblies, he states that men's hopes are often fulfilled, but at other times prove vain (3–6a). No human can know with certainty what the gods have in store for the future (7–9), and many things turn out contrary to men's best judgment: sometimes they are unpleasant, but at other times distress can turn to great happiness (10–12a).

The career of Ergoteles exemplifies adversity proving to be a blessing, for if he had not been exiled from Cnossos, he would not have become a celebrated Panhellenic runner (13–16). Now a victor at Olympia, Delphi, and the Isthmus, he glorifies his new home (17–19).

185

12. ΕΡΓΟΤΕΛΕΙ ΙΜΕΡΑΙΩΙ

ΔΟΛΙΧΟΔΡΟΜΩΙ

Λίσσομαι, παῖ Ζηνὸς Ἐλευθερίου,
Ἱμέραν εὐρυσθενέ᾽ ἀμφιπόλει, σώτειρα Τύχα.
τὶν γὰρ ἐν πόντῳ κυβερνῶνται θοαί
νᾶες, ἐν χέρσῳ τε λαιψηροὶ πόλεμοι
5 κἀγοραὶ βουλαφόροι. αἵ γε μὲν ἀνδρῶν
πόλλ᾽ ἄνω, τὰ δ᾽ αὖ κάτω
6a ψεύδη μεταμώνια τάμνοισαι κυλίνδοντ᾽ ἐλπίδες·

σύμβολον δ᾽ οὔ πώ τις ἐπιχθονίων
πιστὸν ἀμφὶ πράξιος ἐσσομένας εὗρεν θεόθεν,
τῶν δὲ μελλόντων τετύφλωνται φραδαί·
10 πολλὰ δ᾽ ἀνθρώποις παρὰ γνώμαν ἔπεσεν,
ἔμπαλιν μὲν τέρψιος, οἱ δ᾽ ἀνιαραῖς
ἀντικύρσαντες ζάλαις
12a ἐσλὸν βαθὺ πήματος ἐν μικρῷ πεδάμειψαν χρόνῳ.

---

1 Ergoteles won his first Olympic victory in 472 (cf. P. Oxy. 222), but this ode was probably written after his Pythian victory in 466.

12. FOR ERGOTELES OF HIMERA

WINNER, DOLICHOS, 466 B.C.[1]

I entreat you, child of Zeus the Deliverer,	Str.
preserve the might of Himera, Savior Fortune.	
For it is you who on the sea guide swift	
ships, and on land rapid battles	
and assemblies that render counsel. As for men's hopes,	5
they often rise, while at other times they roll down	
as they voyage across vain falsehoods.	6a
No human has yet found a sure sign	Ant.
from the gods regarding an impending action;	
their plans for future events lie hidden from view.[2]	
Many things happen to men counter to their judgment—	10
at times to the reverse of their delight, but then some	
who have encountered grievous storms	
exchange their pain for great good in a short space of	12a
time.	

[2] Others, following the scholiastic gloss of γνώσεις for φραδαί and comparing *Pae.* 7B.18 (τυφλαὶ γὰρ ἀνδρῶν φρένες), translate, "[men's] perceptions of future events are blind."

υἱὲ Φιλάνορος, ἤτοι καὶ τεά κεν
ἐνδομάχας ἅτ' ἀλέκτωρ συγγόνῳ παρ' ἑστίᾳ
15 ἀκλεὴς τιμὰ κατεφυλλορόησε ποδῶν,
εἰ μὴ στάσις ἀντιάνειρα Κνωσίας σ' ἄμερσε
πάτρας.
νῦν δ' Ὀλυμπίᾳ στεφανωσάμενος
καὶ δὶς ἐκ Πυθῶνος Ἰσθμοῖ τ', Ἐργότελες,
θερμὰ Νυμφᾶν λουτρὰ βαστάζεις ὁμι-
λέων παρ' οἰκείαις ἀρούραις.

Son of Philanor, truly would the honor of your feet,   Ep.
like a local fighting cock by its native hearth,
have dropped its leaves ingloriously,   15
had not hostile faction deprived you of your homeland,
    Cnossos.
But now, having won a crown at Olympia,
and twice from Pytho and at the Isthmus, Ergoteles,
you exalt[3] the Nymphs' warm baths, living
    by lands that are your own.

[3] Or *take in your hands* (i.e. bathe in). For the hot springs of
Himera, see Diod. Sic. 5.3.4.

OLYMPIAN 13

The ode opens with Τρισολυμπιονίκαν ("thrice victo-
rious at Olympia"), an imposing compound coined for the
occasion that fills the first verse. It is warranted because
Thessalus, the father of the victor, had won the stadion at
Olympia, while Xenophon achieved the singular feat of
winning both the stadion and the pentathlon in the same
Olympiad. His unique achievement reflects the inventive-
ness of his city, Corinth, for it is credited with the dis-
covery of the dithyramb, the bridle and bit, and temple
decorations. Pindar illustrates Corinthian ingenuity with
the examples of Sisyphus and Medea, but chooses as his
central narrative the discovery of the bridle and bit by
Bellerophon. The athletic success of Xenophon and his
clan, the Oligaethidae, is extraordinary: Pindar credits
them with sixty victories at Nemea and the Isthmus alone.
Pindar also wrote a scolion for Xenophon, twenty lines of
which are preserved as *fr.* 122.

This family with three Olympic victories that is both
kind to citizens and hospitable to foreigners reflects the
qualities of its city, Corinth, where the three Horae (Order,
Justice, and Peace) dwell (1–10). The poet says that he
will boldly proclaim his praise of the Corinthians, includ-
ing their athletic triumphs, inventiveness, and love of the
Muse and Ares (11–23). He prays that Olympian Zeus con-

tinue to bless them with good fortune and receive this
celebration of Xenophon's unprecedented double victory
at Olympia (24–31). There follows an impressive catalog
of Xenophon's and his family's athletic achievements, con-
cluded by the poet's statement that he cannot enumerate
all their victories at Delphi and Nemea, since moderation
should be observed (32–48).

After announcing that he will embark on a public
theme, Pindar praises Corinth for its heroes of the intel-
lect, Sisyphus and Medea, before passing on to the Trojan
war, in which Corinthians fought on both sides, and finally
singling out Glaucus the Lycian, whose ancestor was Bel-
lerophon (49–62). An extensive narrative tells of Bellero-
phon's discovery of the bridle and bit through the help of
Athena, his exploits with Pegasus, and his ultimate fate,
details of which the poet will not provide (63–92).

The poet aims his javelins of praise at the victor's clan,
the Oligaethidae, and provides a catalog of their athletic
victories that includes so many items he must swim away as
if out of a sea (93–114). The poem ends with a prayer to
Zeus to grant them esteem and success (114–115).

13. ΞΕΝΟΦΩΝΤΙ ΚΟΡΙΝΘΙΩΙ

ΣΤΑΔΙΟΔΡΟΜΩΙ ΚΑΙ
ΠΕΝΤΑΘΛΩΙ

Α΄ Τρισολυμπιονίκαν
ἐπαινέων οἶκον ἥμερον ἀστοῖς,
ξένοισι δὲ θεράποντα, γνώσομαι
τὰν ὀλβίαν Κόρινθον, Ἰσθμίου
5 πρόθυρον Ποτειδᾶνος, ἀγλαόκουρον.
ἐν τᾷ γὰρ Εὐνομία ναίει κασι-
γνήτα τε, βάθρον πολίων ἀσφαλές,
Δίκα καὶ ὁμότροφος Εἰ-
ρήνα, τάμι᾽ ἀνδράσι πλούτου,
χρύσεαι παῖδες εὐβούλου Θέμιτος·

ἐθέλοντι δ᾽ ἀλέξειν
10 Ὕβριν, Κόρου ματέρα θρασύμυθον.
ἔχω καλά τε φράσαι, τόλμα τέ μοι

6 κασίγνηταί τε B: κασιγνήτα τε rell.
7 ταμί᾽ Mommsen: ταμίαι codd.

13. FOR XENOPHON OF CORINTH

WINNER, STADION AND PENTATHLON, 464 B.C.

In praising a house with three Olympic victories,   Str. 1
one that is gentle to townsmen
and for foreigners an assiduous host, I shall come to know
prosperous Corinth, portal
of Isthmian Poseidon and city of glorious children.   5
For there dwells Order with her sister Justice,
    firm foundation for cities,
and Peace, steward of wealth for men,
    who was raised with them—
the golden daughters of wise-counseling Themis.[1]

They resolutely ward off   Ant. 1
Hybris, the bold-tongued mother of Excess.[2]   10
I have noble things to tell and straightforward

---

[1] Themis' daughters by Zeus, the Horae (Seasons) are named in the same order at Hes. *Th.* 902.

[2] Hybris is lawless, abusive behavior (the suitors in the *Odyssey* provide good examples); Koros is satiety or excessiveness that becomes cloying. In the normal pairing of *hybris* and *koros*, the relationship is reversed, where excess leads to abusiveness (cf. Theogn. 153).

εὐθεῖα γλῶσσαν ὀρνύει λέγειν,
ἄμαχον δὲ κρύψαι τὸ συγγενὲς ἦθος.
ὔμμιν δέ, παῖδες Ἀλάτα, πολλὰ μὲν
    νικαφόρον ἀγλαΐαν ὤπασαν
15 ἄκραις ἀρεταῖς ὑπερελ-
        θόντων ἱεροῖς ἐν ἀέθλοις,
    πολλὰ δ᾽ ἐν καρδίαις ἀνδρῶν ἔβαλον

Ὧραι πολυάνθεμοι ἀρ-
        χαῖα σοφίσμαθ᾽. ἅπαν δ᾽ εὑρόντος ἔργον.
    ταὶ Διωνύσου πόθεν ἐξέφανεν
    σὺν βοηλάτᾳ χάριτες διθυράμβῳ;
20 τίς γὰρ ἱππείοις ἐν ἔντεσσιν μέτρα,
    ἢ θεῶν ναοῖσιν οἰωνῶν βασιλέα δίδυμον
    ἐπέθηκ᾽; ἐν δὲ Μοῖσ᾽ ἁδύπνοος,
    ἐν δ᾽ Ἄρης ἀνθεῖ νέων
        οὐλίαις αἰχμαῖσιν ἀνδρῶν.

Β΄   ὕπατ᾽ εὐρὺ ἀνάσσων
25 Ὀλυμπίας, ἀφθόνητος ἔπεσσιν
    γένοιο χρόνον ἅπαντα, Ζεῦ πάτερ,
    καὶ τόνδε λαὸν ἀβλαβῆ νέμων
    Ξενοφῶντος εὔθυνε δαίμονος οὖρον·

---

3 The gnome applies both to Pindar's forthright character and to the natural ability of the Corinthians, about to be praised.

4 Aletes was an early Dorian king of Corinth.

5 According to Hdt. 1.23, Arion of Methymna invented the dithyramb and taught it in Corinth. It is called ox-driving because

confidence urges my tongue to speak;
and one cannot conceal the character that is inborn.[3]
Sons of Aletes,[4] upon you have the Horae rich in flowers
    often bestowed the splendor of victory,
when you prevailed with loftiest achievements   15
    in the sacred games,
and often have they put into the hearts of your men

inventions of long ago.   Ep. 1
    All credit belongs to the discoverer.
Whence did the delights of Dionysus appear
with the ox-driving dithyramb?
Who then added the restrainer to the horse's gear   20
or the twin kings of birds to the temples
of the gods?[5] There flourishes the sweet-voiced Muse;
there thrives Ares
    with the young men's deadly spears.

Most exalted, wide-ruling lord   Str. 2
of Olympia, may you not begrudge my words   25
for all time to come, father Zeus,
and, as you guide this people free from harm,
direct the wind of Xenophon's fortune,

oxen served as prizes and were sacrificed during the festival. The
Corinthians initiated the placement of eagles as finials at the apex
of each end of the Doric temple (a schol. claims, however, that
Pindar is referring to the pediments, ἀετώματα, so-called be-
cause they supposedly resemble an eagle's outstretched wings).
The discovery of the bridle and bit will be the subject of the forth-
coming narrative.

PINDAR

δέξαι τέ οἱ στεφάνων ἐγκώμιον
    τεθμόν, τὸν ἄγει πεδίων ἐκ Πίσας,
30 πενταέθλῳ ἅμα σταδίου
    νικῶν δρόμον· ἀντεβόλησεν
    τῶν ἀνὴρ θνατὸς οὔπω τις πρότερον.

δύο δ᾽ αὐτὸν ἔρεψαν
    πλόκοι σελίνων ἐν Ἰσθμιάδεσσιν
    φανέντα· Νεμεά τ᾽ οὐκ ἀντιξοεῖ·
35 πατρὸς δὲ Θεσσαλοῖ ἐπ᾽ Ἀλφεοῦ
    ῥεέθροισιν αἴγλα ποδῶν ἀνάκειται,
    Πυθοῖ τ᾽ ἔχει σταδίου τιμὰν διαύ-
        λου θ᾽ ἁλίῳ ἀμφ᾽ ἑνί, μηνός τέ οἱ
    τωὐτοῦ κρανααῖς ἐν Ἀθά-
        ναισι τρία ἔργα ποδαρκής
    ἁμέρα θῆκε κάλλιστ᾽ ἀμφὶ κόμαις,

40 Ἑλλώτια δ᾽ ἑπτάκις· ἐν
        δ᾽ ἀμφιάλοισι Ποτειδᾶνος τεθμοῖσιν
    Πτοιοδώρῳ σὺν πατρὶ μακρότεραι
    Τερψίᾳ θ᾽ ἕποντ᾽ Ἐριτίμῳ τ᾽ ἀοιδαί·
    ὅσσα τ᾽ ἐν Δελφοῖσιν ἀριστεύσατε
    ἠδὲ χόρτοις ἐν λέοντος, δηρίομαι πολέσιν
45 περὶ πλήθει καλῶν· ὡς μὰν σαφές

42 Τερψίᾳ θ᾽ E. Schmid: τερψία θ᾽ N^{pc}O^{ac}?: τερψίαι θ᾽ B^s:
τέρψιές θ᾽ CO^{pc}B^i: τέρψιες β, sed cf. schol. | Ἐριτίμῳ E.
Schmid: ἐρίτιμοι (ἐριτίμῳ schol.) codd.

196

and receive from him as tribute for his crowns this rite
    of celebration, which he brings from the plains of Pisa,
by winning in both the pentathlon   30
    and the stadion race. He has attained
what no mortal man ever did before.

Two wreaths of wild parsley crowned him   Ant. 2
when he appeared at the Isthmian
festivals, and Nemea offers no opposition.[6]
The foot-racing glory of his father Thessalus   35
is dedicated by the streams of the Alpheus,
and at Pytho he holds the honor of the stadion and
    diaulos won within one sun's course, while in the same
month in rocky Athens one swift-footed day
    placed three fairest
prizes around his hair,

and the Hellotian games[7] did so seven times.   Ep. 2
    But in Poseidon's festivals between the seas
it will take longer songs to keep up with Ptoeodorus, 41
his father, and Terpsias and Eritimus.[8]
And when it comes to all your family's victories at Delphi
and in the lion's fields,[9] I stand opposed to many[10]
concerning the multitude of successes, for truly   45

---

[6] Litotes. Nemea tells the same story.

[7] Games held at Corinth in honor of Athena Hellotis.

[8] The schol. claim that Ptoeodorus and Terpsias were brothers
(and hence father and uncle of Thessalus), while Eritimus was the
son (or grandson) of Terpsias.   [9] Nemea, where Heracles slew
the lion.   [10] I.e. many other eulogists of the family. In lines
98–100 he gives his count of their Nemean and Isthmian victories.

οὐκ ἂν εἰδείην λέγειν
ποντιᾶν ψάφων ἀριθμόν.

Γʹ ἕπεται δ᾽ ἐν ἑκάστῳ
μέτρον· νοῆσαι δὲ καιρὸς ἄριστος.
ἐγὼ δὲ ἴδιος ἐν κοινῷ σταλείς
50 μῆτίν τε γαρύων παλαιγόνων
πόλεμόν τ᾽ ἐν ἡρωίαις ἀρεταῖσιν
οὐ ψεύσομ᾽ ἀμφὶ Κορίνθῳ, Σίσυφον
    μὲν πυκνότατον παλάμαις ὡς θεόν,
καὶ τὰν πατρὸς ἀντία Μή-
    δειαν θεμέναν γάμον αὐτᾷ,
ναῒ σώτειραν Ἀργοῖ καὶ προπόλοις·

55 τὰ δὲ καί ποτ᾽ ἐν ἀλκᾷ
πρὸ Δαρδάνου τειχέων ἐδόκησαν
ἐπ᾽ ἀμφότερα μαχᾶν τάμνειν τέλος,
τοὶ μὲν γένει φίλῳ σὺν Ἀτρέος
Ἑλέναν κομίζοντες, οἱ δ᾽ ἀπὸ πάμπαν
60 εἴργοντες· ἐκ Λυκίας δὲ Γλαῦκον ἐλ-
    θόντα τρόμεον Δαναοί. τοῖσι μέν
ἐξεύχετ᾽ ἐν ἄστεϊ Πει-
    ράνας σφετέρου πατρὸς ἀρχάν
καὶ βαθὺν κλᾶρον ἔμμεν καὶ μέγαρον·

11 I.e. Agamemnon and Menelaus. The Corinthians were un-
der the command of Agamemnon (cf. *Il.* 2.569–577).

I would not know how to state a clear number
    for the pebbles of the sea.

In each matter there comes   Str. 3
due measure, and it is best to recognize what is fitting.
But I, as a private individual embarked upon a public
        mission,
proclaiming their ancestors' intelligence   50
and warfare amidst heroic achievements,
shall tell no lies about Corinth in citing Sisyphus,
    most shrewd in cleverness like a god,
and Medea, who in opposition to her father
    made her own marriage,
to become the savior of the ship Argo and its crew;

and then in former times as well, in their might   Ant. 3
before the walls of Dardanus, they gained the reputation   56
on both sides for determining the outcome of battles,
both those endeavoring with the dear offspring of Atreus[11]
to recover Helen, and those who at every turn were trying
to prevent them: for the Danaans trembled before   60
    Glaucus who came from Lycia. And to them
he boasted that in the city
of Pirene[12] were the kingship
and rich inheritance and the palace of his father,[13]

[12] Corinth, where the fountain of Pirene is located.
[13] This account of Bellerophon is based loosely on the speech
of Glaucus at *Il.* 6.153–211, where the descent is Bellerophon–
Hippolochus–Glaucus. Pindar seems to omit Hippolochus.

ὃς τᾶς ὀφιώδεος υἱ-
  όν ποτε Γοργόνος ἦ πόλλ᾽ ἀμφὶ κρουνοῖς
Πάγασον ζεῦξαι ποθέων ἔπαθεν,
65 πρίν γέ οἱ χρυσάμπυκα κούρα χαλινόν
Παλλὰς ἤνεγκ᾽, ἐξ ὀνείρου δ᾽ αὐτίκα
ἦν ὕπαρ, φώνασε δ᾽· "Εὕδεις Αἰολίδα βασιλεῦ;
ἄγε φίλτρον τόδ᾽ ἵππειον δέκευ,
καὶ Δαμαίῳ νιν θύων
  ταῦρον ἀργάεντα πατρὶ δεῖξον."

Δ΄ κυάναιγις ἐν ὄρφνᾳ
71 κνώσσοντί οἱ παρθένος τόσα εἰπεῖν
ἔδοξεν· ἀνὰ δ᾽ ἔπαλτ᾽ ὀρθῷ ποδί.
παρκείμενον δὲ συλλαβὼν τέρας,
ἐπιχώριον μάντιν ἄσμενος εὗρεν,
75 δεῖξέν τε Κοιρανίδᾳ πᾶσαν τελευ-
  τὰν πράγματος, ὥς τ᾽ ἀνὰ βωμῷ θεᾶς
κοιτάξατο νύκτ᾽ ἀπὸ κεί-
  νου χρήσιος, ὥς τέ οἱ αὐτά
Ζηνὸς ἐγχεικεραύνου παῖς ἔπορεν

δαμασίφρονα χρυσόν.
ἐνυπνίῳ δ᾽ ᾇ τάχιστα πιθέσθαι
80 κελήσατό νιν, ὅταν δ᾽ εὐρυσθενεῖ

79 δ᾽ ᾇ Kayser: δ᾽ ἅ E: δαὶ ζ: δὴ F: δέ᾽ Βγ: δ᾽ ὡς Byz.

---

[14] Pirene.

who once suffered much indeed in his yearning   Ep. 3
    to yoke Pegasus, the snaky Gorgon's
son, beside the spring,[14]
until, that is, the maiden Pallas brought him the bridle   65
with the golden bands, when his dream suddenly
      became
reality and she spoke, "Are you asleep, prince of Aeolus'
      race?[15]
Come, take this horse charm,
and, sacrificing a white bull,
    show it to your father, the Horsetamer."[16]

So much did the maiden of the dark aegis   Str. 4
seem to say to him as he slept   71
in the darkness, and he leapt to his feet.
He took the marvel that lay beside him
and gladly sought out the local seer,
the son of Coeranus,[17] to whom he revealed the entire   75
    outcome of the affair, how he slept the night on the
goddess' altar[18] at the bidding of that seer's oracle,
    and how the very daughter
of Zeus whose spear is the thunderbolt gave him

the spirit-taming gold.   Ant. 4
The seer commanded him to heed the dream
as quickly as possible, and, upon sacrificing   80

---

[15] Aeolus was Bellerophon's great grandfather.

[16] Poseidon; not strictly Bellerophon's father, but ancestor.

[17] Polyidus (cf. *Il.* 13.663).

[18] Sleeping in a temple (*incubatio*) was a means of communication with gods.

καρταίποδ' ἀναρύῃ Γαιαόχῳ,
θέμεν Ἱππίᾳ βωμὸν εὐθὺς Ἀθάνᾳ.
τελεῖ δὲ θεῶν δύναμις καὶ τὰν παρ' ὅρ-
κον καὶ παρὰ ἐλπίδα κούφαν κτίσιν.
ἤτοι καὶ ὁ καρτερὸς ὁρ-
μαίνων ἔλε Βελλεροφόντας,
85   φάρμακον πραῢ τείνων ἀμφὶ γένυι,

ἵππον πτερόεντ'· ἀναβαὶς δ'
εὐθὺς ἐνόπλια χαλκωθεὶς ἔπαιζεν.
σὺν δὲ κείνῳ καί ποτ' Ἀμαζονίδων
αἰθέρος ψυχρῶν ἀπὸ κόλπων ἐρήμου
τοξόταν βάλλων γυναικεῖον στρατὸν
90   καὶ Χίμαιραν πῦρ πνέοισαν καὶ Σολύμους ἔπεφνεν.
διασωπάσομαί οἱ μόρον ἐγώ·
τὸν δ' ἐν Οὐλύμπῳ φάτναι
Ζηνὸς ἀρχαῖαι δέκονται.

Ε΄   ἐμὲ δ' εὐθὺν ἀκόντων
ἱέντα ῥόμβον παρὰ σκοπὸν οὐ χρὴ
95   τὰ πολλὰ βέλεα καρτύνειν χεροῖν.
Μοίσαις γὰρ ἀγλαοθρόνοις ἑκὼν
Ὀλιγαιθίδαισίν τ' ἔβαν ἐπίκουρος.

83 κτίσιν Moschopulus: κτῆσιν vett.
88 ψυχρῶν Schroeder: ψυχρᾶς codd.
96 ἑκών Moschopulus: εἴκων vett.

a strong-footed victim[19] to the mighty Earthholder,
to erect at once an altar to Athena Hippia.[20]
The gods' power easily brings into being even
    what one would swear impossible and beyond hope.
And indeed powerful Bellerophon,
    eagerly stretching
the soothing remedy around its jaws, captured   85

the winged horse. He mounted him, and clad in his armor Ep. 4
    of bronze immediately began to make sport in warfare.
And with that horse thereafter, firing
from the cold recesses of the empty air, he slew
the army of female archers, the Amazons,
and the fire-breathing Chimaera and the Solymi.[21]   90
I shall be silent about his own doom,
but as for the other, Zeus' ancient stalls
    on Olympus still accommodate him.[22]

But I, in casting whirling javelins   Str. 5
on their straight path, must not hurl
those many shafts from my hands beside the mark.   95
For I have come as a willing helper for the Muses
on their splendid thrones, and for the Oligaethidae.[23]

---

[19] I.e. the bull mentioned in 69.

[20] Athena, goddess of horses, who had a cult at Corinth.

[21] For these exploits, see *Il.* 6.179–186.

[22] Bellerophon tried to ride Pegasus to Olympus (*Isth.* 7.44–47) and ended up wandering over the Aleian plain (*Il.* 6.200–202); for Pegasus' reception on Olympus, see Hes. *Th.* 285: ἵετ' ἐς ἀθανάτους· Ζηνὸς δ' ἐν δώμασι ναίει.

[23] The family of Xenophon.

PINDAR

Ἰσθμοῖ τά τ᾽ ἐν Νεμέᾳ παύρῳ ἔπει
　　θήσω φανέρ᾽ ἀθρό᾽, ἀλαθής τέ μοι
ἔξορκος ἐπέσσεται ἑξηκοντάκι δὴ ἀμφοτέρωθεν
100　ἀδύγλωσσος βοὰ κάρυκος ἐσλοῦ.

τὰ δ᾽ Ὀλυμπίᾳ αὐτῶν
ἔοικεν ἤδη πάροιθε λελέχθαι·
τά τ᾽ ἐσσόμενα τότ᾽ ἂν φαίην σαφές.
νῦν δ᾽ ἔλπομαι μέν, ἐν θεῷ γε μάν
105　τέλος· εἰ δὲ δαίμων γενέθλιος ἕρποι,
Δὶ τοῦτ᾽ Ἐννάλίῳ τ᾽ ἐκδώσομεν
　　πράσσειν. τὰ δ᾽ ὑπ᾽ ὀφρύι Παρνασσίᾳ
ἕξ· Ἀργεῖ θ᾽ ὅσσα καὶ ἐν
　　Θήβαις· ὅσα τ᾽ Ἀρκάσιν †ἀνάσσων
μαρτυρήσει Λυκαίου βωμὸς ἄναξ·

Πέλλανά τε καὶ Σικυὼν
　　καὶ Μέγαρ᾽ Αἰακιδᾶν τ᾽ εὐερκὲς ἄλσος
110　ἅ τ᾽ Ἐλευσὶς καὶ λιπαρὰ Μαραθὼν
ταί θ᾽ ὑπ᾽ Αἴτνας ὑψιλόφου καλλίπλουτοι
πόλιες ἅ τ᾽ Εὔβοια· καὶ πᾶσαν κάτα
Ἑλλάδ᾽ εὑρήσεις ἐρευνῶν μάσσον᾽ ἢ ὡς ἰδέμεν.

98 παύρῳ ἔπει θήσω Mommsen: παύρῳ δ᾽ ἔπει θήσω (δ᾽ ἐπιθήσω Bᶜˡ Cᶜˡ Nˡ Oᵃᶜ) codd.
99 δὴ ἀμφ. Boeckh: δ᾽ ἀμφ. codd.　　107 ἕξ· Ἀργεῖ θ᾽ edd.: ἑξ, ἄργει θ᾽ C: ἐν ἀργεῖ θ᾽ NO: ἐξ ἄρατο, ἐν ἄργει δ᾽ B: idem omissis ἐξ ἄρατο β | Ἀρκάσιν ἀνάσσων codd.: Ἀρκάσι βάσσαις Bergk: Ἀρκάσιν ἆσσον Mommsen

204

As for their victories at the Isthmus and Nemea, in a brief
    word I shall reveal their sum, and my true witness
under oath shall be the noble herald's sweet-tongued
shout heard full sixty times from both those places.   100

Their Olympic victories to date   Ant. 5
have, it seems, already been reported;[24]
and those to come I would declare clearly when they
        occur.
At this point I am hopeful, but with the god is
the outcome. But if their family fortune should continue,   105
we will leave it to Zeus and Enyalius[25]
    to accomplish. Their victories beneath Parnassus' brow
number six; and all those at Argos
    and in Thebes, and all those whose witness will be
the Lycaean god's[26] royal altar that rules over the
        Arcadians,

and Pellana and Sicyon and   Ep. 5
    Megara and the well-walled precinct of the Aeacidae,[27]
and Eleusis and shining Marathon   110
and the splendidly rich cities under Aetna's
lofty crest[28] and Euboea—and if you search throughout
all Hellas, you will find more than the eye can see.

---

[24] The three Olympic victories announced by the first word
of the poem, two won by Xenophon (30) and one by Thessalus
(35–36).   [25] Ares.

[26] Zeus'.

[27] In Aegina.

[28] Aetna and Syracuse.

ἄγε κούφοισιν ἔκνευσον ποσίν·
115   Ζεῦ τέλει’, αἰδῶ δίδοι
      καὶ τύχαν τερπνῶν γλυκεῖαν.

114 ἄγε . . . ἔκνευσον (vel ἐκνεύσω) Maas: ἀλλὰ . . . ἐκνεῦ-
σαι codd.: ἄνα . . . ἐκνεῦσαι Kayser
115 αἰδῶ Byz.: αἰδῶ τε codd.

Come, swim out with nimble feet.
Zeus accomplisher, grant them respect   115
    and sweet attainment of success.

OLYMPIAN 14

This is the only ode to a victor from Orchomenus (Erchomenus in Boeotian spelling) and consists mainly of a hymn to the Graces (Χάριτες), associated with the city from ancient times (Paus. 9.35.1–7). Since the date of 476 given by the scholia is not confirmed by P. Oxy. 222, the poem is usually ascribed to 488, the date most likely to have been altered by a scribal error (cf. Gaspar 50). According to the scholia the event (not indicated in the poem) was the stadion in the boys' category. It is the only ode to consist of just two strophes.

The poet invokes the Graces as guardians of Orchomenus and providers of all pleasure for mortals (1–7). They are also present at the gods' festivals and seated beside Apollo (8–12). In the second strophe the poet re-invokes them by name as Aglaia (Splendor), Euphrosyne (Good Cheer), and Thalia (Festivity) and, because she helped bring it about, asks the last of these to look kindly upon the present celebration of Asopichus' Olympic victory (13–20). The sudden appearance of the word μελαντειχέα ("black-walled") casts a shadow over the so-far joyful ode, as the poet asks Echo to convey the news of the young man's victory to his dead father in Hades (20–24).

14. ΑΣΩΠΙΧΩΙ
ΟΡΧΟΜΕΝΙΩΙ
ΣΤΑΔΙΕΙ

Α΄ Καφισίων ὑδάτων
λαχοῖσαι αἵτε ναίετε καλλίπωλον ἕδραν,
ὦ λιπαρᾶς ἀοίδιμοι βασίλειαι
Χάριτες Ἐρχομενοῦ, παλαιγόνων Μιννᾶν ἐπίσκοποι,
5 κλῦτ', ἐπεὶ εὔχομαι· σὺν γὰρ ὑμῖν τά ‹τε› τερπνὰ
καί
τὰ γλυκέ' ἄνεται πάντα βροτοῖς,
εἰ σοφός, εἰ καλός, εἴ τις ἀγλαὸς ἀνήρ.
οὐδὲ γὰρ θεοὶ σεμνᾶν Χαρίτων ἄτερ
κοιρανέοντι χοροὺς
οὔτε δαῖτας· ἀλλὰ πάντων ταμίαι
10 ἔργων ἐν οὐρανῷ, χρυσότοξον θέμεναι πάρα
Πύθιον Ἀπόλλωνα θρόνους,
αἰέναον σέβοντι πατρὸς Ὀλυμπίοιο τιμάν.

5 ‹τε› suppl. Hermann   6 γλυκέ' ἄνεται Kayser e
schol.: γλυκέα γίνεται codd.   8 οὐδὲ Schneidewin: οὔτε
codd.   codd.

14. FOR ASOPICHUS OF ORCHOMENUS

WINNER, STADION

You to whom the waters of Cephisus   Str. 1
belong, and who dwell in a land of fine horses,
O Graces, much sung queens
of shining Orchomenus and guardians of the ancient
    Minyae,[1]
hear my prayer. For with your help all things pleasant   5
and sweet come about for mortals,
whether a man be wise, handsome, or illustrious.
Yes, not even the gods arrange
choruses or feasts
    without the august Graces; but as stewards of all
works in heaven, they have their thrones beside   10
Pythian Apollo of the golden bow,
and worship the Olympian father's[2] ever flowing majesty.

---

[1] The ancient inhabitants of Orchomenus.

[2] Zeus', either as the "father of gods and men" or as the Graces'
father (cf. Hes. *Th.* 907–909, where their names are given in the
same order as in this poem).

211

Β΄ <ὦ> πότνι᾽ Ἀγλαΐα
  φιλησίμολπέ τ᾽ Εὐφροσύνα, θεῶν κρατίστου
15 παῖδες, ἐπακοοῖτε νῦν, Θαλία τε
  ἐρασίμολπε, ἰδοῖσα τόνδε κῶμον ἐπ᾽ εὐμενεῖ τύχᾳ
  κοῦφα βιβῶντα· Λυδῷ γὰρ Ἀσώπιχον ἐν τρόπῳ
  ἐν μελέταις τ᾽ ἀείδων ἔμολον,
  οὕνεκ᾽ Ὀλυμπιόνικος ἁ Μινύεια
20 σεῦ ἕκατι. μελαντειχέα νῦν δόμον
  Φερσεφόνας ἔλθ᾽, Ἀ-
    χοῖ, πατρὶ κλυτὰν φέροισ᾽ ἀγγελίαν,
  Κλεόδαμον ὄφρ᾽ ἰδοῖσ᾽, υἱὸν εἴπῃς ὅτι οἱ νέαν
  κόλποις παρ᾽ εὐδόξοις Πίσας
  ἐστεφάνωσε κυδίμων ἀέθλων πτεροῖσι χαίταν.

13 <ὦ> suppl. Byz.
15 ἐπακοοῖτέ νυν Bergk: ἐπάκοοι νῦν codd.
23 εὐδόξοις Bergk: εὐδόξοιο codd.: εὐδόξου Boeckh

O queenly Aglaia,   Str. 2
and song-loving Euphrosyne, children of the mightiest
of the gods, hear me now—and may you, Thalia,   15
lover of song, look with favor upon this revel band,
stepping lightly in celebration of kindly fortune. For I
    have come,
singing of Asopichus in Lydian mode[3] as I practice my
    art,
since the land of the Minyae is victorious at Olympia
because of you. To the black-walled house   20
of Persephone go now,
    Echo, carrying the glorious news to his father,
so that when you see Cleodamus you can say that his son
has crowned his youthful hair in the famous valley of Pisa
with winged wreaths from the games that bring renown.[4]

[3] For the Lydian mode (or harmony), see *Nem.* 4.45; Aristotle,
Pol. 1342b30–33; and Plato, *Rep.* 398E.
[4] For other examples of dead relatives receiving word of the
victory, see *Ol.* 8.77–84 and *Pyth.* 5.98–103.

213

ΠΥΘΙΟΝΙΚΑΙ

PYTHIAN ODES

PYTHIAN 1

Upon winning the chariot race at the Pythian games in 470, Hieron, ruler of Syracuse, was announced as a citizen of Aetna, thereby publicizing his founding of that city in 476/5 with 5,000 settlers from Syracuse and 5,000 from the Peloponnesus (Diod. Sic. 11.49). The ode celebrates that founding in a broader context of harmonious peace, achieved in the polis by good governance, maintained against foreign aggression by resolute warfare, and, on a cosmic scale, gained and held against the forces of disorder by Zeus' power, exemplified by Typhos' confinement under Mt. Aetna.

There has been much discussion concerning the campaign alluded to in lines 50–55, where Hieron is compared to Philoctetes. One scholion (99a) says that it is Hieron's intervention on behalf of Western Locri against Anaxilas of Rhegium in 477 (cf. *Pyth.* 2.18–20), while many modern scholars have argued that it is Hieron's defeat of Thrasydaeus of Acragas in 472. Most likely it is his victory at Cyme in 474, treated in lines 72–75.

The poem opens with a hymn to the Lyre, which has the power to pacify Zeus' thunderbolt and eagle and calm the spirits of Ares and the other gods (1–12). The effect of the Muses' song on Zeus' enemies is one of terror, especially on Typhos, who, pinned down under Cyme (near Mt. Vesuvius) and Aetna, sends up eruptions of lava in his tor-

216

mented frustration (13–28). In the first of several prayers articulating the poem (cf. 39, 46, 58, 63, 68, and 71), the poet asks for Zeus' favor and tells of Hieron's victory in the Pythian chariot race, which he considers a promising sign of the city's future success (29–38).

Using an analogy from javelin throwing, the poet expresses a hope that he will outdistance his rivals in praising Hieron (41–45), whose family has gained unsurpassed glory in warfare (46–50), while he himself, like Philoctetes, was summoned to campaign although ill (50–55).

An address to the Muse turns attention to Hieron's son, Deinomenes, the titular king of Aetna (58–60). The city was founded in the political tradition established by the Dorian conquest of Greece (61–66); Zeus is asked to assist its rulers in maintaining peace (67–70).

The poet prays that the Carthaginians and Etruscans will remain peaceful (71–72), now that the latter have suffered defeat by Hieron at Cyme (72–75). A brief priamel cites the Athenian victory at Salamis and the Spartan victory at Plataea, and concludes with the Deinomenid victory at Himera against the Carthaginians (75–80).

The final triad turns to Hieron's civic governance, prefaced by a concern that lengthy praise can cause tedium or resentment (81–84). Citing the proverb "envy (for success) is better than pity (for failure)," the poet couches his praise in a series of exhortations to Hieron recommending justice, truthfulness, accountability, and generosity (85–94). Two rulers from the previous century are cited as positive and negative examples: Croesus is well remembered for his generosity, whereas Phalaris' cruelty is abominated (94–98). Best of all is success combined with fame (99–100).

1. ΙΕΡΩΝΙ ΑΙΤΝΑΙΩΙ

ΑΡΜΑΤΙ

Α΄   Χρυσέα φόρμιγξ, Ἀπόλλωνος καὶ ἰοπλοκάμων
σύνδικον Μοισᾶν κτέανον· τᾶς ἀκούει
    μὲν βάσις ἀγλαΐας ἀρχά,
πείθονται δ᾽ ἀοιδοὶ σάμασιν
ἀγησιχόρων ὁπόταν προοιμίων
    ἀμβολὰς τεύχῃς ἐλελιζομένα.
5 καὶ τὸν αἰχματὰν κεραυνὸν σβεννύεις
αἰενάου πυρός. εὕδει δ᾽ ἀνὰ σκά-
    πτῳ Διὸς αἰετός, ὠκεῖ-
αν πτέρυγ᾽ ἀμφοτέρωθεν χαλάξαις,

ἀρχὸς οἰωνῶν, κελαινῶπιν δ᾽ ἐπί οἱ νεφέλαν
ἀγκύλῳ κρατί, γλεφάρων ἀδὺ κλάι-
    θρον, κατέχευας· ὁ δὲ κνώσσων
ὑγρὸν νῶτον αἰωρεῖ, τεαῖς
10 ῥιπαῖσι κατασχόμενος. καὶ γὰρ βια-
τὰς Ἄρης, τραχεῖαν ἄνευθε λιπών
    ἐγχέων ἀκμάν, ἰαίνει καρδίαν
κώματι, κῆλα δὲ καὶ δαιμόνων θέλ-

1. FOR HIERON OF AETNA

WINNER, CHARIOT RACE, 470 B.C.

Golden Lyre, rightful possession[1] of Apollo   Str. 1
and the violet-haired Muses, to you the footstep listens
    as it begins the splendid celebration,
and the singers heed your signals,
whenever with your vibrations you strike up
    the chorus-leading preludes.
You quench even the warring thunderbolt   5
of ever flowing fire; and the eagle sleeps
    on the scepter of Zeus,
    having relaxed his swift wings on either side,

the king of birds, for you have poured   Ant. 1
over his curved head a black-hooded cloud,
    sweet seal for his eyelids. And as he slumbers,
he ripples his supple back, held in check
by your volley of notes. For even powerful   10
    Ares puts aside
his sharp-pointed spears and delights his heart
in sleep; and your shafts enchant

---

[1] Or *possession that speaks on their behalf*. The normal meaning of σύνδικος is "advocate" (cf. *Ol.* 9.98).

γει φρένας ἀμφί τε Λατοί-
δα σοφίᾳ βαθυκόλπων τε Μοισᾶν.

ὅσσα δὲ μὴ πεφίληκε Ζεύς, ἀτύζονται βοάν
Πιερίδων ἀίοντα, γᾶν τε καὶ πόν-
τον κατ' ἀμαιμάκετον,
15 ὅς τ' ἐν αἰνᾷ Ταρτάρῳ κεῖται, θεῶν πολέμιος,
Τυφὼς ἑκατοντακάρανος· τόν ποτε
Κιλίκιον θρέψεν πολυώνυμον ἄντρον· νῦν γε μάν
ταί θ' ὑπὲρ Κύμας ἁλιερκέες ὄχθαι
Σικελία τ' αὐτοῦ πιέζει
στέρνα λαχνάεντα· κίων δ' οὐρανία συνέχει,
20 νιφόεσσ' Αἴτνα, πάνετες χιόνος ὀξείας τιθήνα·

Β΄ τᾶς ἐρεύγονται μὲν ἀπλάτου πυρὸς ἁγνόταται
ἐκ μυχῶν παγαί· ποταμοὶ δ' ἁμέραισιν
μὲν προχέοντι ῥόον καπνοῦ
αἴθων'· ἀλλ' ἐν ὄρφναισιν πέτρας
φοίνισσα κυλινδομένα φλὸξ ἐς βαθεῖ-
αν φέρει πόντου πλάκα σὺν πατάγῳ.
25 κεῖνο δ' Ἀφαίστοιο κρουνοὺς ἑρπετόν
δεινοτάτους ἀναπέμπει· τέρας μὲν
θαυμάσιον προσιδέσθαι,
θαῦμα δὲ καὶ παρεόντων ἀκοῦσαι,

20 πανέτης Christ
26 παρεόντων C, Gellius, Macrobius: παριόντων β

the minds of the deities as well, through the skill
of Leto's son[2] and of the deep-breasted Muses.

But those creatures for whom Zeus has no love are   Ep. 1
    terrified
when they hear the song of the Pierians, those on land
    and in the overpowering sea,
and the one who lies in dread Tartarus, enemy of the   15
    gods,
Typhos[3] the hundred-headed, whom
the famous Cilician cave once reared; now, however,
the sea-fencing cliffs above Cyme
    as well as Sicily weigh upon his shaggy chest,
    and a skyward column constrains him,
snowy Aetna, nurse of biting snow all year round,   20

from whose depths belch forth holiest springs   Str. 2
of unapproachable fire; during the days rivers of lava
    pour forth a blazing stream
of smoke, but in times of darkness
a rolling red flame carries rocks into the deep
    expanse of the sea with a crash.[4]
That monster sends up most terrible springs   25
of Hephaestus' fire—a portent
    wondrous to behold,
    a wonder even to hear of from those present—

---

[2] Apollo; the echo of line 1 reinforces the closure of this part
of the hymn.

[3] Typhos (also called Typhoeus and Typhon) was the last en-
emy of Zeus' reign (cf. Hes. *Th.* 820–880).

[4] The alliteration of π's and ϕ's in the Greek is striking.

οἷον Αἴτνας ἐν μελαμφύλλοις δέδεται κορυφαῖς
καὶ πέδῳ, στρωμνὰ δὲ χαράσσοισ᾿ ἅπαν νῶ-
τον ποτικεκλιμένον κεντεῖ.
εἴη, Ζεῦ, τὶν εἴη ἀνδάνειν,
30   ὃς τοῦτ᾿ ἐφέπεις ὄρος, εὐκάρποιο γαί-
ας μέτωπον, τοῦ μὲν ἐπωνυμίαν
κλεινὸς οἰκιστὴρ ἐκύδανεν πόλιν
γείτονα, Πυθιάδος δ᾿ ἐν δρόμῳ κά-
ρυξ ἀνέειπέ νιν ἀγγέλ-
λων Ἱέρωνος ὑπὲρ καλλινίκου

ἅρμασι. ναυσιφορήτοις δ᾿ ἀνδράσι πρῶτα χάρις
ἐς πλόον ἀρχομένοις πομπαῖον ἐλθεῖν
οὖρον· ἐοικότα γάρ
35   καὶ τελευτᾷ φερτέρου νόστου τυχεῖν. ὁ δὲ λόγος
ταύταις ἐπὶ συντυχίαις δόξαν φέρει
λοιπὸν ἔσσεσθαι στεφάνοισί ν⟨ιν⟩ ἵπποις τε κλυτάν
καὶ σὺν εὐφώνοις θαλίαις ὀνυμαστάν.
Λύκιε καὶ Δάλοι᾿ ἀνάσσων
     Φοῖβε Παρνασσοῦ τε κράναν Κασταλίαν φιλέων,
40   ἐθελήσαις ταῦτα νόῳ τιθέμεν εὔανδρόν τε χώραν.

Γ΄   ἐκ θεῶν γὰρ μαχαναὶ πᾶσαι βροτέαις ἀρεταῖς,
καὶ σοφοὶ καὶ χερσὶ βιαταὶ περίγλωσ-
σοί τ᾿ ἔφυν. ἄνδρα δ᾿ ἐγὼ κεῖνον

34 ἐρχομένοις C(schol. Nem. 1.49)
37 ⟨ιν⟩ suppl. Heyne

such a one is confined within Aetna's dark and leafy peaks   Ant. 2
and the plain; and a jagged bed goads the entire length
   of his back that lies against it.
Grant, O Zeus, grant that I may please you,
you who rule that mountain, the brow of a   30
   fruitful land, whose neighboring city[5] that bears
its name was honored by its illustrious founder,
when at the racecourse of the Pythian festival
   the herald proclaimed it
   in announcing Hieron's splendid victory

with the chariot. For seafaring men the first blessing   Ep. 2
as they set out on a voyage is the coming of a favorable
   wind, since it is likely that they will attain
a more successful return at the end as well. And this   35
     saying,
given the present success, inspires the expectation that
hereafter the city will be renowned for crowns and horses
and its name honored amid tuneful festivities.
Lord of Lycia, O Phoebus, you who rule over Delos
   and who love Parnassus' Castalian spring,[6]
willingly take those things to heart and make this a land   40
   of brave men.

For from the gods come all the means for human   Str. 3
     achievements,
and men are born wise, or strong of hand and eloquent.
   In my eagerness to praise

---

[5] Hieron refounded Catane as Aetna (modern Catania) at the
base of Mt. Aetna in 476/5.   [6] Lycia, Delos, and Delphi (at
Mt. Parnassus) are cult centers of Apollo.

αἰνῆσαι μενοινῶν ἔλπομαι
μὴ χαλκοπάραον ἄκονθ᾽ ὡσείτ᾽ ἀγῶ-
νος βαλεῖν ἔξω παλάμᾳ δονέων,
45 μακρὰ δὲ ῥίψαις ἀμεύσασθ᾽ ἀντίους.
εἰ γὰρ ὁ πᾶς χρόνος ὄλβον μὲν οὕτω
καὶ κτεάνων δόσιν εὐθύ-
νοι, καμάτων δ᾽ ἐπίλασιν παράσχοι·

ἦ κεν ἀμνάσειεν, οἵαις ἐν πολέμοισι μάχαις
τλάμονι ψυχᾷ παρέμειν᾽, ἁνίχ᾽ εὑρί-
σκοντο θεῶν παλάμαις τιμάν
οἵαν οὔτις Ἑλλάνων δρέπει
50 πλούτου στεφάνωμ᾽ ἀγέρωχον. νῦν γε μὰν
τὰν Φιλοκτήταο δίκαν ἐφέπων
ἐστρατεύθη· σὺν δ᾽ ἀνάγκᾳ νιν φίλον
καί τις ἐὼν μεγαλάνωρ ἔσανεν.
φαντὶ δὲ Λαμνόθεν ἕλκει
τειρόμενον μεταβάσοντας ἐλθεῖν

52 μεταβάσοντας anonymus Boeckhii: μεταλ(λ)άσ(σ)οντας codd.

---

[7] Hieron.

[8] Hieron's older brother Gelon joined with Theron of Acragas to defeat a 100,000-man Carthaginian army at the battle of Himera in 480. Hieron defeated the Etruscan navy at the battle of Cyme near Naples in 474 (cf. Diod. Sic. 11.51).

that man,[7] I hope
I may not, as it were, throw outside the lists
    the bronze-cheeked javelin I brandish in my hand,
but cast it far and surpass my competitors.   45
May all time to come keep on course, as heretofore,
    his happiness and the gift of riches,
        and provide him with forgetfulness of his hardships:

surely time would remind him in what battles in the   Ant. 3
        course of wars
he stood his ground with steadfast soul,
    when with divine help he and his family were winning
such honor as no other Hellene enjoys
as a proud crown for wealth.[8] Just now, indeed,   50
    after the fashion of Philoctetes,[9]
he has gone on campaign, and even one who was proud
found it necessary to fawn upon him as a friend.
    They tell that the godlike heroes came to fetch him
    from Lemnos, wasting from his wound,

[9] Philoctetes, son of Poeas, was bitten on the foot by a snake at the beginning of the expedition against Troy. The Greek commanders could not stand his suffering and abandoned him on Lemnos. When all efforts to take the city proved futile, they were forced to retrieve him, for Troy was destined to fall to him with his bow. Like Philoctetes, Hieron, although ill, is summoned from an island to bring salvation to his fellow Greeks. Two scholia (89ab) report that Hieron suffered from kidney stones (or cystitis) and was carried into battle on a litter. The "proud" person cannot be identified.

ἥροας ἀντιθέους Ποίαντος υἱὸν τοξόταν·
ὃς Πριάμοιο πόλιν πέρσεν, τελεύτα-
σέν τε πόνους Δαναοῖς,
55 ἀσθενεῖ μὲν χρωτὶ βαίνων, ἀλλὰ μοιρίδιον ἦν.
οὕτω δ᾽ Ἱέρωνι θεὸς ὀρθωτὴρ πέλοι
τὸν προσέρποντα χρόνον, ὧν ἔραται καιρὸν διδούς.
Μοῖσα, καὶ πὰρ Δεινομένει κελαδῆσαι
πίθεό μοι ποινὰν τεθρίππων·
χάρμα δ᾽ οὐκ ἀλλότριον νικαφορία πατέρος.
60 ἄγ᾽ ἔπειτ᾽ Αἴτνας βασιλεῖ φίλιον ἐξεύρωμεν ὕμνον·

Δ′ τῷ πόλιν κείναν θεοδμάτῳ σὺν ἐλευθερίᾳ
Ὑλλίδος στάθμας Ἱέρων ἐν νόμοις ἔ-
κτισσε· θέλοντι δὲ Παμφύλου
καὶ μὰν Ἡρακλειδᾶν ἔκγονοι
ὄχθαις ὕπο Ταϋγέτου ναίοντες αἰ-
εὶ μένειν τεθμοῖσιν ἐν Αἰγιμιοῦ
65 Δωριεῖς. ἔσχον δ᾽ Ἀμύκλας ὄλβιοι
Πινδόθεν ὀρνύμενοι, λευκοπώλων
Τυνδαριδᾶν βαθύδοξοι
γείτονες, ὧν κλέος ἄνθησεν αἰχμᾶς.

61 κείναν F¹g: κλεινὰν CEF

---

[10] Or *fitting opportunity for*.
[11] Deinomenes is Hieron's son, whom Hieron made king of
Aetna.

Poeas' archer son,   Ep. 3
who destroyed Priam's city and ended
    the Danaans' toils;
he walked with flesh infirm, but it was the work of destiny.   55
In like fashion may the god uphold Hieron
in the time that comes, and give him due measure of[10]
        his desires.
Muse, at the side of Deinomenes[11] too
I bid you sing the reward for the four-horse chariot,
    for a father's victory is no alien joy.
Come then, let us compose a loving hymn for Aetna's   60
        king,

for whom Hieron founded that city with divinely   Str. 4
        fashioned
freedom under the laws of Hyllus' rule,
    because the descendants of Pamphylus
and indeed of Heracles' sons,
who dwell under the slopes of Taygetus, are determined
    to remain forever in the institutions of Aegimius
as Dorians.[12] Blessed with prosperity, they came down   65
from Pindus and took Amyclae, to become much
        acclaimed
    neighbors of the Tyndaridae with white horses,[13]
    and the fame of their spears flourished.

[12] There were three Dorian tribes; one was descended from
Hyllus, Heracles' son, the other two from Pamphylus and Dymas,
the sons of Aegimius. Mt. Taygetus overlooks Sparta.
[13] Pindar sketches the Doric conquest of Greece from the
north (the Pindus range) to Amyclae (near Sparta). The Tyn-
daridae (Castor and Polydeuces) are patrons of Sparta.

Ζεῦ τέλει᾽, αἰεὶ δὲ τοιαύταν Ἀμένα παρ᾽ ὕδωρ
αἶσαν ἀστοῖς καὶ βασιλεῦσιν διακρί-
νειν ἔτυμον λόγον ἀνθρώπων.
σύν τοι τίν κεν ἀγητὴρ ἀνήρ,
70 υἱῷ τ᾽ ἐπιτελλόμενος, δᾶμον γεραί-
ρων τράποι σύμφωνον ἐς ἡσυχίαν.
λίσσομαι νεῦσον, Κρονίων, ἥμερον
ὄφρα κατ᾽ οἶκον ὁ Φοίνιξ ὁ Τυρσα-
νῶν τ᾽ ἀλαλατὸς ἔχῃ, ναυ-
σίστονον ὕβριν ἰδὼν τὰν πρὸ Κύμας,

οἷα Συρακοσίων ἀρχῷ δαμασθέντες πάθον,
ὠκυπόρων ἀπὸ ναῶν ὅ σφιν ἐν πόν-
τῳ βάλεθ᾽ ἁλικίαν,
75 Ἑλλάδ᾽ ἐξέλκων βαρείας δουλίας. ἀρέομαι
πὰρ μὲν Σαλαμῖνος Ἀθαναίων χάριν
μισθόν, ἐν Σπάρτᾳ δ᾽ ἐρέω πρὸ Κιθαιρῶνος μάχαν,
ταῖσι Μήδειοι κάμον ἀγκυλότοξοι,
παρὰ δὲ τὰν εὔυδρον ἀκτὰν
Ἱμέρα παίδεσσιν ὕμνον Δεινομένεος τελέσαις,
80 τὸν ἐδέξαντ᾽ ἀμφ᾽ ἀρετᾷ, πολεμίων ἀνδρῶν
καμόντων.

75 ἀρέομαι Dawes: αἰρέομαι (αἱρέομαι) codd.
77 ἐρέω πρὸ EF: ἐρέω τὰν πρὸ rell.: ἄρα τὰν . . . μαχᾶν
Wilamowitz: ἀπὸ τᾶν Stone

---

[14] Aetna is on the Amenas River.   [15] Or *may the true
report of men always assign such good fortune as this.*

Zeus Accomplisher, determine such good fortune as this   Ant. 4
always for the citizens and their kings by Amenas' water[14]
   to be the true report of men.[15]
For with your help a man who is ruler
and instructs his son can in honoring his people   70
   turn them to harmonious peace.
I beseech you, son of Cronus, grant that the war cry
of the Phoenicians[16] and Etruscans may remain quietly
   at home, now that they have seen their aggression
   bring woe to their fleet before Cyme,

such things did they suffer when overcome by the leader   Ep. 4
of the Syracusans, who cast their youth
   from their swiftly sailing ships into the sea
and delivered Hellas from grievous slavery. I shall earn   75
from Salamis[17] the Athenians' gratitude
as my reward, and at Sparta I shall tell of the battle
   before Cithaeron,[18]
in which conflicts the curve-bowed Medes suffered
   defeat;
but by the well-watered bank of the Himeras I shall pay
   to Deinomenes' sons[19] the tribute of my hymn,
which they won through valor, when their enemies were   80
   defeated.

[16] I.e. Carthaginians.
[17] The Athenians took credit for the Greek victory over the
Persian navy at the battle of Salamis in 480.
· [18] At the battle of Plataea near Mt. Cithaeron, the Spartans
defeated the Persian army in 479.
[19] This Deinomenes is the father of Gelon and Hieron.

Ε΄ καιρὸν εἰ φθέγξαιο, πολλῶν πείρατα συντανύσαις
   ἐν βραχεῖ, μείων ἕπεται μῶμος ἀνθρώ-
      πων· ἀπὸ γὰρ κόρος ἀμβλύνει
   αἰανὴς ταχείας ἐλπίδας,
   ἀστῶν δ᾽ ἀκοὰ κρύφιον θυμὸν βαρύ-
      νει μάλιστ᾽ ἐσλοῖσιν ἐπ᾽ ἀλλοτρίοις.
85 ἀλλ᾽ ὅμως, κρέσσον γὰρ οἰκτιρμοῦ φθόνος,
   μὴ παρίει καλά. νώμα δικαίῳ
      πηδαλίῳ στρατόν· ἀψευ-
   δεῖ δὲ πρὸς ἄκμονι χάλκευε γλῶσσαν.

   εἴ τι καὶ φλαῦρον παραιθύσσει, μέγα τοι φέρεται
   πὰρ σέθεν. πολλῶν ταμίας ἐσσί· πολλοὶ
      μάρτυρες ἀμφοτέροις πιστοί.
   εὐανθεῖ δ᾽ ἐν ὀργᾷ παρμένων,
90 εἴπερ τι φιλεῖς ἀκοὰν ἀδεῖαν αἰ-
      εὶ κλύειν, μὴ κάμνε λίαν δαπάναις·
   ἐξίει δ᾽ ὥσπερ κυβερνάτας ἀνήρ
   ἱστίον ἀνεμόεν. μὴ δολωθῇς,
      ὦ φίλε, κέρδεσιν ἐντραπέ-
   λοις· ὀπιθόμβροτον αὔχημα δόξας

85 κρέσσον Stobaeus cod. S: κρεῖσσον CEˢEⁱF: κρέσσων γ,
Stobaeus codd. MA (κρείσσων Eischol. Thuc.)
92 ἀνεμόεν Callierges: ἀνεμόεν πετάσαις codd. | ἐντραπέ-
λοις CᵃFγ: εὐτραπέλοις CᵇE

If you should speak to the point by combining the   Str. 5
    strands
of many things in brief, less criticism follows from men,
    for cloying excess
dulls eager expectations,
and townsmen are grieved in their secret hearts
    especially when they hear of others' successes.
But nevertheless, since envy is better than pity,[20]   85
do not pass over any noble things. Guide your people
    with a rudder of justice; on an anvil of truth
    forge your tongue.

Even some slight thing, you know, becomes important   Ant. 5
if it flies out from you. You are the steward of many
    things;
    many are the sure witnesses for deeds of both kinds.[21]
Abide in flourishing high spirits,
and if indeed you love always to hear pleasant things said   90
    about you, do not grow too tired of spending,
but let out the sail, like a helmsman,
to the wind. Do not be deceived,
    O my friend, by shameful gains,
    for the posthumous acclaim of fame

[20] Cf. Hdt. 3.52.5.
[21] A euphemism for good and evil deeds.

οἷον ἀποιχομένων ἀνδρῶν δίαιταν μανύει
καὶ λογίοις καὶ ἀοιδοῖς. οὐ φθίνει Κροί-
σου φιλόφρων ἀρετά.
95 τὸν δὲ ταύρῳ χαλκέῳ καυτῆρα νηλέα νόον
ἐχθρὰ Φάλαριν κατέχει παντᾷ φάτις,
οὐδέ νιν φόρμιγγες ὑπωρόφιαι κοινανίαν
μαλθακὰν παίδων ὀάροισι δέκονται.
τὸ δὲ παθεῖν εὖ πρῶτον ἀέθλων·
εὖ δ᾽ ἀκούειν δευτέρα μοῖρ᾽· ἀμφοτέροισι δ᾽ ἀνήρ
100 ὃς ἂν ἐγκύρσῃ καὶ ἕλῃ, στέφανον ὕψιστον δέδεκται.

alone reveals the life of men who are dead and gone   Ep. 5
to both chroniclers and poets. The kindly
    excellence of Croesus[22] does not perish,
but universal execration overwhelms Phalaris,[23] that man   95
of pitiless spirit who burned men in his bronze bull,
and no lyres in banquet halls welcome him
in gentle fellowship with boys' voices.
Success is the first of prizes;
    and renown the second portion; but the man who
meets with both and gains them has won the highest   100
        crown.

[22] Croesus, king of Lydia c. 550, was fabulously wealthy and
a great benefactor of Greeks, especially of Apollo's shrine at Del-
phi (cf. Bacch. 3.23–62).

[23] Phalaris, tyrant of Acragas c. 550, was exceptionally cruel.
He roasted his victims in a bronze bull, so constructed that their
screams sounded like the bellowing of the beast.

PYTHIAN 2

Pythian 2 is one of the most difficult Pindaric odes to interpret. The venue of the chariot victory is not specified, and none of the possibilities proposed by the scholia (Delphi, Nemea, Athens, and Olympia) or by modern scholars (Thebes and Syracuse) is compelling. Furthermore, if the poem's one historical allusion in 18–20 refers (as the scholia claim) to Hieron's protection of Western Locri against Anaxilas of Rhegium in 477, then it merely provides a *terminus post quem* for the poem's composition. Another difficulty is that the extensive narrative of Ixion's ingratitude and punishment seems excessively negative for a celebratory ode; in contrast, in *Ol.* 1 Tantalus' malfeasance is counterbalanced by Pelops' heroic achievement. The meaning of the allusions to this poem as "Phoenician merchandise" (67) and a "Castor song" (69) remains unclear. Finally, the unparalleled concluding section beginning at 69 warns against the dangers posed by slanderers, flatterers, and envious men in a series of rapidly shifting images that contain many obscure details.

The poet says that he comes from Thebes to Syracuse, bringing news of Hieron's chariot victory, in which he was assisted by Artemis, Hermes, and Poseidon (1–12). In a summary priamel Pindar notes that many kings have been praised for their achievements and gives two examples: Cinyras of Cyprus and Hieron (13–20).

Ixion, as he turns on his wheel, advises mortals to repay benefactors (21–24), a lesson he learned when, despite his happy life with the immortals, he tried to rape Hera. Zeus deceived him by fashioning a cloud that looked like Hera, and for his punishment bound him to a four-spoke wheel (25–41). Meanwhile, the cloud bore Centaurus, who mated with Magnesian mares and sired the Centaurs (42–48). The narrative concludes with the observation that the gods fulfill all their designs (49–52).

The poet states that he must avoid being a censurer like Archilochus; instead, he takes god-given wealth as his theme (52–56). Hieron provides him a clear example, whom no Greek has ever surpassed in wealth or honor (57–61). He is extolled for his glorious military campaigns and for his mature wisdom (62–67).

After bidding Hieron farewell in the style of hymns, the poet compares his poem thus far to Phoenician merchandise (perhaps because it is of high quality and was paid for) and asks Hieron to look favorably upon the forthcoming Castor song (67–71). He urges Hieron to imitate Rhadamanthys and not be deceived by slanderers (72–78). The poet declares himself above such behavior (79–80), and abjures deceitful flattery, being instead a straightforward friend or foe of a sort that excels under every form of government (81–88). Envious men are not satisfied with god-given success and injure themselves by their own schemes (88–92). We must accept the constraints of our situation, for resisting is futile; the poet hopes to enjoy the company of good men (93–96).

2. ΙΕΡΩΝΙ ΣΤΡΑΚΟΣΙΩΙ

ΑΡΜΑΤΙ

Α΄ Μεγαλοπόλιες ὦ Συράκοσαι, βαθυπολέμου
    τέμενος Ἄρεος, ἀνδρῶν ἵππων τε σιδαροχαρ-
      μᾶν δαιμόνιαι τροφοί,
    ὕμμιν τόδε τᾶν λιπαρᾶν ἀπὸ Θηβᾶν φέρων
    μέλος ἔρχομαι ἀγγελίαν τετραορίας ἐλελίχθονος,
5 εὐάρματος Ἱέρων ἐν ᾇ κρατέων
    τηλαυγέσιν ἀνέδησεν Ὀρτυγίαν στεφάνοις,
    ποταμίας ἕδος Ἀρτέμιδος, ᾆς οὐκ ἄτερ
    κείνας ἀγαναῖσιν ἐν χερσὶ ποικιλα-
      νίους ἐδάμασσε πώλους.

    ἐπὶ γὰρ ἰοχέαιρα παρθένος χερὶ διδύμᾳ
10 ὅ τ' ἐναγώνιος Ἑρμᾶς αἰγλάεντα τίθησι κόσ-
      μον, ξεστὸν ὅταν δίφρον
    ἔν θ' ἅρματα πεισιχάλινα καταζευγνύῃ
    σθένος ἵππιον, ὀρσοτρίαιναν εὐρυβίαν καλέων θεόν.

---

   [1] An island just off Syracuse, sacred to Artemis (cf. *Nem.* 1.1–
4).   [2] The language perhaps indicates that Hieron closely
supervised the training of the team, not that he himself drove it;

2. FOR HIERON OF SYRACUSE

WINNER, CHARIOT RACE

O great city of Syracuse, sanctuary of   Str. 1
Ares mighty in war, divine nourisher of men
   and horses delighting in steel,
to you I come from shining Thebes bearing this song
and its news of the four-horse chariot that shakes the
      earth,
in which Hieron, possessor of fine chariots, prevailed   5
and with far-shining garlands crowned Ortygia,[1]
abode of the river goddess Artemis, with whose help
he mastered in his gentle hands
   those fillies with their embroidered reins,[2]

because with both hands the virgin archeress[3]   Ant. 1
and Hermes, lord of the games, place on them the shining   10
   harness, whenever he yokes the strong horses
to the polished car and to the chariot that controls the bit,
and calls upon the wide-ruling god who wields the
      trident.[4]

rich men retained their own charioteers (cf. *Pyth.* 5.26–53). The
only mention of a victor driving his own chariot is at *Isth.* 1.15.

  [3] Artemis.

  [4] Poseidon, a patron god of horses.

ἄλλοις δέ τις ἐτέλεσσεν ἄλλος ἀνήρ
εὐαχέα βασιλεῦσιν ὕμνον ἄποιν' ἀρετᾶς.
15 κελαδέοντι μὲν ἀμφὶ Κινύραν πολλάκις
φᾶμαι Κυπρίων, τὸν ὁ χρυσοχαῖτα προ-
φρόνως ἐφίλησ' Ἀπόλλων,

ἱερέα κτίλον Ἀφροδίτας· ἄγει δὲ χάρις
φίλων ποί τινος ἀντὶ ἔργων ὀπιζομένα·
σὲ δ', ὦ Δεινομένειε παῖ, Ζεφυρία πρὸ δόμων
Λοκρὶς παρθένος ἀπύει,
πολεμίων καμάτων ἐξ ἀμαχάνων
20 διὰ τεὰν δύναμιν δρακεῖσ' ἀσφαλές.
θεῶν δ' ἐφετμαῖς Ἰξίονα φαντὶ ταῦτα βροτοῖς
λέγειν ἐν πτερόεντι τροχῷ
παντᾷ κυλινδόμενον·
τὸν εὐεργέταν ἀγαναῖς
ἀμοιβαῖς ἐποιχομένους τίνεσθαι.

Β΄ ἔμαθε δὲ σαφές. εὐμενέσσι γὰρ παρὰ Κρονίδαις
26 γλυκὺν ἑλὼν βίοτον, μακρὸν οὐχ ὑπέμεινεν ὄλ-
βον, μαινομέναις φρασίν
Ἥρας ὅτ' ἐράσσατο, τὰν Διὸς εὐναὶ λάχον
πολυγαθέες· ἀλλά νιν ὕβρις εἰς ἀνάταν ὑπεράφανον
ὦρσεν· τάχα δὲ παθὼν ἐοικότ' ἀνήρ

17 ποί τινος codd.: ποίνιμος Spigel
28 πολυγαθέες ζ: πολυγαθέος β | ὑπερφίαλον ζ: ὑπερά-
φανον rell.

238

Various men pay the tribute of a resounding hymn
to various kings as recompense for their excellence.
The voices of the Cyprians often celebrate   15
Cinyras,[5] whom golden-haired Apollo
    heartily befriended,

the priestly favorite of Aphrodite, for reverent gratitude   Ep. 1
    goes forth in one way or another in return for some-
        one's friendly deeds.
But you, O son of Deinomenes, the maiden of Western
Locri invokes in front of her house,
    for after desperate toils of war
she has a look of security in her eyes thanks to your   20
    power.[6]
They say that by the gods' commands Ixion speaks
these words to mortals as he turns
in every direction on his winged wheel:
go and repay your benefactor
    with deeds of gentle recompense.

He learned this clearly, for having won a pleasant   Str. 2
    existence
among Cronus' beneficent children, he could not sustain   26
    his happiness for long, when in his maddened mind
he fell in love with Hera, who belonged to Zeus for joyous
acts of love. But insolence drove him to arrogant delusion,
and quickly suffering what was fitting, the man

---

[5] A mythical king of Cyprus, the island sacred to Aphrodite.
[6] According to the scholia, when Anaxilas of Rhegium threat-
ened Locri with war (in 477), Hieron sent Chromius to tell him to
stop or Hieron would attack him.

PINDAR

30 ἐξαίρετον ἕλε μόχθον. αἱ δύο δ᾽ ἀμπλακίαι
φερέπονοι τελέθοντι· τὸ μὲν ἥρως ὅτι
ἐμφύλιον αἷμα πρώτιστος οὐκ ἄτερ
τέχνας ἐπέμειξε θνατοῖς,

ὅτι τε μεγαλοκευθέεσσιν ἔν ποτε θαλάμοις
Διὸς ἄκοιτιν ἐπειρᾶτο. χρὴ δὲ κατ᾽ αὐτὸν αἰ-
εὶ παντὸς ὁρᾶν μέτρον.
35 εὐναὶ δὲ παράτροποι ἐς κακότατ᾽ ἀθρόαν
ἔβαλον· ποτὶ καὶ τὸν ἵκοντ᾽· ἐπεὶ
νεφέλᾳ παρελέξατο
ψεῦδος γλυκὺ μεθέπων ἄιδρις ἀνήρ·
εἶδος γὰρ ὑπεροχωτάτᾳ πρέπεν Οὐρανιᾶν
θυγατέρι Κρόνου· ἅντε δόλον αὐτῷ θέσαν
40 Ζηνὸς παλάμαι, καλὸν πῆμα. τὸν δὲ τε-
τράκναμον ἔπραξε δεσμόν

ἑὸν ὄλεθρον ὅγ᾽· ἐν δ᾽ ἀφύκτοισι γυιοπέδαις
πεσὼν τὰν πολύκοινον ἀνδέξατ᾽ ἀγγελίαν.
ἄνευ οἱ Χαρίτων τέκεν γόνον ὑπερφίαλον
μόνα καὶ μόνον οὔτ᾽ ἐν ἀν-
δράσι γερασφόρον οὔτ᾽ ἐν θεῶν νόμοις·
τὸν ὀνύμαζε τράφοισα Κένταυρον, ὅς

30 ἕλε Moschopulus: ἔχε Thomas Magister: ἔσχε vett.
34 κατ᾽ αὐτὸν Thiersch: καθ᾽ αὐτὸν codd.
36 ποτὶ καὶ τὸν ἵκοντ᾽ codd.: alii alia (locus conclamatus, Schroeder)
38 οὐρανιᾶν codd.: οὐρανίου schol.: Οὐρανίδα Mommsen

240

won an extraordinary torment. His two offenses   30
bring this pain: the one, because that hero
was the very first to bring upon mortals the stain of
    kindred blood, not without guile;[7]

the other, because once in the great depths of her   Ant. 2
    chambers
he made an attempt on Zeus' wife. One must always
    measure everything by one's own station.
Aberrant acts of love cast one into the thick   35
of trouble; they came upon him too, because he
    lay with a cloud,
an ignorant man in pursuit of a sweet lie,
for it resembled in looks the foremost heavenly goddess,
Cronus' daughter. Zeus' wiles set it
as a snare for him, a beautiful affliction. The man made   40
    that binding to the four spokes

his own destruction.[8] After falling into inescapable   Ep. 2
    fetters, he received that message meant for everyone.
Without the Graces' blessing, that unique mother[9]
bore a unique son, who was overbearing and respected
    neither among men nor in the ways of the gods.
She who reared him called him Centaurus. He mated

[7] To avoid paying the price for his bride, Ixion contrived to have his father-in-law Deioneus fall into a pit of burning charcoal.

[8] Ixion's punishment mimics the iynx, a love charm consisting of a wryneck bound to a wheel with four spokes (cf. *Pyth.* 4.213–219).

[9] The cloud.

45　ἵπποισι Μαγνητίδεσσιν ἐμείγνυτ᾽ ἐν Παλίου
　　σφυροῖς, ἐκ δ᾽ ἐγένοντο στρατός
　　θαυμαστός, ἀμφοτέροις
　　ὁμοῖοι τοκεῦσι, τὰ μα-
　　　τρόθεν μὲν κάτω, τὰ δ᾽ ὕπερθε πατρός.

Γ　θεὸς ἅπαν ἐπὶ ἐλπίδεσσι τέκμαρ ἀνύεται,
50　θεός, ὃ καὶ πτερόεντ᾽ αἰετὸν κίχε, καὶ θαλασ-
　　　σαῖον παραμείβεται
　　δελφῖνα, καὶ ὑψιφρόνων τιν᾽ ἔκαμψε βροτῶν,
　　ἑτέροισι δὲ κῦδος ἀγήραον παρέδωκ᾽. ἐμὲ δὲ χρεών
　　φεύγειν δάκος ἀδινὸν κακαγοριᾶν·
　　εἶδον γὰρ ἑκὰς ἐὼν τὰ πόλλ᾽ ἐν ἀμαχανίᾳ
55　ψογερὸν Ἀρχίλοχον βαρυλόγοις ἔχθεσιν
　　πιαινόμενον· τὸ πλουτεῖν δὲ σὺν τύχᾳ
　　　πότμου σοφίας ἄριστον.

　　τὺ δὲ σάφα νιν ἔχεις ἐλευθέρᾳ φρενὶ πεπαρεῖν,
　　πρύτανι κύριε πολλᾶν μὲν εὐστεφάνων ἀγυι-
　　　ᾶν καὶ στρατοῦ. εἰ δέ τις
　　ἤδη κτεάτεσσί τε καὶ περὶ τιμᾷ λέγει
60　ἕτερόν τιν᾽ ἀν᾽ Ἑλλάδα τῶν πάροιθε γενέσθαι
　　　ὑπέρτερον,
　　χαύνᾳ πραπίδι παλαιμονεῖ κενεά.
　　εὐανθέα δ᾽ ἀναβάσομαι στόλον ἀμφ᾽ ἀρετᾷ
　　κελαδέων. νεότατι μὲν ἀρήγει θράσος
　　δεινῶν πολέμων· ὅθεν φαμὶ καὶ σὲ τὰν
　　　ἀπείρονα δόξαν εὑρεῖν,

with Magnesian mares in the foothills of Pelion,   45
and from them issued a wondrous
herd of offspring
similar to both parents,
    with the mother's features below, the father's above.

The god accomplishes every purpose just as he wishes,   Str. 3
the god, who overtakes the winged eagle   50
    and surpasses the seagoing
dolphin, and bows down many a haughty mortal,
while to others he grants ageless glory. But I must
flee the persistent bite of censure,
for standing at a far remove I have seen
Archilochus[10] the blamer often in straits as he fed on   55
dire words of hatred. And possessing wealth that is
    granted by destiny is the best object of wisdom.

You clearly have it to display with a liberal spirit,   Ant. 3
lord and master of many streets with their fine
    battlements and of a host of men. If anyone
at this time claims that in point of wealth and honor
any other man in Hellas from the past is your superior,   60
with an empty mind he wrestles in vain.
I shall embark upon a garlanded ship[11] to celebrate
your excellence. Courage is a help to youth
in fearsome wars, and from them I proclaim that you
    have won that boundless fame of yours,

---

[10] Archilochus (fl. c. 650 B.C.) was notorious for his bitter
invective.   [11] Pindar compares his singing Hieron's praise to
sailing on a festive ship. He later uses the analogy of a Phoenician
merchant ship (67).

PINDAR

65 τὰ μὲν ἐν ἱπποσόαισιν ἄνδρεσσι μαρνάμενον,
    τὰ δ' ἐν πεζομάχαισι· βουλαὶ δὲ πρεσβύτεραι
    ἀκίνδυνον ἐμοὶ ἔπος ⟨σὲ⟩ ποτὶ πάντα λόγον
    ἐπαινεῖν παρέχοντι. χαῖ-
    ρε· τόδε μὲν κατὰ Φοίνισσαν ἐμπολάν
    μέλος ὑπὲρ πολιᾶς ἁλὸς πέμπεται·
    τὸ Καστόρειον δ' ἐν Αἰολίδεσσι χορδαῖς θέλων
70 ἄθρησον χάριν ἑπτακτύπου
    φόρμιγγος ἀντόμενος.
    γένοι᾽, οἷος ἐσσὶ μαθών.
    καλός τοι πίθων παρὰ παισίν, αἰεί

Δ' καλός. ὁ δὲ Ῥαδάμανθυς εὖ πέπραγεν, ὅτι φρενῶν
    ἔλαχε καρπὸν ἀμώμητον, οὐδ' ἀπάταισι θυ-
    μὸν τέρπεται ἔνδοθεν,
75 οἷα ψιθύρων παλάμαις ἕπετ᾽ αἰεὶ βροτῷ.
    ἄμαχον κακὸν ἀμφοτέροις διαβολιᾶν ὑποφάτιες,
    ὀργαῖς ἀτενὲς ἀλωπέκων ἴκελοι.
    κέρδει δὲ τί μάλα τοῦτο κερδαλέον τελέθει;
    ἅτε γὰρ ἐννάλιον πόνον ἐχοίσας βαθύν
80 σκευᾶς ἑτέρας, ἀβάπτιστος εἶμι φελ-
    λὸς ὣς ὑπὲρ ἕρκος ἅλμας.

66 ⟨σὲ⟩ suppl. Bergk   72 γένοι᾽ Triclinius: γένοι δ᾽ B:
γένοιο δ᾽ ζβ   75 βροτῷ Heindorf: βροτῶν codd.
79 βαθύν Bergk: βαθύ codd.
80 εἶμι Schnitzer: εἰμὶ codd.

12 "This song" apparently refers to the preceding part of the

244

while campaigning both among horse-driving cavalrymen   Ep. 3
    and among infantrymen. And your counsels, mature
beyond your years, permit me to give you words of praise   66
without any risk up to the full account. Farewell.
    This song[12] is being sent like Phoenician
merchandise over the gray sea,
but as for the Castor song in Aeolic strains, may you
        gladly
look with favor upon it, the glory of[13] the seven-stringed   70
lyre, as you greet it.
Become such as you are, having learned what that is.
    Pretty is an ape in the eyes of children, always

pretty, but Rhadamanthys has fared well[14] because   Str. 4
he was allotted the blameless fruit of good judgment
    and within his heart takes no delight in deceptions,
such as ever attend a mortal through whisperers' wiles.   75
Purveyors of slander are a deadly evil to both parties,[15]
with temperaments just like those of foxes.
But what profit really results from that cunning?
None, for just as when the rest of the tackle labors
in the depths of the sea, like a cork I shall go undipped   80
    over the surface of the brine.[16]

ode, whereas the *Castoreion*, a song in celebration of an eques-
trian victory (cf. *Isth.* 1.16), presumably refers to the remainder
of the poem. One implication may be that the first part is "contrac-
tual," the second sent "gratis."   [13] Or *in honor of*.
[14] Cf. *Ol.* 2.75–76. According to Plato, *Gorgias* 523E, he be-
came one of the judges in Hades along with Aeacus and Minos.
[15] I.e. to those whom they slander and to those who believe
them.   [16] The image is that of a cork floating on the surface
while the weights and nets sink into the sea.

PINDAR

ἀδύνατα δ᾽ ἔπος ἐκβαλεῖν κραταιὸν ἐν ἀγαθοῖς
δόλιον ἀστόν· ὅμως μὰν σαίνων ποτὶ πάντας ἄ-
ταν πάγχυ διαπλέκει.
οὔ οἱ μετέχω θράσεος. φίλον εἴη φιλεῖν·
ποτὶ δ᾽ ἐχθρὸν ἅτ᾽ ἐχθρὸς ἐὼν λύκοιο
δίκαν ὑποθεύσομαι,
85 ἄλλ᾽ ἄλλοτε πατέων ὁδοῖς σκολιαῖς.
ἐν πάντα δὲ νόμον εὐθύγλωσσος ἀνὴρ προφέρει,
παρὰ τυραννίδι, χὠπόταν ὁ λάβρος στρατός,
χὤταν πόλιν οἱ σοφοὶ τηρέωντι. χρὴ
δὲ πρὸς θεὸν οὐκ ἐρίζειν,

ὃς ἀνέχει τοτὲ μὲν τὰ κείνων, τότ᾽ αὖθ᾽ ἑτέροις
ἔδωκεν μέγα κῦδος. ἀλλ᾽ οὐδὲ ταῦτα νόον
90 ἰαίνει φθονερῶν· στάθμας δέ τινος ἑλκόμενοι
περισσᾶς ἐνέπαξαν ἕλ-
κος ὀδυνηρὸν ἑᾷ πρόσθε καρδίᾳ,
πρὶν ὅσα φροντίδι μητίονται τυχεῖν.
φέρειν δ᾽ ἐλαφρῶς ἐπαυχένιον λαβόντα ζυγὸν
ἀρήγει· ποτὶ κέντρον δέ τοι
95 λακτιζέμεν τελέθει
ὀλισθηρὸς οἶμος· ἁδόν-
τα δ᾽ εἴη με τοῖς ἀγαθοῖς ὁμιλεῖν.

82 ἄταν Heyne: ἄγαν codd.
90 τινες Sheppard
90–91 ἑλκόμενος . . . ἐνέπαξεν Βζ

246

PYTHIAN 2

The deceitful citizen cannot utter an effective word   Ant. 4
among good men, but nonetheless he fawns on all
    and weaves his utter ruin.
I have no part in his impudence. Let me befriend a
        friend,
but against an enemy, I shall, as his enemy,
    run him down as a wolf does,
stalking now here, now there, on twisting paths.   85
And under every regime the straight-talking man excels:
in a tyranny, when the boisterous people rule,
or when the wise watch over the city.
    One must not contend with a god,

who at one time raises these men's fortunes, then at   Ep. 4
        other times
    gives great glory to others. But not even that
soothes the mind of envious men; by pulling, as it were,   90
a measuring line too far,
    they fix a painful wound in their own hearts,[17]
before they gain all that they contrive in their thoughts.
It helps to bear lightly the yoke one has taken upon one's
neck, and kicking against the goad,
you know, becomes   95
a slippery path. May it be mine
    to find favor with the good and keep their company.

[17] "The measuring-line has two sharp pegs. The measurer fastens one into the ground and pulls the cord tight, in order to stretch it over more space than it ought to cover ($\pi\epsilon\rho\iota\sigma\sigma\hat{a}s$). In so doing he runs the peg into his own heart" (Gildersleeve). Others see here the image of a plumbline.

247

PYTHIAN 3

The occasion of this ode is not a recent victory, but Hieron's illness. The poem was probably classed among the epinicia by the Alexandrian editors because of the passing mention of a former Pythian victory won by Hieron's horse Pherenicus (73–74). It was composed sometime between 476, when Hieron founded Aetna (cf. 69), and 467, when he died.

The first 79 lines comprise an elaborate sequence in ring form that begins with the poet's impossible wish that Chiron were still alive and ends with his stated intention to pray to the Mother Goddess, presumably for Hieron's health. In between, he tells the stories of Coronis, mother of Asclepius, and of Asclepius himself, narratives that show the dire consequences of discontent with one's lot and motivate some of Pindar's best known verses: "Do not, my soul, strive for the life of the immortals . . . " (61–62). The last part of the ode (80–115) offers consolation to Hieron.

The poet wishes that Chiron the Centaur still lived on Pelion, as when he raised the healer Asclepius (1–7). Coronis was killed by Artemis before giving birth to Asclepius, Apollo's son, because she slept with Ischys the Arcadian after becoming pregnant with the god's child— she was like many who foolishly despise what is nearby and seek what is distant and futile (8–23). When Apollo

248

learned of her perfidy, he sent Artemis to cause a plague that killed her and many others, but rescued his son from her body as it lay on the burning pyre and gave him to Chiron to instruct in medicine (24–46). Asclepius was a very successful healer, but when he fell prey to the allure of gold and brought a man back to life, Zeus destroyed patient and physician with a thunderbolt (47–58).

Mortals should know their limits, and the poet urges his soul to be content with what is in its power (59–62). If, however, Chiron were alive, and if Pindar could have charmed him with his songs to provide another Asclepius, he would have come to Syracuse, bringing Hieron health and a victory celebration as in the past (63–76). But as it is, he will offer his prayers to the Mother Goddess (77–79).

Pindar reminds Hieron of what former poets (i.e. Homer) have taught: that the gods grant two evils for each good. Fools find this hard to bear, but good men make the best of their good fortune (80–83). As a ruler, Hieron has had a great portion of happiness (84–86). Not even Peleus and Cadmus, whose weddings were attended by the gods, experienced unlimited good; they suffered through the misfortunes of their offspring (86–103). A man must make do with what the gods give him, for nothing remains constant (103–106). In a series of first person statements of general import, the poet declares that he shall be small or great, depending on fortune, but hopes to use what wealth he has to gain fame (107–111). The names of Nestor and Sarpedon endure through epic poetry; few are those whose excellence is preserved in song (112–115).

3. ΙΕΡΩΝΙ ΣΤΡΑΚΟΣΙΩΙ

ΚΕΛΗΤΙ

Α΄   Ἤθελον Χείρωνά κε Φιλλυρίδαν,
    εἰ χρεὼν τοῦθ᾽ ἁμετέρας ἀπὸ γλώσσας
        κοινὸν εὔξασθαι ἔπος,
    ζώειν τὸν ἀποιχόμενον,
    Οὐρανίδα γόνον εὐρυμέδοντα Κρόνου,
        βάσσαισί τ᾽ ἄρχειν Παλίου φῆρ᾽ ἀγρότερον
5   νόον ἔχοντ᾽ ἀνδρῶν φίλον· οἷος ἐὼν θρέψεν ποτέ
    τέκτονα νωδυνίας
        ἥμερον γυιαρκέος Ἀσκλαπιόν,
    ἥροα παντοδαπᾶν ἀλκτῆρα νούσων.

    τὸν μὲν εὐίππου Φλεγύα θυγάτηρ
    πρὶν τελέσσαι ματροπόλῳ σὺν Ἐλειθυί-
        ᾳ, δαμεῖσα χρυσέοις
10 τόξοισιν ὕπ᾽ Ἀρτέμιδος
    εἰς Ἀΐδα δόμον ἐν θαλάμῳ κατέβα,
        τέχναις Ἀπόλλωνος. χόλος δ᾽ οὐκ ἀλίθιος
    γίνεται παίδων Διός. ἁ δ᾽ ἀποφλαυρίξαισά νιν

1 Χείρωνα codd.: Χίρωνα Schroeder

250

3. FOR HIERON OF SYRACUSE

WINNER, SINGLE–HORSE RACE

I wish that Chiron—	Str. 1
if it is right for my tongue to utter	
that common prayer—	
were still living, the departed son of Philyra	
and wide-ruling offspring of Uranus' son Cronus,	
and still reigned in Pelion's glades, that wild creature	
who had a mind friendly to men. I would have him be	5
as he was when he once reared the gentle craftsman	
of body-strengthening relief from pain, Asclepius,	
the hero and protector from diseases of all sorts.	
Before the daughter[1] of the horseman Phlegyas	Ant. 1
could bring him to term with the help of Eleithyia,	
goddess of childbirth, she was overcome	
by the golden arrows of Artemis	10
in her chamber and went down to the house of Hades	
through Apollo's designs. The anger of Zeus' children	
is no vain thing. Yet she made light of it	

---

[1] His mother, Coronis (cf. Hes. *frr.* 59–60 and *h. Hom.* 16).

ἀμπλακίαισι φρενῶν,
  ἄλλον αἴνησεν γάμον κρύβδαν πατρός,
πρόσθεν ἀκερσεκόμᾳ μιχθεῖσα Φοίβῳ,

15 καὶ φέροισα σπέρμα θεοῦ καθαρόν·
οὐκ ἔμειν' ἐλθεῖν τράπεζαν νυμφίαν,
οὐδὲ παμφώνων ἰαχὰν ὑμεναίων, ἅλικες
οἷα παρθένοι φιλέοισιν ἑταῖραι
ἑσπερίαις ὑποκουρίζεσθ' ἀοιδαῖς· ἀλλά τοι
20 ἤρατο τῶν ἀπεόντων· οἷα καὶ πολλοὶ πάθον·
ἔστι δὲ φῦλον ἐν ἀνθρώποισι ματαιότατον,
ὅστις αἰσχύνων ἐπιχώρια παπταίνει τὰ πόρσω,
μεταμώνια θηρεύων ἀκράντοις ἐλπίσιν.

Β΄ ἔσχε τοι ταύταν μεγάλαν ἀάταν
25 καλλιπέπλου λῆμα Κορωνίδος· ἐλθόν-
  τος γὰρ εὐνάσθη ξένου
λέκτροισιν ἀπ' Ἀρκαδίας.
οὐδ' ἔλαθε σκοπόν· ἐν δ' ἄρα μηλοδόκῳ
  Πυθῶνι τόσσαις ἄιεν ναοῦ βασιλεύς
Λοξίας, κοινᾶνι παρ' εὐθυτάτῳ γνώμαν πιθών,
πάντα ἰσάντι νόῳ·
  ψευδέων δ' οὐχ ἅπτεται, κλέπτει τέ μιν
30 οὐ θεὸς οὐ βροτὸς ἔργοις οὔτε βουλαῖς.

18 ἑταίρᾳ (vel ἑταίραις) West
24 ταύταν codd.: τοιαύτας Cᵃᶜ: τοιαύταν schol.
28 γνώμᾳ(ι) ζ

252

in the folly of her mind and
    unknown to her father consented to another union,
although she had previously lain with long-haired
      Phoebus

and was carrying the god's pure seed.   Ep. 1
But she could not wait for the marriage feast to come   16
or for the sound of full-voiced nuptial hymns with such
endearments as unmarried companions are wont to utter
in evening songs. No, she was in love with things
remote—such longings as many others have suffered,   20
for there is among mankind a very foolish kind of person,
who scorns what is at hand and peers at things far away,
chasing the impossible with hopes unfulfilled.

Indeed, headstrong Coronis of the beautiful robes   Str. 2
fell victim to that great delusion, for she slept   25
    in the bed of a stranger,
who came from Arcadia.
But she did not elude the watching god, for although he
    was in flock-receiving Pytho as lord of his temple,
Loxias perceived it, convinced by the surest confidant,
his all-knowing mind.[2]
    He does not deal in falsehoods, and neither god
nor mortal deceives him by deeds or designs.   30

    [2] According to Hes. *fr.* 60, a raven told Apollo; Pindar's Apollo
is omniscient.

PINDAR

καὶ τότε γνοὺς Ἴσχυος Εἰλατίδα
ξεινίαν κοίταν ἄθεμίν τε δόλον, πέμ-
    ψεν κασιγνήταν μένει
θυίοισαν ἀμαιμακέτῳ
ἐς Λακέρειαν, ἐπεὶ παρὰ Βοιβιάδος
    κρημνοῖσιν ᾤκει παρθένος· δαίμων δ' ἕτερος
35 ἐς κακὸν τρέψαις ἐδαμάσσατό νιν, καὶ γειτόνων
πολλοὶ ἐπαῦρον, ἁμᾶ
    δ' ἔφθαρεν· πολλὰν δ' ὄρει πῦρ ἐξ ἑνός
σπέρματος ἐνθορὸν ἀίστωσεν ὕλαν.

ἀλλ' ἐπεὶ τείχει θέσαν ἐν ξυλίνῳ
σύγγονοι κούραν, σέλας δ' ἀμφέδραμεν
40 λάβρον Ἀφαίστου, τότ' ἔειπεν Ἀπόλλων· "Οὐκέτι
τλάσομαι ψυχᾷ γένος ἀμὸν ὀλέσσαι
οἰκτροτάτῳ θανάτῳ ματρὸς βαρείᾳ σὺν πάθᾳ."
ὣς φάτο· βάματι δ' ἐν πρώτῳ κιχὼν παῖδ' ἐκ νεκροῦ
ἅρπασε· καιομένα δ' αὐτῷ διέφαινε πυρά.
45 καί ῥά νιν Μάγνητι φέρων πόρε Κενταύρῳ διδάξαι
πολυπήμονας ἀνθρώποισιν ἰᾶσθαι νόσους.

Γ' τοὺς μὲν ὦν, ὅσσοι μόλον αὐτοφύτων
ἑλκέων ξυνάονες, ἢ πολιῷ χαλκῷ μέλη τετρωμένοι
ἢ χερμάδι τηλεβόλῳ,

33 θυίοισαν Wilhelm Schulze: θύοισαν codd.
36 ὄρει Moschopulus: ἐν ὄρει vett.
41 ἀμὸν C^{ac}D: ἁμὸν BC^{pc}: ἐμὸν EF

254

And at this time, when he knew of her sleeping with the   Ant. 2
stranger Ischys, son of Elatus, and her impious deceit,
    he sent his sister
raging with irresistible force
to Lacereia, for the maiden was living
    by the banks of Lake Boebias.[3] An adverse fortune
turned her to ruin and overcame her; and many neighbors 35
shared her fate and perished with her.
    Fire that springs from one
spark onto a mountain can destroy a great forest.

But when her relatives had placed the girl   Ep. 2
within the pyre's wooden wall and the fierce blaze
of Hephaestus ran around it, then Apollo said: "No longer 40
shall I endure in my soul to destroy my own offspring
by a most pitiful death along with his mother's heavy
        suffering."
Thus he spoke, and with his first stride came and
        snatched the child
from the corpse, while the burning flame parted for him.
He took him and gave him to the Magnesian Centaur 45
for instruction in healing the diseases that plague men.

Now all who came to him afflicted with natural sores   Str. 3
or with limbs wounded by gray bronze
or by a far-flung stone,

[3] In southeastern Thessaly, near Magnesia, where Chiron
lived.

PINDAR

50 ἢ θερινῷ πυρὶ περθόμενοι δέμας ἢ
        χειμῶνι, λύσαις ἄλλον ἀλλοίων ἀχέων
     ἔξαγεν, τοὺς μὲν μαλακαῖς ἐπαοιδαῖς ἀμφέπων,
     τοὺς δὲ προσανέα πί-
        νοντας, ἢ γυίοις περάπτων πάντοθεν
     φάρμακα, τοὺς δὲ τομαῖς ἔστασεν ὀρθούς.

     ἀλλὰ κέρδει καὶ σοφίᾳ δέδεται.
55 ἔτραπεν καὶ κεῖνον ἀγάνορι μισθῷ
        χρυσὸς ἐν χερσὶν φανείς
     ἄνδρ' ἐκ θανάτου κομίσαι
     ἤδη ἁλωκότα· χερσὶ δ' ἄρα Κρονίων
        ῥίψαις δι' ἀμφοῖν ἀμπνοὰν στέρνων κάθελεν
     ὠκέως, αἴθων δὲ κεραυνὸς ἐνέσκιμψεν μόρον.
     χρὴ τὰ ἐοικότα πὰρ
        δαιμόνων μαστευέμεν θναταῖς φρασίν
60 γνόντα τὸ πὰρ ποδός, οἵας εἰμὲν αἴσας.

     μή, φίλα ψυχά, βίον ἀθάνατον
     σπεῦδε, τὰν δ' ἔμπρακτον ἄντλει μαχανάν.
     εἰ δὲ σώφρων ἄντρον ἔναι' ἔτι Χείρων, καί τί οἱ
     φίλτρον ⟨ἐν⟩ θυμῷ μελιγάρυες ὕμνοι
65 ἁμέτεροι τίθεν, ἰατρά τοί κέν νιν πίθον
     καί νυν ἐσλοῖσι παρασχεῖν ἀνδράσιν θερμᾶν νόσων
     ἤ τινα Λατοΐδα κεκλημένον ἢ πατέρος.
     καί κεν ἐν ναυσὶν μόλον Ἰονίαν τάμνων θάλασσαν
     Ἀρέθοισαν ἐπὶ κράναν παρ' Αἰτναῖον ξένον,

256

or with bodies wracked by summer fever   50
    or winter chill, he relieved of their various ills and
restored them; some he tended with calming
      incantations,
while others drank soothing potions,
    or he applied remedies to all parts
of their bodies; still others he raised up with surgery.

But even wisdom is enthralled to gain.   Ant. 3
Gold appearing in his hands   55
    with its lordly wage
prompted even him to bring back from death a man
already carried off. But then, with a cast from his hands,
    Cronus' son took the breath from both men's breasts
in an instant; the flash of lightning hurled down doom.
It is necessary to seek what is proper from the gods
    with our mortal minds,
by knowing what lies at our feet and what kind of destiny   60
    is ours.

Do not, my soul, strive for the life of the immortals,   Ep. 3
but exhaust the practical means at your disposal.
Yet if wise Chiron were still living in his cave, and if
my honey-sounding hymns could put a charm in his heart,
I would surely have persuaded him to provide a healer   65
now as well to cure the feverish illnesses of good men,
someone called a son of Apollo or of Zeus.
And I would have come, cleaving the Ionian sea in a ship,
to the fountain of Arethusa and to my Aetnaean host,

---

64 ⟨ἐν⟩ suppl. Moschopulus

PINDAR

Δ′ ὃς Συρακόσσαισι νέμει βασιλεύς,
71 πραῢς ἀστοῖς, οὐ φθονέων ἀγαθοῖς, ξεί-
        νοις δὲ θαυμαστὸς πατήρ.
    τῷ μὲν διδύμας χάριτας
    εἰ κατέβαν ὑγίειαν ἄγων χρυσέαν
        κῶμόν τ᾽ ἀέθλων Πυθίων αἴγλαν στεφάνοις,
    τοὺς ἀριστεύων Φερένικος ἕλεν Κίρρᾳ ποτέ,
75   ἀστέρος οὐρανίου
        φαμὶ τηλαυγέστερον κείνῳ φάος
    ἐξικόμαν κε βαθὺν πόντον περάσαις.

    ἀλλ᾽ ἐπεύξασθαι μὲν ἐγὼν ἐθέλω
    Ματρί, τὰν κοῦραι παρ᾽ ἐμὸν πρόθυρον σὺν
        Πανὶ μέλπονται θαμά
    σεμνὰν θεὸν ἐννύχιαι.
80 εἰ δὲ λόγων συνέμεν κορυφάν, Ἱέρων,
        ὀρθὰν ἐπίστᾳ, μανθάνων οἶσθα προτέρων
    ἓν παρ᾽ ἐσλὸν πήματα σύνδυο δαίονται βροτοῖς
    ἀθάνατοι. τὰ μὲν ὦν
        οὐ δύνανται νήπιοι κόσμῳ φέρειν,
    ἀλλ᾽ ἀγαθοί, τὰ καλὰ τρέψαντες ἔξω.

---

4 Probably in 478 (cf. Bacch. 5.37–41). Pherenicus' Olympic victory is celebrated in *Ol.* 1 and Bacch. 5.

5 It is not clear why Pindar prays to the Mother of the gods, Magna Mater (Rhea, Cybele, or perhaps Demeter), or what his relationship to her was. The scholiasts, biographers, and

who rules as king over Syracuse,   Str. 4
gentle to townsmen, not begrudging to good men,   71
   and to guests a wondrous father.
And if I had landed, bringing him
two blessings, golden health and a victory revel·
   to add luster to the crowns from the Pythian games
which Pherenicus once won when victorious at Cirrha,[4]
I swear that I would have come for that man   75
   as a saving light outshining any heavenly star,
upon crossing the deep sea.

But for my part, I wish to pray   Ant. 4
to the Mother, to whom, along with Pan, the maidens
   often sing before my door at night,
for she is a venerable goddess.[5]
But, Hieron, if you can understand the true point   80
   of sayings, you know the lesson of former poets:
the immortals apportion to humans a pair of evils
for every good.[6] Now fools
   cannot bear them gracefully,
but good men can, by turning the noble portion
      outward.[7]

Pausanias (9.25.3) all claim that Pindar had a shrine to her and
Pan by his house.

[6] Cf. *Il.* 24.527–528: δοιοὶ γάρ τε πίθοι κατακείαται ἐν Διὸς
οὔδει | δώρων οἷα δίδωσι κακῶν, ἕτερος δὲ ἑάων. Pindar inter-
prets the text to mean that there were two urns of evil gifts and
one of good. Most scholars follow Plato's interpretation, according
to which only two urns are at issue (*Rep.* 379D).

[7] That is, by letting people see only the good (cf. *fr.* 42).

PINDAR

τὶν δὲ μοῖρ' εὐδαιμονίας ἕπεται.
85 λαγέταν γάρ τοι τύραννον δέρκεται,
εἴ τιν' ἀνθρώπων, ὁ μέγας πότμος. αἰὼν δ' ἀσφαλής
οὐκ ἔγεντ' οὔτ' Αἰακίδᾳ παρὰ Πηλεῖ
οὔτε παρ' ἀντιθέῳ Κάδμῳ· λέγονται μὰν βροτῶν
ὄλβον ὑπέρτατον οἳ σχεῖν, οἵτε καὶ χρυσαμπύκων
90 μελπομενᾶν ἐν ὄρει Μοισᾶν καὶ ἐν ἑπταπύλοις
ἄιον Θήβαις, ὁπόθ' Ἁρμονίαν γᾶμεν βοῶπιν,
ὁ δὲ Νηρέος εὐβούλου Θέτιν παῖδα κλυτάν,

Ε΄ καὶ θεοὶ δαίσαντο παρ' ἀμφοτέροις,
καὶ Κρόνου παῖδας βασιλῆας ἴδον χρυ-
σέαις ἐν ἕδραις, ἕδνα τε
95 δέξαντο· Διὸς δὲ χάριν
ἐκ προτέρων μεταμειψάμενοι καμάτων
ἔστασαν ὀρθὰν καρδίαν. ἐν δ' αὖτε χρόνῳ
τὸν μὲν ὀξείαισι θύγατρες ἐρήμωσαν πάθαις
εὐφροσύνας μέρος αἱ
τρεῖς· ἀτὰρ λευκωλένῳ γε Ζεὺς πατήρ
ἤλυθεν ἐς λέχος ἱμερτὸν Θυώνᾳ.

88 μὰν Byz.: γε μὰν vett.

---

8 Peleus and Thetis were married on Mt. Pelion, Cadmus and Harmonia in Thebes.
9 Cf. Nem. 4.65–68.

Your share of happiness attends you,   Ep. 4
for truly if great destiny looks with favor upon any man,   85
it is upon a people-guiding ruler. But an untroubled life
did not abide with Aeacus' son Peleus
or with godlike Cadmus; yet they are said to have attained
the highest happiness of any men, for they even heard
the golden-crowned Muses singing on the mountain and   90
in seven-gated Thebes, when one married ox-eyed
      Harmonia,
the other Thetis, wise-counseling Nereus' famous
      daughter;[8]

the gods feasted with both of them,   Str. 5
and they beheld the regal children of Cronus
   on their golden thrones and received
their wedding gifts.[9] By the grace of Zeus,   95
they recovered from their earlier hardships
   and they raised up their hearts. But then in time,
the bitter suffering of his three daughters[10]
deprived the one of a part of his joy,
   although father Zeus did
come to the longed-for bed of white-armed Thyone.[11]

[10] Cadmus and Harmonia had four daughters: Ino, Autonoë, Agaue, and Semele. Pindar here refers to the first three. Ino's husband Athamas slew one of their sons, Learchus, and Ino flung herself into the sea with the other, Melicertes. Autonoë's son Actaeon was killed by his own hunting dogs. Agaue killed her son Pentheus in a bacchic frenzy.

[11] Usually called Semele, mother by Zeus of Dionysus (cf. *Ol.* 2.22–30).

100 τοῦ δὲ παῖς, ὅνπερ μόνον ἀθανάτα
τίκτεν ἐν Φθίᾳ Θέτις, ἐν πολέμῳ τό-
    ξοις ἀπὸ ψυχὰν λιπών
ὦρσεν πυρὶ καιόμενος
ἐκ Δαναῶν γόον. εἰ δὲ νόῳ τις ἔχει
    θνατῶν ἀλαθείας ὁδόν, χρὴ πρὸς μακάρων
    τυγχάνοντ᾽ εὖ πασχέμεν. ἄλλοτε δ᾽ ἀλλοῖαι πνοαί
105 ὑψιπετᾶν ἀνέμων.
    ὄλβος οὐκ ἐς μακρὸν ἀνδρῶν ἔρχεται
σάος, πολὺς εὖτ᾽ ἂν ἐπιβρίσαις ἔπηται.

σμικρὸς ἐν σμικροῖς, μέγας ἐν μεγάλοις
ἔσσομαι, τὸν δ᾽ ἀμφέποντ᾽ αἰεὶ φρασίν
δαίμον᾽ ἀσκήσω κατ᾽ ἐμὰν θεραπεύων μαχανάν.
110 εἰ δέ μοι πλοῦτον θεὸς ἁβρὸν ὀρέξαι,
ἐλπίδ᾽ ἔχω κλέος εὑρέσθαι κεν ὑψηλὸν πρόσω.
Νέστορα καὶ Λύκιον Σαρπηδόν᾽, ἀνθρώπων φάτις,
ἐξ ἐπέων κελαδεννῶν, τέκτονες οἷα σοφοί
ἅρμοσαν, γινώσκομεν· ἁ δ᾽ ἀρετὰ κλειναῖς ἀοιδαῖς
115 χρονία τελέθει· παύροις δὲ πράξασθ᾽ εὐμαρές.

105 ὄλβος Triclinius: ὄλβος δ᾽ vett.
106 σάος Emperius, Schroeder: ὃς codd.

But the other's son,[12] the only child immortal   Ant. 5
Thetis bore him in Phthia,   101
   lost his life to an arrow in war,
and as he was consumed by the fire, he raised
a lament from the Danaans. If any mortal understands
   the way of truth, he must be happy with what good
the blessed gods allot him. Now here, now there blow
the gusts of the high-flying winds.   105
   Men's happiness does not come for long
unimpaired, when it accompanies them, descending with
     full weight.

I shall be small in small times, great in great ones;   Ep. 5
I shall honor with my mind whatever fortune attends
   me,
by serving it with the means at my disposal.
And if a god should grant me luxurious wealth,   110
I hope that I may win lofty fame hereafter.
We know of Nestor and Lycian Sarpedon,[13] still the talk
     of men,
from such echoing verses as wise craftsmen
constructed. Excellence endures in glorious songs
for a long time. But few can win them easily.   115

[12] Achilles.
[13] Two heroes at Troy, one a Greek, the other a Trojan ally.

263

PYTHIAN 4

Arcesilas IV was the eighth ruler in a dynasty that be-
gan with Battus I, who colonized Cyrene from Thera c.
630 B.C. Under the Battidae, the city became a powerful
commercial center, whose main export, an extract from a
plant known as silphium, had medicinal properties. Since
Cyrene was also famous for its doctors, the many refer-
ences to healing in this poem are especially appropriate.

The ode is by far the longest in the collection, owing to
its epic-like narrative of Jason's quest for the golden fleece,
a topic relevant to Arcesilas because the Battidae claimed
Euphamus, one of the Argonauts, as their ancestor. A sur-
prising feature is the plea at the end for Arcesilas to take
back Damophilus, a young Cyrenaean living in exile. The
closing remark about Damophilus' discovery of a spring of
verses while being hosted in Thebes suggests that he com-
missioned the ode. The date of the victory was 462; within
a few years Arcesilas was deposed and his dynasty came to
an end.

The Muse is asked to celebrate Arcesilas and Apollo,
who had once prophesied that Battus would colonize
Libya and fulfill Medea's prediction uttered seventeen
generations before (1–11). Medea's words to the Argo-
nauts are quoted at length (11–56). Pindar announces his
intention to sing of Arcesilas, victorious at Pytho, and of
the golden fleece (64–69).

An oracle had warned Pelias to beware of a man with

264

one sandal (71–78). When Jason arrives in the agora at Iolcus, his appearance stuns the onlookers (78–92). Pelias hastens to meet him and Jason declares that he has come to reclaim the kingship Pelias had usurped from Jason's father. He recounts that when he was born his parents feigned his death and sent him to be raised by Chiron (93–119). After celebrating with his relatives, Jason goes with them to confront Pelias (120–136). Jason offers to let Pelias retain the herds and property, but asks for the scepter and throne (136–155). Pelias agrees, but requests that Jason first bring back the golden fleece (156–167).

Many heroes, inspired by Hera, join Jason and the expedition sets sail (171–202). After passing through the Symplegades, they reach Colchis, where Aphrodite devises the iynx for Jason to seduce Medea (203–219). With Medea's help, Jason accomplishes the task set by her father, Aeetes, of plowing with the fire-breathing bulls (220–241). Aeetes tells Jason where the golden fleece is kept, but does not expect him to retrieve it, because it is guarded by a huge serpent (241–246).

Pressed for time, the poet briefly recounts that after Jason slew the serpent the Argonauts slept with the women on Lemnos on their way home. From this union came the race of Euphamus, Arcesilas' ancestors, who eventually colonized Libya (247–262).

To lead up to the mention of Damophilus, the poet proposes an allegory for Arcesilas to ponder: an oak tree stripped of its boughs can still perform service as firewood or as a beam (263–269). Arcesilas has an opportunity to heal the wounds of his disordered city (270–276). The poet reminds Arcesilas of the virtues of Damophilus, who wishes to return in peace to Cyrene, bringing the song he found while a guest at Thebes (277–299).

4. ΑΡΚΕΣΙΛΑΩΙ ΚΥΡΗΝΑΙΩΙ

ΑΡΜΑΤΙ

Α΄ Σάμερον μὲν χρή σε παρ᾽ ἀνδρὶ φίλῳ
στᾶμεν, εὐίππου βασιλῆι Κυράνας,
    ὄφρα κωμάζοντι σὺν Ἀρκεσίλᾳ,
Μοῖσα, Λατοΐδαισιν ὀφειλόμενον Πυ-
    θῶνί τ᾽ αὔξῃς οὖρον ὕμνων,
ἔνθα ποτὲ χρυσέων Διὸς αἰετῶν πάρεδρος
5 οὐκ ἀποδάμου Ἀπόλλωνος τυχόντος ἱέρεα
    χρῆσεν οἰκιστῆρα Βάττον
    καρποφόρου Λιβύας, ἱερὰν
νᾶσον ὡς ἤδη λιπὼν κτίσσειεν εὐάρματον
πόλιν ἐν ἀργινόεντι μαστῷ,

καὶ τὸ Μηδείας ἔπος ἀγκομίσαι
10 ἑβδόμᾳ καὶ σὺν δεκάτᾳ γενεᾷ Θή-
    ραιον, Αἰήτα τό ποτε ζαμενὴς

8 ἀργεννόεντι Schroeder
9 ἀγκομίσαι Β¹(E¹G¹): ἀγκομίσαιθ᾽ (ἐγκομίσαιθ᾽ C) ζν

---

[1] Artemis and Apollo, the patron god of Delphi (Pytho).
[2] The priestess who spoke the oracles was known as the Pythia.

4. FOR ARCESILAS OF CYRENE

WINNER, CHARIOT RACE, 462 B.C.

Today, Muse, you must stand beside a man who is a   Str. 1
friend, the king of Cyrene with its fine horses,
    so that while Arcesilas is celebrating
you may swell the breeze of hymns
    owed to Leto's children[1] and to Pytho,
where long ago the priestess who sits beside the golden
eagles of Zeus[2] prophesied when Apollo was not away[3]   5
that Battus would be the colonizer
    of fruit-bearing Libya, and that
he should at once leave the holy island[4] to found a city
of fine chariots on the white breast of a hill,[5]

and to fulfill in the seventeenth generation that word   Ant. 1
spoken on Thera by Medea,   10
    which the high-spirited daughter of Aeetes

Strabo (9.3.6) reports that Pindar had told how Zeus released two
eagles from east and west that came together at the center of the
world, where the "navel" at Delphi was located.

[3] Apollo visited other cult centers, including the Hyperbo-
reans (cf. *Pyth.* 10.34–36); his presence would assure the efficacy
of the oracle.   [4] Thera.

[5] Cyrene was built on a chalk cliff (Gildersleeve).

παῖς ἀπέπνευσ᾽ ἀθανάτου στόματος, δέσ-
    ποινα Κόλχων. εἶπε δ᾽ οὕτως
ἡμιθέοισιν Ἰάσονος αἰχματᾶο ναύταις·
"Κέκλυτε, παῖδες ὑπερθύμων τε φωτῶν καὶ θεῶν·
φαμὶ γὰρ τᾶσδ᾽ ἐξ ἁλιπλά-
    κτου ποτὲ γᾶς Ἐπάφοιο κόραν
15 ἀστέων ῥίζαν φυτεύσεσθαι μελησιμβρότων
Διὸς ἐν Ἄμμωνος θεμέθλοις.

ἀντὶ δελφίνων δ᾽ ἐλαχυπτερύγων ἵπ-
    πους ἀμείψαντες θοάς,
ἀνία τ᾽ ἀντ᾽ ἐρετμῶν δί-
    φρους τε νωμάσοισιν ἀελλόποδας.
κεῖνος ὄρνις ἐκτελευτάσει μεγαλᾶν πολίων
20 ματρόπολιν Θήραν γενέσθαι, τόν ποτε
    Τριτωνίδος ἐν προχοαῖς
λίμνας θεῷ ἀνέρι εἰδομένῳ γαῖαν διδόντι
ξείνια πρῴραθεν Εὔφαμος καταβαὶς
δέξατ᾽—αἰσίαν δ᾽ ἐπί οἱ Κρονίων
    Ζεὺς πατὴρ ἔκλαγξε βροντάν—

15 μελησιμβρότων Barrett: μελησίμβροτον codd.
23 αἰσίαν Schroeder: αἴσιον codd.

268

and queen of the Colchians had once breathed forth
    from her immortal mouth. Such were her words
to the demigods who sailed with spear-bearing Jason:[6]
"Hear me, sons of great-hearted men and gods.
I declare that one day from this sea-beaten land[7]
    the daughter[8] of Epaphus
will have planted within her a root of famous cities   15
at the foundations of Zeus Ammon.[9]

In place of short-finned dolphins   Ep. 1
    they will take swift horses
and instead of oars they will ply reins
    and chariots that run like a storm.
This sign will bring it to pass that Thera
will become the mother-city of great cities—the token   20
    which Euphamus once received at the outflow
of Lake Tritonis,[10] when he descended from the prow
and accepted earth proffered as a guest-present by a god
in the guise of a man—and father Zeus, son of Cronus,
    pealed for him an auspicious thunderclap—

[6] On the expedition of the Argo.

[7] Thera.

[8] Libya.

[9] Although at a considerable distance from the capital, the oracle of Zeus Ammon was a noted feature of the region of Cyrene.

[10] Pindar's account of the Argonauts' return is as follows. After leaving Colchis (on the southeastern end of the Black Sea) by the Phasis River, they crossed Oceanus and the Red Sea (perhaps the Indian Ocean and our Red Sea), returned to Oceanus, traveled overland for twelve days to Libya and Lake Tritonis, through whose outflow they reached the Mediterranean, stopping at Thera and Lemnos on their way to Iolcus.

Β΄   ἁνίκ' ἄγκυραν ποτὶ χαλκόγενυν
25 ναῒ κριμνάντων ἐπέτοσσε, θοᾶς Ἀρ-
        γοῦς χαλινόν· δώδεκα δὲ πρότερον
    ἁμέρας ἐξ Ὠκεανοῦ φέρομεν νώ-
        των ὕπερ γαίας ἐρήμων
    ἐννάλιον δόρυ, μήδεσιν ἀνσπάσσαντες ἁμοῖς.
    τουτάκι δ' οἰοπόλος δαίμων ἐπῆλθεν, φαιδίμαν
    ἀνδρὸς αἰδοίου πρόσοψιν
        θηκάμενος· φιλίων δ' ἐπέων
30 ἄρχετο, ξείνοις ἅτ' ἐλθόντεσσιν εὐεργέται
    δεῖπν' ἐπαγγέλλοντι πρῶτον.

    ἀλλὰ γὰρ νόστου πρόφασις γλυκεροῦ
    κώλυεν μεῖναι. φάτο δ' Εὐρύπυλος Γαι-
        αόχου παῖς ἀφθίτου Ἐννοσίδα
    ἔμμεναι· γίνωσκε δ' ἐπειγομένους· ἂν
        δ' εὐθὺς ἁρπάξαις ἀρούρας
35 δεξιτερᾷ προτυχὸν ξένιον μάστευσε δοῦναι.
    οὐδ' ἀπίθησέ νιν, ἀλλ' ἥρως ἐπ' ἀκταῖσιν θορών,
    χειρί οἱ χεῖρ' ἀντερείσαις
        δέξατο βώλακα δαιμονίαν.
    πεύθομαι δ' αὐτὰν κατακλυσθεῖσαν ἐκ δούρατος
    ἐναλίαν βᾶμεν σὺν ἅλμᾳ

26 ἐρήμου EF(paraphr.)
30 ἄρχετο BF(schol.): ἄρχεται ΖΕγ
36 ἀπίθησέ νιν codd.: ἀπίθησέ(ν) ἰν Hermann
39 ἐναλίαν Thiersch: ἐναλία codd.

when he came upon us hanging the bronze-jawed   Str. 2
anchor, swift Argo's bridle,   25
    against the ship. Before that, we had drawn up
the sea-faring bark from Oceanus in accordance
    with my instructions, and for twelve days
had been carrying it across desolate stretches of land.
At that point the solitary god approached us,
having assumed the radiant face of a respectful man,
    and he began with the friendly words
which generous men first utter when offering dinner   30
to strangers upon their arrival.

The excuse, however, of our sweet return home   Ant. 2
prevented our tarrying. He said that he was Eurypylus,
    son of the immortal Holder and Shaker of the Earth,[11]
and he recognized that we were in a hurry.
    He immediately picked up some earth
in his right hand and sought to give it as a makeshift   35
       guest-gift.
Nor did he fail to persuade him, but the hero leapt
upon the shore, pressed his hand into the stranger's,
    and accepted the divine clod.
I have heard that it was washed off the ship
by a wave during the evening and passed

[11] Triton, son of Poseidon, calls himself here by the name of
Libya's first king, Eurypylus. Lake Tritonis means "Triton's Lake."

PINDAR

40 ἑσπέρας ὑγρῷ πελάγει σπομέναν. ἦ
    μάν νιν ὤτρυνον θαμά
λυσιπόνοις θεραπόντεσ-
    σιν φυλάξαι· τῶν δ᾽ ἐλάθοντο φρένες·
καί νυν ἐν τᾷδ᾽ ἄφθιτον νάσῳ κέχυται Λιβύας
    εὐρυχόρου σπέρμα πρὶν ὥρας. εἰ γὰρ οἴ-
    κοι νιν βάλε πὰρ χθόνιον
Ἀίδα στόμα, Ταίναρον εἰς ἱερὰν Εὔφαμος ἐλθών,
45 υἱὸς ἱππάρχου Ποσειδάωνος ἄναξ,
    τόν ποτ᾽ Εὐρώπα Τιτυοῦ θυγάτηρ
    τίκτε Καφισοῦ παρ᾽ ὄχθαις,

Γ' τετράτων παίδων κ᾽ ἐπιγεινομένων
    αἷμά οἱ κείναν λάβε σὺν Δαναοῖς εὐ-
    ρεῖαν ἄπειρον· τότε γὰρ μεγάλας
    ἐξανίστανται Λακεδαίμονος Ἀργεί-
    ου τε κόλπου καὶ Μυκηνᾶν.
50 νῦν γε μὲν ἀλλοδαπᾶν κριτὸν εὑρήσει γυναικῶν
    ἐν λέχεσιν γένος, οἵ κεν τάνδε σὺν τιμᾷ θεῶν
    νᾶσον ἐλθόντες τέκωνται
    φῶτα κελαινεφέων πεδίων
δεσπόταν· τὸν μὲν πολυχρύσῳ ποτ᾽ ἐν δώματι
Φοῖβος ἀμνάσει θέμισσιν

50 μὲν Byz.: μὰν vett.

---

12 Thera.
13 Near Orchomenus in Boeotia (cf. *Ol.* 14.1–5).

into the sea, borne on the watery main. In truth,   Ep. 2
    I frequently urged
the servants who relieve our toils   41
    to guard it, but their minds were forgetful;
and now the immortal seed of spacious Libya has been
shed upon this island[12] prematurely. For if Euphamus,
    the royal son of horse-ruling Poseidon,
whom Europa, Tityus' daughter, once bore by the banks
of the Cephisus,[13] had gone home to holy Taenarus[14]   45
and cast the clod at the earth's
    entrance to Hades,

the blood of the fourth generation of children   Str. 3
born to him would have taken that broad mainland
    with the Danaans, for at that time
they are to set out from great Lacedaemon,
    from the gulf of Argos, and from Mycenae.[15]
Now, however, he will find in the beds of foreign women[16]   50
a chosen race, who will come honored by the gods
to this island and beget a man[17]
    to be ruler of the plains with dark clouds.[18]
And when, at a later time, he enters the temple at Pytho,
within his house filled with gold

[14] At the southern tip of Lacedaemon, where an entrance to
Hades was supposed to be.

[15] As part of the mass migrations of the twelfth century.

[16] The women of Lemnos, with whom the Argonauts slept on
their way home to Iolcus (cf. 254–257).

[17] Battus.

[18] Unlike much of the surrounding area, Cyrene receives
some rainfall.

55 Πύθιον ναὸν καταβάντα χρόνῳ
ὑστέρῳ, νάεσσι πολεῖς ἀγαγὲν Νεί-
λοιο πρὸς πῖον τέμενος Κρονίδα."
ἦ ῥα Μηδείας ἐπέων στίχες· ἔπτα-
ξαν δ᾽ ἀκίνητοι σιωπᾷ
ἥροες ἀντίθεοι πυκινὰν μῆτιν κλύοντες.
ὦ μάκαρ υἱὲ Πολυμνάστου, σὲ δ᾽ ἐν τούτῳ λόγῳ
60 χρησμὸς ὤρθωσεν μελίσσας
Δελφίδος αὐτομάτῳ κελάδῳ·
ἅ σε χαίρειν ἐστρὶς αὐδάσαισα πεπρωμένον
βασιλέ᾽ ἄμφανεν Κυράνᾳ,

δυσθρόου φωνᾶς ἀνακρινόμενον ποι-
νὰ τίς ἔσται πρὸς θεῶν.
ἦ μάλα δὴ μετὰ καὶ νῦν,
ὥτε φοινικανθέμου ἦρος ἀκμᾷ,
65 παισὶ τούτοις ὄγδοον θάλλει μέρος Ἀρκεσίλας·
τῷ μὲν Ἀπόλλων ἅ τε Πυθὼ κῦδος ἐξ
Ἀμφικτιόνων ἔπορεν
ἱπποδρομίας. ἀπὸ δ᾽ αὐτὸν ἐγὼ Μοίσαισι δώσω
καὶ τὸ πάγχρυσον νάκος κριοῦ· μετὰ γάρ
κεῖνο πλευσάντων Μινυᾶν, θεόπομ-
ποί σφισιν τιμαὶ φύτευθεν.

55 χρόνῳ E. Schmid: χρόνῳ δ᾽ codd.   56 ἀγαγεῖν C
62 κυράνας B   64 ὥτε Bergk: ὥστε B: om. ζβ
66 ἀμφικτιόνων Boeckh: ἀμφικτυόνων codd.

19 Battus.   20 The Pythia, the priestess through whom

274

Phoebus will admonish him through oracles Ant. 3
to convey many people in ships
to the fertile domain of Cronus' son on the Nile."
Such were the verses of Medea's speech;
the godlike heroes shrank down in silence
and without moving listened to her astute counsel.
O blessed son of Polymnastus,[19] it was you
whom the oracle, in accordance with that speech, exalted
through the spontaneous cry of the Delphic Bee,[20]
who thrice bade you hail and revealed you to be
the destined king of Cyrene,

when you were asking what requital would come Ep. 3
from the gods for your stammering voice.
Yes, indeed, now in later time as well,
as at the height of red-flowered spring,
the eighth generation of those sons flourishes in Arcesilas,
to whom Apollo and Pytho granted glory
from the hands of the Amphictyons[21]
in horse racing. And for my part, I shall entrust to the Muses
both him and the all-golden fleece of the ram, for when
the Minyae sailed in quest of it, god-sent honors
were planted for them.[22]

Apollo conveyed his oracles. "Spontaneous" indicates that she answered before she was asked the question. For Battus' stammer and consultation of the Pythia, see Hdt. 4.155.

[21] The officials overseeing the Pythian games (schol). Others treat as lowercase and translate as "from the surrounding people."

[22] The Minyae, the Battidae, or both. The Minyae were from Orchomenus (cf. *Ol.* 14.4).

Δ΄ τίς γὰρ ἀρχὰ δέξατο ναυτιλίας,
71 τίς δὲ κίνδυνος κρατεροῖς ἀδάμαντος
   δῆσεν ἅλοις; θέσφατον ἦν Πελίαν
ἐξ ἀγαυῶν Αἰολιδᾶν θανέμεν χεί-
   ρεσσιν ἢ βουλαῖς ἀκνάμπτοις.
ἦλθε δέ οἱ κρυόεν πυκινῷ μάντευμα θυμῷ,
πὰρ μέσον ὀμφαλὸν εὐδένδροιο ῥηθὲν ματέρος
75 τὸν μονοκρήπιδα πάντως
   ἐν φυλακᾷ σχεθέμεν μεγάλᾳ,
εὖτ᾽ ἂν αἰπεινῶν ἀπὸ σταθμῶν ἐς εὐδείελον
χθόνα μόλῃ κλειτᾶς Ἰαολκοῦ,

ξεῖνος αἴτ᾽ ὢν ἀστός. ὁ δ᾽ ἦρα χρόνῳ
ἵκετ᾽ αἰχμαῖσιν διδύμαισιν ἀνὴρ ἔκ-
   παγλος· ἐσθὰς δ᾽ ἀμφοτέρα νιν ἔχεν,
80 ἅ τε Μαγνήτων ἐπιχώριος ἁρμό-
   ζοισα θαητοῖσι γυίοις,
ἀμφὶ δὲ παρδαλέᾳ στέγετο φρίσσοντας ὄμβρους·
οὐδὲ κομᾶν πλόκαμοι κερθέντες ᾤχοντ᾽ ἀγλαοί,
ἀλλ᾽ ἅπαν νῶτον καταίθυσ-
   σον. τάχα δ᾽ εὐθὺς ἰὼν σφετέρας
ἐστάθη γνώμας ἀταρβάκτοιο πειρώμενος
85 ἐν ἀγορᾷ πλήθοντος ὄχλου.

τὸν μὲν οὐ γίνωσκον· ὀπιζομένων δ᾽ ἔμ-
   πας τις εἶπεν καὶ τόδε·

78 ἦρα Schroeder: ἄρα codd.: ἆρα Boeckh

276

What beginning took them on their voyage,	Str. 4
and what danger bound them with strong nails	71
of adamant? It was fated that Pelias	

would perish because of the proud Aeolidae, at their hands
   or through their inflexible counsels.
And an oracle came to him that chilled his crafty heart,
spoken at the central navel of the tree-clad mother,[23]
to be greatly on guard in every way against   75
   the man with one sandal,
when he should come from the high dwelling places
into the sunny land of famous Iolcus,

whether he be a stranger or a townsman. And so in time	Ant. 4

he came, an awesome man with two spears,
   and clothing of both kinds was covering him:
native garb of the Magnesians[24] closely fitted   80
   his marvelous limbs, but around it he protected
himself from chilly showers with a leopard skin;
nor were the splendid locks of his hair cut off and lost,
but they rippled down the length of his back.
   Putting his intrepid resolve to the test,
he quickly went straight ahead and stood
in the agora as a crowd was thronging.   85

They did not recognize him, but, awestruck as they were,	Ep. 4
one of them nevertheless said, among other things:	

[23] Delphi, the navel of Gaea, Earth.   [24] Magnesia was the easternmost district of Thessaly, between the Peneius River and the Gulf of Pagasae, including Iolcus and Mt. Pelion.

---

79 ἀμφοτέρα EF: ἀμφότερον rell.

"Οὔ τί που οὗτος Ἀπόλλων,
  οὐδὲ μὰν χαλκάρματός ἐστι πόσις
Ἀφροδίτας· ἐν δὲ Νάξῳ φαντὶ θανεῖν λιπαρᾷ
Ἰφιμεδείας παῖδας, Ὦτον καὶ σέ, τολ-
    μάεις Ἐπιάλτα ἄναξ.
90 καὶ μὰν Τιτυὸν βέλος Ἀρτέμιδος θήρευσε κραιπνόν,
  ἐξ ἀνικάτου φαρέτρας ὀρνύμενον,
ὄφρα τις τᾶν ἐν δυνατῷ φιλοτά-
    των ἐπιψαύειν ἔραται."

Ε΄ τοὶ μὲν ἀλλάλοισιν ἀμειβόμενοι
  γάρυον τοιαῦτ'· ἀνὰ δ' ἡμιόνοις ξε-
    στᾷ τ' ἀπήνᾳ προτροπάδαν Πελίας
95 ἵκετο σπεύδων· τάφε δ' αὐτίκα παπτά-
    ναις ἀρίγνωτον πέδιλον
δεξιτερῷ μόνον ἀμφὶ ποδί. κλέπτων δὲ θυμῷ
δεῖμα προσήνεπε· "Ποίαν γαῖαν, ὦ ξεῖν', εὔχεαι
πατρίδ' ἔμμεν; καὶ τίς ἀνθρώ-
    πων σε χαμαιγενέων πολιᾶς
ἐξανῆκεν γαστρός; ἐχθίστοισι μὴ ψεύδεσιν
100 καταμιάναις εἰπὲ γένναν."

    89 ἐπιάλτα Schroeder e schol. Harl. Od. 11.309: ἐφιάλτ(α)
ζν

"He surely is not Apollo,
   nor certainly is he Aphrodite's husband
of the bronze chariot;[25] and they say that in shining Naxos
Iphimedeia's sons died, Otus and you, bold
   king Ephialtes;[26]
and certainly Artemis' swift arrow hunted down Tityus,   90
as it sped from her invincible quiver,
warning a person to desire to attain loves
   within his power."[27]

While they were saying such things in turn   Str. 5
to one another, Pelias came
   on his polished mule car
in precipitous haste. He was stunned as soon as   95
   he caught sight of the single sandal in clear view
upon his right foot, but he hid his panic in his heart
and addressed him, "What land, O stranger, do you claim
to be your fatherland? And what mortal
   born upon the earth delivered you forth
from her gray womb?[28] Tell me your lineage
and do not stain it with most hateful lies."   100

[25] Ares.

[26] Two gigantic brothers who tried to scale heaven by piling Ossa on Olympus and Pelion on them; they were killed by Apollo (cf. *Od.* 11.307–320) or Artemis (cf. Apollod. 1.7.4).

[27] The giant Tityus was slain by Artemis (and confined in Hades) for attempting to rape her mother Leto on her way to Delphi (cf. *Od.* 11.576–581).

[28] The scholia gloss πολιᾶς as "old," hence respectful in tone, but others take it to be insulting.

τὸν δὲ θαρσήσαις ἀγανοῖσι λόγοις
ὧδ' ἀμείφθη· "Φαμὶ διδασκαλίαν Χεί-
  ρωνος οἴσειν. ἀντρόθε γὰρ νέομαι
πὰρ Χαρικλοῦς καὶ Φιλύρας, ἵνα Κενταύ-
  ρου με κοῦραι θρέψαν ἀγναί.
εἴκοσι δ' ἐκτελέσαις ἐνιαυτοὺς οὔτε ἔργον
105 οὔτ' ἔπος ἐκτράπελον κείνοισιν εἰπὼν ἱκόμαν
οἴκαδ', ἀρχαίαν κομίζων
  πατρὸς ἐμοῦ, βασιλευομέναν
οὐ κατ' αἶσαν, τάν ποτε Ζεὺς ὤπασεν λαγέτᾳ
Αἰόλῳ καὶ παισὶ τιμάν.

πεύθομαι γάρ νιν Πελίαν ἄθεμιν λευ-
  καῖς πιθήσαντα φρασίν
110 ἀμετέρων ἀποσυλᾶ-
  σαι βιαίως ἀρχεδικᾶν τοκέων·
τοί μ', ἐπεὶ πάμπρωτον εἶδον φέγγος, ὑπερφιάλου
ἀγεμόνος δείσαντες ὕβριν, κᾶδος ὡσ-
  είτε φθιμένου δνοφερὸν
ἐν δώμασι θηκάμενοι μίγα κωκυτῷ γυναικῶν,
κρύβδα πέμπον σπαργάνοις ἐν πορφυρέοις,
115 νυκτὶ κοινάσαντες ὁδόν, Κρονίδᾳ
  δὲ τράφεν Χείρωνι δῶκαν.

105 ἐκτράπελον Heyne e schol.: ἐντράπελον codd.
113 μίγα CᵖᶜVEᵖᶜFγ (μέσα Cᵃᶜ, μέγα Eᵃᶜ): μετὰ B

Taking courage, he answered him with gentle words   Ant. 5
in this way: "I claim that I shall manifest the teachings
   of Chiron, for I come
from the side of Chariclo and Philyra[29] and from the cave
   where the Centaur's holy daughters raised me.
After completing twenty years without doing
or saying anything untoward to them, I have come   105
home to reclaim my father's ancient honor
   of kingship, now being wielded
unjustly, which long ago Zeus granted
to Aeolus, leader of the people, and to his sons,[30]

for I am told that lawless Pelias   Ep. 5
   gave in to his white wits[31]
and usurped it   110
   by force from my justly ruling parents,
who, as soon as I saw the light,
fearing the violence of the overbearing ruler,
   made a dark funeral
in the house and added women's wailing as if I had died,
but secretly sent me away in my purple swaddling clothes,
and, entrusting the journey to the night, gave me   115
   to Chiron, son of Cronus, to raise.

[29] Chariclo was Chiron's wife, Philyra his mother.
[30] See Appendix, genealogy of Aeolus. Tyro was married to her
uncle Cretheus, thus making Aeson and Pelias half-brothers.
[31] The meaning of the phrase is in doubt. Glosses include
"evil" (Hesychius), "shallow" (schol.), or "empty" (schol.).

Ϛ΄ ἀλλὰ τούτων μὲν κεφάλαια λόγων
    ἴστε. λευκίππων δὲ δόμους πατέρων, κε-
        δνοὶ πολῖται, φράσσατέ μοι σαφέως·
    Αἴσονος γὰρ παῖς ἐπιχώριος οὐ ξεί-
        ναν ἱκάνω γαῖαν ἄλλων.
    φὴρ δέ με θεῖος Ἰάσονα κικλήσκων προσαύδα."
120 ὣς φάτο· τὸν μὲν ἐσελθόντ᾽ ἔγνον ὀφθαλμοὶ πατρός·
    ἐκ δ᾽ ἄρ᾽ αὐτοῦ πομφόλυξαν
        δάκρυα γηραλέων γλεφάρων,
    ἃν περὶ ψυχὰν ἐπεὶ γάθησεν ἐξαίρετον
    γόνον ἰδὼν κάλλιστον ἀνδρῶν.

    καὶ κασίγνητοί σφισιν ἀμφότεροι
125 ἤλυθον κείνου γε κατὰ κλέος· ἐγγὺς
        μὲν Φέρης κράναν Ὑπερῇδα λιπών,
    ἐκ δὲ Μεσσάνας Ἀμυθάν· ταχέως δ᾽ Ἄ-
        δματος ἷκεν καὶ Μέλαμπος
    εὐμενέοντες ἀνεψιόν. ἐν δαιτὸς δὲ μοίρᾳ
    μειλιχίοισι λόγοις αὐτοὺς Ἰάσων δέγμενος
    ξείνι᾽ ἁρμόζοντα τεύχων
        πᾶσαν εὐφροσύναν τάννεν
130 ἀθρόαις πέντε δραπὼν νύκτεσσιν ἔν θ᾽ ἁμέραις
    ἱερὸν εὐζοίας ἄωτον.

        118 ἱκάνω Madvig: ἱκόμαν codd.: μὲν ἵκω Christ
        120 ἔγνον Byz.: ἔγνων vett.
        129 πᾶσαν B(schol.): πᾶσαν ἐς ζβ

But now you know the principal elements of my story.   Str. 6
Dear fellow citizens, show me clearly
    the home of my fathers who rode white horses,
for I come here as the son of Aeson, a native,
    to no strangers' land.
The divine creature called me by the name Jason."
Thus he spoke. When he entered his home, his father's   120
eyes recognized him and then tears burst forth
    from under his aged eyelids,
as he rejoiced in his soul to see his extraordinary
offspring, fairest of men.

Both of his father's brothers   Ant. 6
arrived when they heard the news about him: Pheres   125
    came from the nearby Hyperian spring[32]
and Amythaon came from Messene; Admetus
    and Melampus also came quickly,
out of good will, to their cousin. During the feasting
Jason received them with gentle words
and, providing fitting hospitality,
    extended all manner of festivity
for five whole nights and days, culling   130
the sacred excellence of joyous living.

[32] In the Thessalian city of Pherae (Strabo 9.5.18).

ἀλλ' ἐν ἔκτᾳ πάντα λόγον θέμενος σπου-
    δαῖον ἐξ ἀρχᾶς ἀνήρ
συγγενέσιν παρεκοινᾶθ'
οἱ δ' ἐπέσποντ'. αἶψα δ' ἀπὸ κλισιᾶν
ὦρτο σὺν κείνοισι· καί ῥ' ἦλθον Πελία μέγαρον·
135 ἐσσύμενοι δ' εἴσω κατέσταν· τῶν δ' ἀκού-
    σαις αὐτὸς ὑπαντίασεν
Τυροῦς ἐρασιπλοκάμου γενεά· πραῢν δ' Ἰάσων
μαλθακᾷ φωνᾷ ποτιστάζων ὄαρον
βάλλετο κρηπῖδα σοφῶν ἐπέων·
    "Παῖ Ποσειδᾶνος Πετραίου,

Ζ´ ἐντὶ μὲν θνατῶν φρένες ὠκύτεραι
140 κέρδος αἰνῆσαι πρὸ δίκας δόλιον τρα-
    χεῖαν ἑρπόντων πρὸς ἔπιβδαν ὅμως·
ἀλλ' ἐμὲ χρὴ καὶ σὲ θεμισσαμένους ὀρ-
    γὰς ὑφαίνειν λοιπὸν ὄλβον.
εἰδότι τοι ἐρέω· μία βοῦς Κρηθεῖ τε μάτηρ
καὶ θρασυμήδεϊ Σαλμωνεῖ· τρίταισιν δ' ἐν γοναῖς
ἄμμες αὖ κείνων φυτευθέν-
    τες σθένος ἀελίου χρύσεον
145 λεύσσομεν. Μοῖραι δ' ἀφίσταντ', εἴ τις ἔχθρα πέλει
ὁμογόνοις αἰδῶ καλύψαι.

οὐ πρέπει νῷν χαλκοτόροις ξίφεσιν

    133 πᾶσι κοινᾶθ' ζΒ: παρεκοινᾶθ' rell.
    134 ἦλθε(ν) ζ

284

But on the sixth day, the hero laid out in earnest   Ep. 6
    the whole story from the beginning
and shared it with his relatives,
    who joined him. At once he rose with them
from the couches, and they went to Pelias' palace.
They hastened straight in and took a stand. When he   135
    heard them, the son of lovely-haired Tyro
met them face to face. In a soft voice
Jason distilled soothing speech
and laid the foundation of wise words:
    "Son of Poseidon of the Rock,[33]

the minds of mortals are all too swift   Str. 7
to commend deceitful gain above justice, even though   140
    they are headed for a rough reckoning the day after.
You and I, however, must rule our tempers with law
    and weave our future happiness.
You know what I am about to say: one heifer[34] was mother
to Cretheus and bold-counseling Salmoneus; we in turn
were born in the third generation from them
    and behold the golden strength
of the sun. The Fates withdraw, if any feuding arises   145
to make kinsmen hide their mutual respect.

It is not proper for the two of us to divide the great honor Ant. 7

[33] Poseidon was called Πετραῖος by the Thessalians for split-
ting the mountains to create the valley of Tempe (schol.).
[34] Enarea, wife of Aeolus.

---

145 ἀφίσαντ' BH: ἀφίσταιντ' V, Chaeris: ἀμφίσταντ'
CEFG

οὐδ᾿ ἀκόντεσσιν μεγάλαν προγόνων τι-
   μὰν δάσασθαι. μῆλά τε γάρ τοι ἐγώ
καὶ βοῶν ξανθὰς ἀγέλας ἀφίημ᾿ ἀ-
   γρούς τε πάντας, τοὺς ἀπούρας
150 ἀμετέρων τοκέων νέμεαι πλοῦτον πιαίνων·
κοὔ με πονεῖ τεὸν οἶκον ταῦτα πορσύνοντ᾿ ἄγαν·
   ἀλλὰ καὶ σκᾶπτον μόναρχον
   καὶ θρόνος, ᾧ ποτε Κρηθεΐδας
ἐγκαθίζων ἱππόταις εὔθυνε λαοῖς δίκας—
   τὰ μὲν ἄνευ ξυνᾶς ἀνίας

155 λῦσον, ἄμμιν μή τι νεώτερον ἐξ αὐ-
   τῶν ἀναστάῃ κακόν."
ὣς ἄρ᾿ ἔειπεν, ἀκᾷ δ᾿ ἀντ-
   αγόρευσεν καὶ Πελίας· "Ἔσομαι
τοῖος· ἀλλ᾿ ἤδη με γηραιὸν μέρος ἁλικίας
ἀμφιπολεῖ· σὸν δ᾿ ἄνθος ἥβας ἄρτι κυ-
   μαίνει· δύνασαι δ᾿ ἀφελεῖν
μᾶνιν χθονίων. κέλεται γὰρ ἑὰν ψυχὰν κομίξαι
160 Φρίξος ἐλθόντας πρὸς Αἰήτα θαλάμους
   δέρμα τε κριοῦ βαθύμαλλον ἄγειν,
   τῷ ποτ᾿ ἐκ πόντου σαώθη

Η´ ἔκ τε ματρυιᾶς ἀθέων βελέων.

155 ἀναστάῃ Wilhelm Schulze: ἀναστήσῃς (ἀναστήσας
Ε) ζν: ἀναστήσῃ Β^{pc}(Σ^c): ἀνασταίη Σ^a: ἀναστῄη Hermann:
ἀναστάσῃς Schnitzer

of our forefathers with bronze-piercing swords
    or javelins. For I give over to you the sheep,
the tawny herds of cattle, and all the fields
    which you stole
from my parents and administer to fatten your wealth—   150
I do not mind if these overly enrich your house—
but, as for the scepter of sole rule
    and the throne upon which Cretheus' son[35] once
sat and rendered straight justice to his people of
        horsemen,
these you must give up without grief

on both sides, lest some more troubling evil   Ep. 7
    arise for us from them."
Thus he spoke, and Pelias   156
    responded calmly, "I shall be
such as you wish, but already the aged portion of life
attends me, whereas your flower of youth
    is just cresting; and you are capable of removing
the anger of those in the underworld. For Phrixus orders
us to go to the halls of Aeetes to bring back his soul[36]   160
and to recover the thick-fleeced hide of the ram
    by which he was once preserved from the sea

and from the impious weapons of his stepmother.[37]   Str. 8

[35] Aeson.

[36] I.e. call back his soul to rest in a cenotaph at home.

[37] Ino, who in some versions falsely accused Phrixus of being
in love with her; he escaped across the sea to Colchis on the back
of the ram with the golden fleece.

PINDAR

ταῦτά μοι θαυμαστὸς ὄνειρος ἰὼν φω-
   νεῖ. μεμάντευμαι δ' ἐπὶ Κασταλίᾳ,
εἰ μετάλλατόν τι· καὶ ὡς τάχος ὀτρύ-
   νει με τεύχειν ναΐ πομπάν.
165 τοῦτον ἄεθλον ἑκὼν τέλεσον· καί τοι μοναρχεῖν
καὶ βασιλευέμεν ὄμνυμι προήσειν. καρτερός
   ὅρκος ἄμμιν μάρτυς ἔστω
      Ζεὺς ὁ γενέθλιος ἀμφοτέροις."
σύνθεσιν ταύταν ἐπαινήσαντες οἱ μὲν κρίθεν·
ἀτὰρ Ἰάσων αὐτὸς ἤδη

170 ὤρινεν κάρυκας ἐόντα πλόον
φαινέμεν παντᾷ. τάχα δὲ Κρονίδαο
   Ζηνὸς υἱοὶ τρεῖς ἀκαμαντομάχαι
ἦλθον Ἀλκμήνας θ' ἑλικογλεφάρου Λή-
   δας τε, δοιοὶ δ' ὑψιχαῖται
ἀνέρες, Ἐννοσίδα γένος, αἰδεσθέντες ἀλκάν,
ἔκ τε Πύλου καὶ ἀπ' ἄκρας Ταινάρου· τῶν μὲν κλέος
175 ἐσλὸν Εὐφάμου τ' ἐκράνθη
   σόν τε, Περικλύμεν' εὐρυβία.
ἐξ Ἀπόλλωνος δὲ φορμιγκτὰς ἀοιδᾶν πατήρ
ἔμολεν, εὐαίνητος Ὀρφεύς.

πέμπε δ' Ἑρμᾶς χρυσόραπις διδύμους υἱ-
   οὺς ἐπ' ἄτρυτον πόνον,

176 φορμικτὰς v

288

Such things does a wondrous dream come and tell
    to me. I have inquired of the oracle at Castalia
if some expedition must be made, and it orders me
    to provide conveyance by ship as soon as possible.
Willingly accomplish this task and I swear   165
that I will hand over to you sole rule and kingship.
As a mighty pledge, let our witness be
    Zeus, progenitor of both our families."
After agreeing to this pact, they parted.
But Jason himself at once began

sending heralds everywhere to announce that a voyage   Ant. 8
was in the making. Swiftly came Cronian Zeus'   171
    three tireless warrior sons, born to
bright-eyed Alcmene and to Leda,[38]
    and the two men with hair piled on high,
offspring of Earthshaker, out of respect for their valor,
from Pylos and the headland of Taenarus, whose noble
glory was fulfilled, that of Euphamus   175
    and yours, mighty Periclymenus.[39]
And from Apollo came the father of songs,
the widely praised minstrel Orpheus.

And Hermes of the golden wand sent his twin sons   Ep. 8
    for the endless toil,

[38] Heracles, son of Alcmene, and Castor and Polydeuces, sons of Leda.

[39] Euphamus is from Taenarus (cf. 43–44); Periclymenus is the son of Neleus from Pylos. Their hair was presumably tied up in a knot; others render "high-plumed."

τὸν μὲν Ἐχίονα, κεχλά-
δοντας ἥβᾳ, τὸν δ᾽ Ἔρυτον. ταχέες
180 ἀμφὶ Παγγαίου θεμέθλοις ναιετάοντες ἔβαν,
καὶ γὰρ ἑκὼν θυμῷ γελανεῖ θᾶσσον ἔν-
τυνεν βασιλεὺς ἀνέμων
Ζήταν Κάλαΐν τε πατὴρ Βορέας, ἄνδρας πτεροῖσιν
νῶτα πεφρίκοντας ἄμφω πορφυρέοις.
τὸν δὲ παμπειθῆ γλυκὺν ἡμιθέοι-
σιν πόθον ἔνδαιεν Ἥρα

Θ´ ναὸς Ἀργοῦς, μή τινα λειπόμενον
186 τὰν ἀκίνδυνον παρὰ ματρὶ μένειν αἰ-
ῶνα πέσσοντ᾽, ἀλλ᾽ ἐπὶ καὶ θανάτῳ
φάρμακον κάλλιστον ἑᾶς ἀρετᾶς ἅ-
λιξιν εὑρέσθαι σὺν ἄλλοις.
ἐς δ᾽ Ἰαολκὸν ἐπεὶ κατέβα ναυτᾶν ἄωτος,
λέξατο πάντας ἐπαινήσαις Ἰάσων. καί ῥά οἱ
190 μάντις ὀρνίχεσσι καὶ κλά-
ροισι θεοπροπέων ἱεροῖς
Μόψος ἄμβασε στρατὸν πρόφρων· ἐπεὶ δ᾽ ἐμβόλου
κρέμασαν ἀγκύρας ὕπερθεν,

χρυσέαν χείρεσσι λαβὼν φιάλαν
ἀρχὸς ἐν πρύμνᾳ πατέρ᾽ Οὐρανιδᾶν ἐγ-
χεικέραυνον Ζῆνα, καὶ ὠκυπόρους

179 ταχέες Boeckh: ταχέες δ᾽ codd.
180 θεμέθλοις Boeckh: θέμεθλα ζΒᵇEF: om. Bᵃγ(schol.)

290

one Echion, the other Erytus, both
    swelling with youthfulness. Swift
to come were those dwelling at the base of Pangaeum,[40]   180
for with a cheerful heart their willing father Boreas,
    king of the winds, swiftly equipped[41]
Zetes and Calaïs, men whose backs both
rippled with wings of purple.
And Hera enkindled in these demigods
    that all-persuasive, sweet longing

for the ship Argo, so that no one might be left behind   Str. 9
to remain with his mother and coddle a life   186
    without risk, but rather, even if it meant death,
to gain the most noble remedy[42] for his own achievement
    in the company of others of his age.
When the pick of the sailors came down to Iolcus,
Jason praised and mustered them all. Then the seer
Mopsus, prophesying for them by means of birds   190
    and sacred lots,
gladly sent the host on board. And when they had slung
the anchors above the prow,

the captain took a golden bowl in his hands   Ant. 9
and, standing on the stern, called upon Zeus,
    father of the Uranidae and wielder of lightning,

[40] A mountain in Thrace.
[41] Or *spurred on*.
[42] I.e. fame. Others translate, "remedy to effect his own excellence."

---

184 ἔνδαιεν C^bB¹Fγ: ἔδαιεν ζBE: ἐνέδαιεν Turyn

195　κυμάτων ῥιπὰς ἀνέμους τ᾽ ἐκάλει νύ-
　　　κτας τε καὶ πόντου κελεύθους
　　ἄματά τ᾽ εὔφρονα καὶ φιλίαν νόστοιο μοῖραν·
　　ἐκ νεφέων δέ οἱ ἀντάυσε βροντᾶς αἴσιον
　　φθέγμα· λαμπραὶ δ᾽ ἦλθον ἀκτῖ-
　　　νες στεροπᾶς ἀπορηγνύμεναι.
　　ἀμπνοὰν δ᾽ ἥρωες ἔστασαν θεοῦ σάμασιν
200　πιθόμενοι· κάρυξε δ᾽ αὐτοῖς

　　ἐμβαλεῖν κώπαισι τερασκόπος ἀδεί-
　　　ας ἐνίπτων ἐλπίδας·
　　εἰρεσία δ᾽ ὑπεχώρη-
　　　σεν ταχειᾶν ἐκ παλαμᾶν ἄκορος.
　　σὺν Νότου δ᾽ αὔραις ἐπ᾽ Ἀξείνου στόμα πεμπόμενοι
　　ἤλυθον· ἔνθ᾽ ἁγνὸν Ποσειδάωνος ἔσ-
　　　σαντ᾽ ἐνναλίου τέμενος,
205　φοίνισσα δὲ Θρηϊκίων ἀγέλα ταύρων ὑπᾶρχεν,
　　καὶ νεόκτιστον λίθων βωμοῖο θέναρ.
　　ἐς δὲ κίνδυνον βαθὺν ἱέμενοι
　　　δεσπόταν λίσσοντο ναῶν,

Ι´　συνδρόμων κινηθμῶν ἀμαιμάκετον
　　ἐκφυγεῖν πετρᾶν. δίδυμαι γὰρ ἔσαν ζω-
　　　αί, κυλινδέσκοντό τε κραιπνότεραι
210　ἢ βαρυγδούπων ἀνέμων στίχες· ἀλλ᾽ ἤ-
　　　δη τελευτὰν κεῖνος αὐταῖς

and upon the rushing waves and winds to be swift-   195
    moving and the nights and paths of the sea and days
to be propitious and their homecoming favorable.
And from the clouds there answered him an auspicious
clap of thunder, and bright flashes of lightning
    came bursting forth.
The heroes took fresh courage, trusting
the god's signs. The seer bade them   200

fall to the oars, as he expressed   Ep. 9
    cheerful expectations.
From under their swift hands the rowing
    proceeded tirelessly.
Sped by the breezes of the South Wind, they came
to the mouth of the Inhospitable Sea,[43] where they
    established a sacred precinct for Poseidon of the Sea,
and there was at hand a tawny herd of Thracian bulls   205
and a newly built stone altar with a hollow.[44]
As they sped on to grave danger,
    they prayed to the lord of ships[45]

for escape from the irresistible movement   Str. 10
of the clashing rocks,[46] for the two of them were alive
    and would roll more swiftly
than the ranks of loudly roaring winds.   210
    That voyage of the demigods, however, finally

[43] The Black Sea, also called (euphemistically) the Hospitable
(Euxine) Sea.   [44] The hollowed top of the altar held the fire
upon which the animal parts were burned.   [45] Poseidon.
[46] The Symplegades. At *Od.* 12.61–72 Homer refers to Jason's
passing through the "Planctae" on his return voyage.

PINDAR

ἡμιθέων πλόος ἄγαγεν. ἐς Φᾶσιν δ᾽ ἔπειτεν
ἤλυθον, ἔνθα κελαινώπεσσι Κόλχοισιν βίαν
μεῖξαν Αἰήτα παρ᾽ αὐτῷ.
πότνια δ᾽ ὀξυτάτων βελέων
ποικίλαν ἴυγγα τετράκναμον Οὐλυμπόθεν
215 ἐν ἀλύτῳ ζεύξαισα κύκλῳ

μαινάδ᾽ ὄρνιν Κυπρογένεια φέρεν
πρῶτον ἀνθρώποισι λιτάς τ᾽ ἐπαοιδὰς
ἐκδιδάσκησεν σοφὸν Αἰσονίδαν,
ὄφρα Μηδείας τοκέων ἀφέλοιτ᾽ αἰ-
δῶ, ποθεινὰ δ᾽ Ἑλλὰς αὐτάν
ἐν φρασὶ καιομέναν δονέοι μάστιγι Πειθοῦς.
220 καὶ τάχα πείρατ᾽ ἀέθλων δείκνυεν πατρωίων·
σὺν δ᾽ ἐλαίῳ φαρμακώσαισ᾽
ἀντίτομα στερεᾶν ὀδυνᾶν
δῶκε χρίεσθαι. καταίνησάν τε κοινὸν γάμον
γλυκὺν ἐν ἀλλάλοισι μεῖξαι.

ἀλλ᾽ ὅτ᾽ Αἰήτας ἀδαμάντινον ἐν μέσ-
σοις ἄροτρον σκίμψατο
225 καὶ βόας, οἳ φλόγ᾽ ἀπὸ ξαν-
θᾶν γενύων πνέον καιομένοιο πυρός,
χαλκέαις δ᾽ ὁπλαῖς ἀράσσεσκον χθόν᾽ ἀμειβόμενοι·

213 ὠκυτάτων v (sed cf. schol.)

294

put an end to them. Next they came to the Phasis,[47]
where they matched strength with the dark-faced
Colchians in the presence of Aeetes himself.

But the Cyprus-born queen of sharpest arrows
bound the dappled wryneck to the four spokes
of the inescapable wheel   215

and brought from Olympus that bird of madness[48]   Ant. 10
for the first time to men, and she taught
    the son of Aeson to be skillful in prayers and charms,
so that he might take away Medea's respect
    for her parents, and so that desire for Hellas might set
her mind afire and drive her with the whip of Persuasion.
And right away she showed him the ways to accomplish   220
her father's trials, and she concocted with oil
    antidotes for terrible pains and gave them to him
for anointing—and so they agreed to join with one
another in a sweet marriage of mutual consent.

But after Aeetes positioned in their midst the plow   Ep. 10
    made of adamant
and the oxen that were breathing the flame of blazing fire   225
    from their tawny jaws
and pawing the ground in turn with brazen hoofs,

[47] River at the eastern end of the Black Sea where Colchis is
located.
[48] The iynx, a love charm intended to instill a responsive pas-
sion in the person desired as a lover, consisted of a wryneck at-
tached to a small wheel.

PINDAR

τοὺς ἀγαγὼν ζεύγλᾳ πέλασσεν μοῦνος. ὀρ-
θὰς δ᾽ αὔλακας ἐντανύσαις
ἤλαυν᾽, ἀνὰ βωλακίας δ᾽ ὀρόγυιαν σχίζε νῶτον
γᾶς. ἔειπεν δ᾽ ὧδε· "Τοῦτ᾽ ἔργον βασιλεύς,
230 ὅστις ἄρχει ναός, ἐμοὶ τελέσαις
ἄφθιτον στρωμνὰν ἀγέσθω,

IA´ κῶας αἰγλᾶεν χρυσέῳ θυσάνῳ."
ὣς ἄρ᾽ αὐδάσαντος ἀπὸ κρόκεον ῥί-
ψαις Ἰάσων εἷμα θεῷ πίσυνος
εἴχετ᾽ ἔργου· πῦρ δέ νιν οὐκ ἐόλει παμ-
φαρμάκου ξείνας ἐφετμαῖς.
σπασσάμενος δ᾽ ἄροτρον, βόεους δήσαις ἀνάγκᾳ
235 ἔντεσιν αὐχένας ἐμβάλλων τ᾽ ἐριπλεύρῳ φυᾷ
κέντρον αἰανὲς βιατὰς
ἐξεπόνησ᾽ ἐπιτακτὸν ἀνήρ
μέτρον. ἴυξεν δ᾽ ἀφωνήτῳ περ ἔμπας ἄχει
δύνασιν Αἰήτας ἀγασθείς.

πρὸς δ᾽ ἑταῖροι καρτερὸν ἄνδρα φίλας
240 ὤρεγον χεῖρας, στεφάνοισί τέ νιν ποί-
ας ἔρεπτον, μειλιχίοις τε λόγοις

228 ἀνὰ βωλακίας δ᾽ Fᵖᶜ: ἀναβωλακίαις δ᾽ EF: ἀνὰ βω-
λάκι᾽ ἐς δ᾽ Braswell
234 βόεους ζ: βόεοις [B]βCⁱ | δήσαις Heyne: δῆσεν ζ[B?]
Bⁱ: δήσας Cⁱβ | ἀνάγκᾳ Σγρ: ἀνάγκας ζ[B?]γ: ἐν ἀνάγκαις F
(ι inserto) Eᵖᶜ: ἀνάγκαις paraphr.
235 ἐμβάλλων B(?): ἐμβαλὼν ζBᵐβ(paraphr.)

296

he led them and brought them to the yoke-strap single-
     handedly.
He stretched straight furrows as he drove them
and split open the stretch of clodded earth a fathom
deep. Then he spoke thus, "When the king, whoever it is
who captains the ship, completes this task for me,   230
     let him take away the immortal bedding,

the fleece that gleams with golden fringe."   Str. 11
When he had spoken thus, Jason flung off his saffron
     cloak, and putting his trust in the god, took on the task.
The fire did not make him flinch, owing to the commands
     of the hospitable woman skilled in all medicines.
He grasped the plow, bound the necks of the oxen
by force in their harness, and by thrusting   235
the ruthless goad into their strong-ribbed bulk,
     the powerful man accomplished the appointed
measure of toil. Aeetes cried out, although in
     inarticulate pain,
astonished at the power he beheld.

But his comrades were stretching forth their hands   Ant. 11
to the mighty man, covering him with crowns of leaves,[49]   240
     and greeting him with words

___

[49] Some follow schol. 427b in seeing here a φυλλοβολία
"showering with leaves" (cf. *Pyth.* 9.123–124).

ἀγαπάζοντ'. αὐτίκα δ' Ἀελίου θαυ-
    μαστὸς υἱὸς δέρμα λαμπρόν
ἔννεπεν, ἔνθα νιν ἐκτάνυσαν Φρίξου μάχαιραι·
ἔλπετο δ' οὐκέτι οἱ κεῖνόν γε πράξασθαι πόνον.
κεῖτο γὰρ λόχμᾳ, δράκοντος
    δ' εἴχετο λαβροτατᾶν γενύων,
245 ὃς πάχει μάκει τε πεντηκόντερον ναῦν κράτει,
τέλεσεν ἂν πλαγαὶ σιδάρου.

μακρά μοι νεῖσθαι κατ' ἀμαξιτόν· ὥρα
    γὰρ συνάπτει· καί τινα
οἶμον ἴσαμι βραχύν· πολ-
    λοῖσι δ' ἅγημαι σοφίας ἑτέροις.
κτεῖνε μὲν γλαυκῶπα τέχναις ποικιλόνωτον ὄφιν,
250 ὦ Ἀρκεσίλα, κλέψεν τε Μήδειαν σὺν αὐ-
    τᾷ, τὰν Πελιαοφόνον·
ἔν τ' Ὠκεανοῦ πελάγεσσι μίγεν πόντῳ τ' ἐρυθρῷ
Λαμνιᾶν τ' ἔθνει γυναικῶν ἀνδροφόνων·
ἔνθα καὶ γυίων ἀέθλοις ἐπεδεί-
    ξαντο ἷν' ἐσθᾶτος ἀμφίς,

ΙΒ΄ καὶ συνεύνασθεν. καὶ ἐν ἀλλοδαπαῖς

246 τέλεσεν Mommsen e schol.: (ἐ)τέλεσ(σ)αν ζνΣ^{γρ}
250 αὐτῷ CΣ^{γρ} | Πελιαοφόνον edd.: πελιαοφονον variis ac-
centibus codd.: Πελίαο φόνον Chaeris: Πελίαο φονόν Wacker-
nagel
253 ἷν' Kayser: κρίσιν codd.

of kindness. At once the wondrous son of Helius[50]
    told him where Phrixus' sacrificial knives
had stretched out the shining hide,
but he did not expect him to perform that further trial,
    because it lay in a thicket
    and was right by the ferocious jaws of a serpent,
which exceeded in breadth and length a ship of fifty oars,   245
which strokes of iron have fashioned.

But it is too far for me to travel on the highway,   Ep. 11
    because the hour is pressing and I know
a short path—and I lead the way
    in wise skill for many others.
He cunningly slew the green-eyed snake with spotted
        back,
O Arcesilas, and with her own help stole away Medea,   250
    the slayer of Pelias.[51]
They came to the expanses of Oceanus, to the Red Sea,
and to the race of man-slaying Lemnian women.
There they also displayed the strength of their limbs
    in games for the prize of a cloak[52]

and slept with the women. Then it was in those foreign   Str. 12

[50] Aeetes (cf. *Od.* 10.135–139).

[51] She tricked Pelias' daughters into boiling him in an attempt to rejuvenate him.

[52] The games held by Hypsipyle (cf. *Ol.* 4.19–23). Before the Argonauts arrived the women of Lemnos had killed their husbands (cf. Aesch. *Cho.* 631 ff.).

255 σπέρμ᾽ ἀρούραις τουτάκις ὑμετέρας ἀ-
κτῖνος ὄλβου δέξατο μοιρίδιον
ἆμαρ ἢ νύκτες· τόθι γὰρ γένος Εὐφά-
μου φυτευθὲν λοιπὸν αἰεί
τέλλετο· καὶ Λακεδαιμονίων μιχθέντες ἀνδρῶν
ἤθεσιν ἔν ποτε Καλλίσταν ἀπῴκησαν χρόνῳ
νᾶσον· ἔνθεν δ᾽ ὔμμι Λατοί-
δας ἔπορεν Λιβύας πεδίον
260 σὺν θεῶν τιμαῖς ὀφέλλειν, ἄστυ χρυσοθρόνου
διανέμειν θεῖον Κυράνας

ὀρθόβουλον μῆτιν ἐφευρομένοις.
γνῶθι νῦν τὰν Οἰδιπόδα σοφίαν· εἰ
γάρ τις ὄζους ὀξυτόμῳ πελέκει
ἐξερείψειεν μεγάλας δρυός, αἰσχύ-
νοι δέ οἱ θαητὸν εἶδος,
265 καὶ φθινόκαρπος ἐοῖσα διδοῖ ψᾶφον περ᾽ αὐτᾶς,
εἴ ποτε χειμέριον πῦρ ἐξίκηται λοίσθιον,
ἢ σὺν ὀρθαῖς κιόνεσσιν
δεσποσύναισιν ἐρειδομένα
μόχθον ἄλλοις ἀμφέπει δύστανον ἐν τείχεσιν,
ἑὸν ἐρημώσαισα χῶρον.

255 σπέρμ᾽ ἀρούραις . . . ἀκτῖνος Hermann: περ ἀρού-
ραισι . . . ἀκτῖνας codd. | ὄλβου VBEFᵃᶜ: ὄλβον C: ὄλβῳ
γ(schol.)
258 ἔν Chaeris: ἄν ζν: ἄν schol.
264 ἐξερείψειεν Thiersch: ἐξερ(ε)ίψαι κε codd. | αἰσχύνοι
Moschopulus: αἰσχύνῃ vett.

300

furrows[53] that the fated days or nights received the seed   255
    of your family's radiant
prosperity, for there the race of Euphamus
    was planted and continued ever after.
And, after coming to the abodes of Lacedaemonian men,
in time they settled on the island formerly called
Calliste.[54] And from there the son of Leto gave your family
    the plain of Libya
to make prosper through honors coming from the gods,   260
and the divine city of golden-throned Cyrene to govern,

to you who have devised policy based on right counsel.   Ant. 12
Now come to know the wisdom of Oedipus:[55] if someone
    with a sharp-bladed axe
should strip the boughs from a great oak tree
    and ruin its splendid appearance,
although it cannot bear foliage, it gives an account of   265
    itself,
if ever it comes at last to a winter's fire,
or if, supported by upright columns
    belonging to a master,
it performs a wretched labor within alien walls,[56]
having left its own place desolate.

[53] I.e. women's wombs.
[54] "Fairest," i.e. Thera (cf. Hdt. 4.147.4).
[55] Proverbial for his ability to understand riddles.
[56] If Arcesilas does not recall Damophilus, he will serve a master in another city.

270 ἐσσὶ δ' ἰατὴρ ἐπικαιρότατος, Παι-
    άν τέ σοι τιμᾷ φάος.
    χρὴ μαλακὰν χέρα προσβάλ-
    λοντα τρῶμαν ἕλκεος ἀμφιπολεῖν.
    ῥᾴδιον μὲν γὰρ πόλιν σεῖσαι καὶ ἀφαυροτέροις·
    ἀλλ' ἐπὶ χώρας αὖτις ἕσσαι δυσπαλὲς
        δὴ γίνεται, ἐξαπίνας
    εἰ μὴ θεὸς ἁγεμόνεσσι κυβερνατὴρ γένηται.
275 τὶν δὲ τούτων ἐξυφαίνονται χάριτες.
    τλᾶθι τᾶς εὐδαίμονος ἀμφὶ Κυρά-
        νας θέμεν σπουδὰν ἅπασαν.

ΙΓ΄ τῶν δ' Ὁμήρου καὶ τόδε συνθέμενος
    ῥῆμα πόρσυν'· ἄγγελον ἐσλὸν ἔφα τι-
        μὰν μεγίσταν πράγματι παντὶ φέρειν·
    αὔξεται καὶ Μοῖσα δι' ἀγγελίας ὀρ-
        θᾶς. ἐπέγνω μὲν Κυράνα
280 καὶ τὸ κλεεννότατον μέγαρον Βάττου δικαιᾶν
    Δαμοφίλου πραπίδων. κεῖνος γὰρ ἐν παισὶν νέος,
    ἐν δὲ βουλαῖς πρέσβυς ἐγκύρ-
        σαις ἑκατονταετεῖ βιοτᾷ,
    ὀρφανίζει μὲν κακὰν γλῶσσαν φαεννᾶς ὀπός,
    ἔμαθε δ' ὑβρίζοντα μισεῖν,

285 οὐκ ἐρίζων ἀντία τοῖς ἀγαθοῖς,
    οὐδὲ μακύνων τέλος οὐδέν. ὁ γὰρ και-
        ρὸς πρὸς ἀνθρώπων βραχὺ μέτρον ἔχει.

302

But you are a most fitting healer, and Paean[57]   Ep. 12
    honors your saving light.
One must apply a gentle hand to tend   271
    a sore wound.
For easily can even weaklings shake a city;
but to set it back in place again is a difficult
    struggle indeed, unless suddenly
a god becomes a helmsman for the leaders.
But for you the blessings of such things are unfolding.   275
Dare to devote all your serious effort
    to the cause of blessed Cyrene.

And among the sayings of Homer, take this one to heart   Str. 13
and heed it: he said that a good messenger
    brings the greatest honor to every affair.[58]
The Muse, too, gains distinction through true
    reporting. Cyrene and the most celebrated house
of Battus have learned to know the just mind   280
of Damophilus. For that man, a youth among boys,
but in counsels an elder
    who has attained a life of one hundred years,
deprives a malicious tongue of its shining voice
and has learned to hate the person who is violent,

not striving against the noble   Ant. 13
nor delaying any accomplishment, since opportunity   286
    in men's affairs has a brief span.

[57] Apollo the healer.
[58] Cf. *Il.* 15.207.

εὖ νιν ἔγνωκεν· θεράπων δέ οἱ, οὐ δρά-
στας ὀπαδεῖ. φαντὶ δ᾽ ἔμμεν
τοῦτ᾽ ἀνιαρότατον, καλὰ γινώσκοντ᾽ ἀνάγκᾳ
ἐκτὸς ἔχειν πόδα. καὶ μὰν κεῖνος Ἄτλας οὐρανῷ
290   προσπαλαίει νῦν γε πατρῴ-
ας ἀπὸ γᾶς ἀπό τε κτεάνων·
λῦσε δὲ Ζεὺς ἄφθιτος Τιτᾶνας. ἐν δὲ χρόνῳ
μεταβολαὶ λήξαντος οὔρου

ἱστίων. ἀλλ᾽ εὔχεται οὐλομέναν νοῦ-
σον διαντλήσαις ποτέ
οἶκον ἰδεῖν, ἐπ᾽ Ἀπόλλω-
νός τε κράνᾳ συμποσίας ἐφέπων
295   θυμὸν ἐκδόσθαι πρὸς ἥβαν πολλάκις, ἔν τε σοφοῖς
δαιδαλέαν φόρμιγγα βαστάζων πολί-
ταις ἡσυχίᾳ θιγέμεν,
μήτ᾽ ὦν τινι πῆμα πορών, ἀπαθὴς δ᾽ αὐτὸς πρὸς
ἀστῶν·
καί κε μυθήσαιθ᾽, ὁποίαν, Ἀρκεσίλα,
εὗρε παγὰν ἀμβροσίων ἐπέων,
πρόσφατον Θήβᾳ ξενωθείς.

He has come to know it well; he serves it
    as an attendant, not as a hireling. They say
that the most distressing thing is to know the good,
but to be forced to stand away. Yes, that Atlas[59]
is wrestling even now with the sky   290
    away from his homeland and from his possessions;
yet immortal Zeus released the Titans. In the course of
        time
sails are changed when the wind

dies down. But he prays that, having drained   Ep. 13
    his accursed disease to the end,
he may some day see his home; that he may join
    the symposia at Apollo's fountain,[60]
often give his heart over to youthful enjoyment, and,   295
taking up the ornate lyre among his cultured citizens,
    may attain peace,
neither doing harm to anyone, nor suffering it from his
        townsmen.
And he would tell, Arcesilas,
what a spring of ambrosial verses he found,
    when he was recently a guest at Thebes.[61]

[59] I.e. Damophilus.

[60] In Cyrene (cf. Hdt. 6.158 and Call. *Hymn* 2.88).

[61] The immortal verses are Pindar's. The closing lines constitute a *sphragis*, in which the poet alludes to himself and predicts the immortality of his poem through future performance (cf. Bacch. 3.96–98).

PYTHIAN 5

This ode celebrates the same Pythian chariot victory as the preceding poem, but is a much more straightforward encomium of Arcesilas. The winter storm briefly mentioned in line 10 probably refers to the political turmoil associated with Damophilus' exile treated in *Pyth.* 4. The praise of the driver Carrhotus is the most extensive tribute to a charioteer in the odes. The scholia report that he was Arcesilas' brother-in-law, but there is no independent evidence to confirm this. The poem appears to have been performed during the Carneian festival for Apollo, who figures very prominently in the ode (as he does in the other two odes to Cyrenaeans, *Pyth.* 4 and 9). At the end of the poem Pindar prays for an Olympic victory. According to a scholion on *Pyth.* 4 (inscr. b, 2.92.11 Dr.) Arcesilas won an Olympic victory in 460, but sometime afterward he was killed in a democratic revolution and his dynasty came to an end.

Wealth is powerful when divinely granted and used virtuously to make friends (1–4). Such is true in the case of Arcesilas, who has been favored by Castor, the patron of chariot racing (5–11). A wise and just king, he is blessed with the present celebration of his victory at Pytho (12–23), earned by his charioteer Carrhotus, who kept his chariot unscathed (while forty other drivers fell) and dedicated it in a shrine at Delphi (23–53).

Although no individual is free from adversity, the prosperity of Battus continues to bless Cyrene (54–57). A catalog of Apollo's powers indirectly lists his benefactions to the city: as colony founder who aided Battus; as healing god who provides medicinal remedies; as god of poetry who fosters peaceful order; and as oracular god who helped settle the Dorians in the Peloponnesus (57–72).

The poet states that his forefathers, the Spartan Aegeidae, colonized Thera, whence derives the present Carneian festival (72–81). The colonists from Thera still honor an earlier group of settlers, the sons of Antenor, who came from Troy after its destruction (82–88). The poet relates that Battus enlarged the city's sanctuaries and built a paved road for processions in honor of Apollo (89–93); he surmises that Battus and the successive kings in their tombs along the way share in this celebration of their offspring, Arcesilas (93–107).

Pindar praises Arcesilas by briefly recounting what everyone says: he is wise, courageous, appreciative of poetry, and an expert in chariot racing; he has sought all the distinctions his homeland offers (107–117). Pindar prays that Arcesilas' success may continue and that Zeus may grant him a chariot victory in the Olympic games (117–124).

5. ΑΡΚΕΣΙΛΑΩΙ ΚΥΡΗΝΑΙΩΙ

ΑΡΜΑΤΙ

Α΄ Ὁ πλοῦτος εὐρυσθενής,
    ὅταν τις ἀρετᾷ κεκραμένον καθαρᾷ
    βροτήσιος ἀνὴρ πότμου παραδόντος αὐτὸν ἀνάγῃ
    πολύφιλον ἐπέταν.
5 ὦ θεόμορ᾽ Ἀρκεσίλα,
    σύ τοί νιν κλυτᾶς
    αἰῶνος ἀκρᾶν βαθμίδων ἄπο
    σὺν εὐδοξίᾳ μετανίσεαι
    ἕκατι χρυσαρμάτου Κάστορος·
10 εὐδίαν ὃς μετὰ χειμέριον ὄμβρον τεάν
    καταιθύσσει μάκαιραν ἑστίαν.

    σοφοὶ δέ τοι κάλλιον
    φέροντι καὶ τὰν θεόσδοτον δύναμιν.
    σὲ δ᾽ ἐρχόμενον ἐν δίκᾳ πολὺς ὄλβος ἀμφινέμεται·
15 τὸ μέν, ὅτι βασιλεύς
    ἐσσὶ μεγαλᾶν πολίων·
    ἐπεὶ συγγενής
    ὀφθαλμὸς αἰδοιότατον γέρας

5. FOR ARCESILAS OF CYRENE

WINNER, CHARIOT RACE, 462 B.C.

Wealth has wide strength,	Str. 1
when, conjoined with flawless excellence,	
a mortal man receives it from destiny and takes it	
as a companion which brings many friends.	
O Arcesilas, favored by heaven,	5
truly have you, from the very first steps	
of your glorious life,	
been seeking it along with fame,	
thanks to Castor of the golden chariot,	
who, after a winter rainstorm, sheds fair weather	10
over your blessed hearth.	

Truly, wise men sustain more nobly	Ant. 1
even their god-given power.	
And as you travel the path of justice, great prosperity	
surrounds you:	
first, because you are king	15
of great cities	
(since that privilege, most venerable	
when combined with your understanding,	

---

17 ἐπεὶ Hermann: ἔχει codd.

τεᾷ τοῦτο μειγνύμενον φρενί·
20 μάκαρ δὲ καὶ νῦν, κλεεννᾶς ὅτι
εὖχος ἤδη παρὰ Πυθιάδος ἵπποις ἑλών
δέδεξαι τόνδε κῶμον ἀνέρων,

Ἀπολλώνιον ἄθυρμα· τῶ σε μὴ λαθέτω,
Κυράνᾳ γλυκὺν ἀμφὶ κᾶ-
πον Ἀφροδίτας ἀειδόμενον,
25 παντὶ μὲν θεὸν αἴτιον ὑπερτιθέμεν,
φιλεῖν δὲ Κάρρωτον ἔξοχ᾽ ἑταίρων·
ὃς οὐ τὰν Ἐπιμαθέος ἄγων
ὀψινόου θυγατέρα Πρόφασιν Βαττιδᾶν
ἀφίκετο δόμους θεμισκρεόντων·
30 ἀλλ᾽ ἀρισθάρματον
ὕδατι Κασταλίας ξενω-
θεὶς γέρας ἀμφέβαλε τεαῖσιν κόμαις,

Β´ ἀκηράτοις ἀνίαις
ποδαρκέων δώδεκ᾽ ἂν δρόμων τέμενος.
κατέκλασε γὰρ ἐντέων σθένος οὐδέν· ἀλλὰ κρέμαται
35 ὁπόσα χεριαρᾶν
τεκτόνων δαίδαλ᾽ ἄγων

23 σε μὴ E. Schmid: μή σε codd.
24 Κυράνᾳ E. Schmid: κυράνα ζν: Κυράνας Schroeder
33 δώδεκ᾽ ἂν δρόμων Thiersch: δώδεκαδρόμων v.l. in βζ:
δυώδεκαδρόμων Βγ: δωδεκάδρομον v.l. in ζ
36 δαίδαλ᾽ Pauw: δαιδάλματ᾽ codd.

is an inherited glory);[1]
and you are blessed now too, because in the glorious   20
Pythian festival you have lately gained a triumph with
    your horses
and have welcomed this victory revel of men,

in which Apollo delights. Therefore, do not forget,   Ep. 1
as you are being sung of at the sweet garden
    of Aphrodite in Cyrene,
to give credit to the god for everything,   25
but to cherish above all comrades Carrhotus,
who did not bring with him Prophasis, daughter
of late-thinking Epimetheus,[2] when he came
to the palace of the justly ruling Battidae.
But instead, after receiving hospitality   30
by the water of Castalia, he placed around your hair
    the prize for the first-place chariot,

won with his reins intact   Str. 2
in the sanctuary with its twelve swift-footed courses.
For he broke none of his strong equipment, but it is hung
in dedication—all that ornate handiwork   35
of skilled craftsmen

[1] The text of 17–19 as transmitted in the MSS produces nonsense. Hermann's ἐπεί for ἔχει at least yields a tolerable meaning. I have understood the inherited "glory" (literally "eye," ὀφθαλμός) and "privilege" (γέρας) to be the tradition of eight generations of rule in Cyrene from Battus to Arcesilas IV.

[2] Excuse, daughter of Hindsight; for Epimetheus, see Hes. *Op.* 83–89.

PINDAR

Κρισαῖον λόφον
ἄμειψεν ἐν κοιλόπεδον νάπος
θεοῦ· τό σφ᾽ ἔχει κυπαρίσσινον
40 μέλαθρον ἀμφ᾽ ἀνδριάντι σχεδόν,
Κρῆτες ὃν τοξοφόροι τέγεϊ Παρνασσίῳ
καθέσσαντο μονόδροπον φυτόν.

ἑκόντι τοίνυν πρέπει
νόῳ τὸν εὐεργέταν ὑπαντιάσαι.
45 Ἀλεξιβιάδα, σὲ δ᾽ ἠύκομοι φλέγοντι Χάριτες.
μακάριος, ὃς ἔχεις
καὶ πεδὰ μέγαν κάματον
λόγων φερτάτων
μναμήι᾽· ἐν τεσσαράκοντα γάρ
50 πετόντεσσιν ἀνιόχοις ὅλον
δίφρον κομίξαις ἀταρβεῖ φρενί,
ἦλθες ἤδη Λιβύας πεδίον ἐξ ἀγλαῶν
ἀέθλων καὶ πατρωίαν πόλιν.

πόνων δ᾽ οὔ τις ἀπόκλαρός ἐστιν οὔτ᾽ ἔσεται·
55 ὁ Βάττου δ᾽ ἕπεται παλαι-
ὸς ὄλβος ἔμπαν τὰ καὶ τὰ νέμων,
πύργος ἄστεος ὄμμα τε φαεννότατον
ξένοισι. κεῖνόν γε καὶ βαρύκομποι
λέοντες περὶ δείματι φύγον,

49 μναμήι᾽ Boeckh: μνημήια β(paraphr.): μνημήιον ζΒ
52 ἀγλαῶν Moschopulus: ἀγαθῶν v: ἀγανῶν V

312

which he drove past the hill of Crisa[3]
on his way to the hollow valley
of the god. And so, the shrine of cypress wood
holds it beside the statue hewn from a single trunk,   40
which the bow-bearing Cretans
set up in the chamber on Parnassus.

Therefore, it is fitting to greet one's benefactor   Ant. 2
with an eager mind.
Son of Alexibius,[4] the fair-haired Graces are setting you   45
     ablaze.
Blessed are you in having,
though after great toil,
a memorial of finest words of praise,
for among forty
charioteers who fell, you preserved   50
your chariot intact with your unflinching mind,
and now you have come to the plain of Libya
from the splendid games and to your native city.

No one is without his share of toil, nor will be.   Ep. 2
But the ancient prosperity of Battus continues,   55
     nevertheless, as it bestows now this, now that,
bastion for the city and most splendid light[5]
for foreigners. Even loudly roaring lions
fled in fear from that man,

[3] The chariot races were held at Crisa, down the slope from
the sanctuary in the hollow valley under Mt. Parnassus.
[4] Carrhotus.
[5] Literally, eye (cf. ὀφθαλμός, 18).

PINDAR

γλῶσσαν ἐπεί σφιν ἀπένεικεν ὑπερποντίαν·
60 ὁ δ᾽ ἀρχαγέτας ἔδωκ᾽ Ἀπόλλων
θῆρας αἰνῷ φόβῳ,
ὄφρα μὴ ταμίᾳ Κυρά-
     νας ἀτελὴς γένοιτο μαντεύμασιν.

Γ΄ ὁ καὶ βαρειᾶν νόσων
ἀκέσματ᾽ ἄνδρεσσι καὶ γυναιξὶ νέμει,
65 πόρεν τε κίθαριν, δίδωσί τε Μοῖσαν οἷς ἂν ἐθέλῃ,
ἀπόλεμον ἀγαγών
ἐς πραπίδας εὐνομίαν,
μυχόν τ᾽ ἀμφέπει
μαντήιον· τῷ Λακεδαίμονι
70 ἐν Ἄργει τε καὶ ζαθέᾳ Πύλῳ
ἔνασσεν ἀλκάεντας Ἡρακλέος
ἐκγόνους Αἰγιμιοῦ τε. τὸ δ᾽ ἐμὸν γαρύειν
ἀπὸ Σπάρτας ἐπήρατον κλέος,

ὅθεν γεγενναμένοι
75 ἵκοντο Θήρανδε φῶτες Αἰγεΐδαι,
ἐμοὶ πατέρες, οὐ θεῶν ἄτερ, ἀλλὰ Μοῖρά τις ἄγεν·

69 τῷ Pauw: τῷ καὶ codd.
72 γαρύειν Hermann: γαρύετ᾽ Vv: γαρύεντ᾽ dett.: γαρύει
Wilamowitz

---

[6] Battus ("Stammerer") was cured of his impediment when he
encountered a lion in Cyrene and cried out in fear (Paus. 10.15.7).

314

PYTHIAN 5

when he conveyed to them his outlandish speech.⁶
It was Apollo the colony founder   60
who gave over the beasts to panic,
so that he might not fail to fulfill his oracles
    for the steward of Cyrene.⁷

He also bestows remedies for grievous illnesses   Str. 3
upon men and women; he has provided
the cithara and confers the Muse on whomever he   65
        pleases,
after putting peaceful good governance
into their minds;
and he rules over
his oracular shrine, through which he settled
in Lacedaemon and in Argos and holy Pylos   70
the valiant descendants of Heracles
and Aegimius.⁸ And mine it is to proclaim⁹
the delightful glory that comes from Sparta,

whence men born   Ant. 3
as Aegeidae, my forefathers,¹⁰ came to Thera,   75
not without divine favor, but some Fate led them.

---

⁷ I.e. Battus.   ⁸ For the establishment of the Dorians in
the Peloponnesus, see *Pyth.* 1.65–67.   ⁹ Others read γαρύει
with Wilamowitz: "he (Apollo) proclaims."
¹⁰ The Theban Aegeidae assisted in the establishment of the
Dorians in Amyclae (cf. *Isth.* 7.14–15). I take the sentence to
refer to the poet's announcement of his personal connection with
the Spartan Aegeidae who subsequently emigrated to Thera. Others
argue that he is speaking for the chorus of Cyrenaeans, with whom
he associates himself in the following lines.

315

πολύθυτον ἔρανον
ἔνθεν ἀναδεξάμενοι,
Ἄπολλον, τεᾷ,
80 Καρνήϊ', ἐν δαιτὶ σεβίζομεν
Κυράνας ἀγακτιμέναν πόλιν·
ἔχοντι τὰν χαλκοχάρμαι ξένοι
Τρῶες Ἀντανορίδαι· σὺν Ἑλένᾳ γὰρ μόλον,
καπνωθεῖσαν πάτραν ἐπεὶ ἴδον

85 ἐν Ἄρει· τὸ δ' ἐλάσιππον ἔθνος ἐνδυκέως
δέκονται θυσίαισιν ἄν-
    δρες οἰχνέοντές σφε δωροφόροι,
τοὺς Ἀριστοτέλης ἄγαγε ναυσὶ θοαῖς
ἁλὸς βαθεῖαν κέλευθον ἀνοίγων.
κτίσεν δ' ἄλσεα μείζονα θεῶν,
90 εὐθύτομόν τε κατέθηκεν Ἀπολλωνίαις
ἀλεξιμβρότοις πεδιάδα πομπαῖς
ἔμμεν ἱππόκροτον
σκυρωτὰν ὁδόν, ἔνθα πρυ-
    μνοῖς ἀγορᾶς ἔπι δίχα κεῖται θανών.

Δ΄ μάκαρ μὲν ἀνδρῶν μέτα
95 ἔναιεν, ἥρως δ' ἔπειτα λαοσεβής.
ἄτερθε δὲ πρὸ δωμάτων ἕτεροι λαχόντες Ἀίδαν
βασιλέες ἱεροί

---

11 For the transfer of the Carnean festival from Sparta to

PYTHIAN 5

From there we have received
the communal banquet with its many sacrifices,
and in your feast,
Carnean Apollo,[11] we venerate   80
the nobly built city of Cyrene,
which the sons of Antenor, Trojan foreigners delighting
in bronze armor, still hold,[12] for they came with Helen
after they saw their homeland go up in smoke

during war. And warmly is that race of chariot drivers[13]   Ep. 3
welcomed with sacrifices   86
    and greeted with gifts by those men
whom Aristoteles[14] brought in swift ships,
when he opened a deep path through the salt sea.
He founded larger sanctuaries for the gods,
and laid down a paved road, straight and level,   90
to echo with horses' hoofs
in processions that honor Apollo
and bring succor to mortals. And there, at the end
    of the agora, he has lain apart since his death.

He was blessed while he dwelt among men,   Str. 4
and afterwards a hero worshiped by his people.   95
Apart from him before the palace are the other
sacred kings whose lot is Hades;

Thera to Cyrene and its connections with the Theban Oedipodae,
see Call. *Hymn* 2.71–79.
[12] The Trojan Antenoridae had settled the city before the
colonization from Thera.   [13] The Antenoridae.
[14] Another name for Battus; his descendants still honor the
Antenoridae.

ἐντί· μεγαλᾶν δ᾽ ἀρετᾶν
δρόσῳ μαλθακᾷ
100 ῥανθεισᾶν κώμων ὑπὸ χεύμασιν,
ἀκούοντί ποι χθονίᾳ φρενί,
σφὸν ὄλβον υἱῷ τε κοινὰν χάριν
ἔνδικόν τ᾽ Ἀρκεσίλᾳ· τὸν ἐν ἀοιδᾷ νέων
πρέπει χρυσάορα Φοῖβον ἀπύειν,

105 ἔχοντα Πυθωνόθεν
τὸ καλλίνικον λυτήριον δαπανᾶν
μέλος χαρίεν. ἄνδρα κεῖνον ἐπαινέοντι συνετοί·
λεγόμενον ἐρέω·
κρέσσονα μὲν ἁλικίας
110 νόον φέρβεται
γλῶσσάν τε· θάρσος δὲ τανύπτερος
ἐν ὄρνιξιν αἰετὸς ἔπλετο·
ἀγωνίας δ᾽, ἕρκος οἷον, σθένος·
ἔν τε Μοίσαισι ποτανὸς ἀπὸ ματρὸς φίλας,
115 πέφανταί θ᾽ ἁρματηλάτας σοφός·

ὅσαι τ᾽ εἰσὶν ἐπιχωρίων καλῶν ἔσοδοι,
τετόλμακε. θεός τέ οἱ
τὸ νῦν τε πρόφρων τελεῖ δύνασιν,
καὶ τὸ λοιπὸν ὁμοῖα, Κρονίδαι μάκαρες,

98–100 μεγαλᾶν δ᾽ ἀρετᾶν . . . ῥανθεισᾶν edd.: μεγαλαν δ᾽
ἀρεταν . . . ῥανθεισαν variis accentibus codd.; schol. inter acc.
sing. et gen. pl. fluctuant

318

and perhaps they hear with their minds beneath the earth
of the great achievements
sprinkled with soft dew   100
beneath the outpourings of revel songs—
their own happiness and a glory justly shared
with their son Arcesilas. It is fitting for him in a song
by young men to call upon Phoebus of the golden lyre,[15]

since he has obtained from Pytho,   Ant. 4
in recompense for his expenditures,   106
the gracious victory song. Experts praise that man;
I shall tell the common report:
he cultivates a mind
beyond his years,   110
and tongue as well; in courage he is a long-winged
eagle among birds;
his strength in competition is like a bulwark;
he soars among the Muses from his dear mother;[16]
he has shown himself to be a skillful charioteer;   115

and he has boldly essayed all the avenues to his   Ep. 4
homeland's noble achievements. A god graciously
    brings his power to fulfillment now,
and in the future may you blessed children of Cronus

[15] Or *sword*.
[16] It is ambiguous whether he was taught by his mother or was
famous from his earliest years (schol.).

---

100 κώμων Byz.: κώμων θ' vett.
107 ἐπαινέοντι Moschopulus: αἰνέοντι vett.
118 ὁμοῖα Hartung: ὦ Vv

διδοῖτ' ἐπ' ἔργοισιν ἀμφί τε βουλαῖς
120 ἔχειν, μὴ φθινοπωρὶς ἀνέμων
χειμερία κατὰ πνοὰ δαμαλίζοι χρόνον.
Διός τοι νόος μέγας κυβερνᾷ
δαίμον' ἀνδρῶν φίλων.
εὔχομαί νιν Ὀλυμπίᾳ
    τοῦτο δόμεν γέρας ἔπι Βάττου γένει.

124 ἔπι Triclinius: ἐπὶ vett.

permit him to have like success in his deeds and counsels,
that no stormy blast of autumn winds   120
may disrupt his lifetime.
Truly the great mind of Zeus steers
the fortune of men who are dear to him.
I pray that he grant another such prize at Olympia
    to the race of Battus.

PYTHIAN 6

Although the occasion of the ode is a Pythian chariot victory (also mentioned at *Ol.* 2.49–51) won by Xenocrates of Acragas, younger brother of Theron, probably in 490 B.C., most of the poem is devoted to praise of his son Thrasybulus. A tradition going back to the scholia claims that Thrasybulus drove the chariot, but this is probably fabricated to explain his prominence in the poem. *Isth.* 2, composed after Xenocrates' death, also contains extended praise of Thrasybulus.

The opening lines suggest that the poem is meant to accompany a procession to Apollo's temple at Delphi, whose way was lined with treasuries belonging to various cities (the Athenians' has been reconstructed), but as the poem continues, the actual treasuries are replaced by a metaphorical storehouse of songs (cf. *Ol.* 6.1–4 for another example of a poem portrayed as a building).

The poet invokes Aphrodite and the Graces as he approaches Apollo's temple (1–4). Here a treasury of Pythian hymns has been erected for the Emmenidae of Acragas and for Xenocrates, one which neither rain nor wind can destroy (5–14), and whose façade proclaims the victory of Thrasybulus' father (14–18).

The remainder of the poem contains praise of Thrasybulus for following the counsel that Chiron gave to Achilles, namely to honor Zeus and one's parents (19–27). A brief narrative in ring composition recounts how Antilochus gave his life to save his father from Memnon's attack (28–43). In the present generation Thrasybulus comes closest to the ideal of such filial devotion (44–45). He emulates his uncle Theron, uses his wealth intelligently, is not insolent, enjoys poetry, is devoted to horse racing, and makes a pleasant companion (46–54).

6. ΞΕΝΟΚΡΑΤΕΙ
ΑΚΡΑΓΑΝΤΙΝΩΙ
ΑΡΜΑΤΙ

Α΄   Ἀκούσατ'· ἦ γὰρ ἑλικώπιδος Ἀφροδίτας
    ἄρουραν ἢ Χαρίτων
    ἀναπολίζομεν, ὀμφαλὸν ἐριβρόμου
    χθονὸς ἐς νάιον προσοιχόμενοι·
5 Πυθιόνικος ἔνθ' ὀλβίοισιν Ἐμμενίδαις
    ποταμίᾳ τ' Ἀκράγαντι καὶ μὰν Ξενοκράτει
    ἑτοῖμος ὕμνων
    θησαυρὸς ἐν πολυχρύσῳ
    Ἀπολλωνίᾳ τετείχισται νάπᾳ·

Β΄   τὸν οὔτε χειμέριος ὄμβρος, ἐπακτὸς ἐλθών
11 ἐριβρόμου νεφέλας
    στρατὸς ἀμείλιχος, οὔτ' ἄνεμος ἐς μυχούς
    ἁλὸς ἄξοισι παμφόρῳ χεράδει
    τυπτόμενον. φάει δὲ πρόσωπον ἐν καθαρῷ

4 νάιον Hermann: ναὸν codd.
12 ἄνεμοι E(paraphr.)   14 τυπτόμενον Dawes: τυπτό-
μενοι v(paraphr.): τυπτόμενος V

324

6. FOR XENOCRATES
OF ACRAGAS

WINNER, CHARIOT RACE, 490 B.C.

Listen! for indeed we are plowing once again	Str. 1
the field of bright-eyed Aphrodite	
or of the Graces, as we proceed to the enshrined	
navel of the loudly rumbling earth,[1]	
where at hand for the fortunate Emmenidae	5
and for Acragas on its river, yes, and for Xenocrates,	
a Pythian victor's	
treasure house of hymns	
has been built in Apollo's valley rich in gold,	

one which neither winter rain, coming from abroad	Str. 2
as a relentless army	11
from a loudly rumbling cloud, nor wind shall buffet	
and with their deluge of silt carry into the depths	
of the sea. But in clear light its front	

[1] Delphi was considered to be the navel of the earth; see *Pyth.* 4.5, note 2.

15 πατρὶ τεῷ, Θρασύβουλε, κοινάν τε γενεᾷ
    λόγοισι θνατῶν
    εὔδοξον ἅρματι νίκαν
    Κρισαίαις ἐνὶ πτυχαῖς ἀπαγγελεῖ.

Γ΄   σύ τοι σχεθών νιν ἐπὶ δεξιὰ χειρός, ὀρθάν
20   ἄγεις ἐφημοσύναν,
    τά ποτ᾽ ἐν οὔρεσι φαντὶ μεγαλοσθενεῖ
    Φιλύρας υἱὸν ὀρφανιζομένῳ
    Πηλεΐδα παραινεῖν· μάλιστα μὲν Κρονίδαν,
    βαρύοπαν στεροπᾶν κεραυνῶν τε πρύτανιν,
25   θεῶν σέβεσθαι·
    ταύτας δὲ μή ποτε τιμὰς
    ἀμείρειν γονέων βίον πεπρωμένον.

Δ΄   ἔγεντο καὶ πρότερον Ἀντίλοχος βιατάς
    νόημα τοῦτο φέρων,
30   ὃς ὑπερέφθιτο πατρός, ἐναρίμβροτον
    ἀναμείναις στράταρχον Αἰθιόπων
    Μέμνονα. Νεστόρειον γὰρ ἵππος ἅρμ᾽ ἐπέδα
    Πάριος ἐκ βελέων δαϊχθείς· ὁ δ᾽ ἔφεπεν
    κραταιὸν ἔγχος·

        15 κοινᾷ V   21 τά E. Schmid: τάν codd.
        24 βαρύοπα Maas
        25 θεὸν B

    ² Or *it*, the precept (schol.). Some understand νιν to refer to
    personified Victory.

will proclaim a chariot victory,   15
famous in men's speech,
shared by your father, Thrasybulus, and your clan,
won in the dells of Crisa.

Truly, by keeping him[2] at your right hand,   Str. 3
you uphold the precept,   20
whose words of advice they say Philyra's son[3]
once gave to the mighty son of Peleus in the mountains,[4]
when he was away from his parents: above all gods
to revere Cronus' son, loud-voiced lord
of lightning and thunder,   25
and never to deprive of like honor
one's parents during their allotted lifetime.[5]

In the past as well, mighty Antilochus   Str. 4
bore such thoughts in mind,
who died to save his father by standing up to   30
the man-slaughtering general of the Ethiopians,
Memnon.[6] For Nestor's chariot had become entangled
when his horse was struck by Paris' arrows, and he[7]
was brandishing his powerful spear.

[3] Chiron.
[4] Achilles, when under the tutelage of Chiron on Mt. Pelion (cf. *Nem.* 3.43–52).
[5] The scholiast says that this comes from "The Precepts of Chiron" (Χείρωνος Ὑποθῆκαι), attributed to Hesiod (*fr.* 283).
[6] This episode comes from the *Aethiopis* by Arctinus. At *Il.* 8.80–117 Diomedes rescues Nestor from Hector; Antilochus' death is briefly mentioned at *Od.* 4.187–188. Xen. *Cyn.* 1.14 shows how well known the story was.   [7] Memnon.

35 Μεσσανίου δὲ γέροντος
    δονηθεῖσα φρὴν βόασε παῖδα ὅν,

Ε΄ χαμαιπετὲς δ᾽ ἄρ᾽ ἔπος οὐκ ἀπέριψεν· αὐτοῦ
    μένων δ᾽ ὁ θεῖος ἀνήρ
    πρίατο μὲν θανάτοιο κομιδὰν πατρός,
40 ἐδόκησέν τε τῶν πάλαι γενεᾷ
    ὁπλοτέροισιν ἔργον πελώριον τελέσαις
    ὕπατος ἀμφὶ τοκεῦσιν ἔμμεν πρὸς ἀρετάν.
    τὰ μὲν παρίκει·
    τῶν νῦν δὲ καὶ Θρασύβουλος
45 πατρῴαν μάλιστα πρὸς στάθμαν ἔβα,

Ϝ΄ πάτρῳ τ᾽ ἐπερχόμενος ἀγλαΐαν ἄπασαν.
    νόῳ δὲ πλοῦτον ἄγει,
    ἄδικον οὔθ᾽ ὑπέροπλον ἥβαν δρέπων,
    σοφίαν δ᾽ ἐν μυχοῖσι Πιερίδων·
50 τίν τ᾽, Ἐλέλιχθον, ἄρχεις ὃς ἱππιᾶν ἐσόδων,
    μάλα ἁδόντι νόῳ, Ποσειδάν, προσέχεται.
    γλυκεῖα δὲ φρήν
    καὶ συμπόταισιν ὁμιλεῖν
    μελισσᾶν ἀμείβεται τρητὸν πόνον.

46 ἀγλαΐαν Bergk²: ἀγλαΐαν ἔδειξεν codd.

50 ἄρχεις Bowra: ὀργαῖς πάσαις codd.: ὤπασας Wilamo-
witz: ὀρθοῖς Erbse | ἱππιᾶν ἐσόδων M. Schmidt (ἱππικὰς
ἀμίλλας paraphr.): ἱππείαν ἔσοδον codd.

51 προσέχεται E. Schmid: προσέρχεται codd.

In panic the mind of the old man   35
from Messene shouted to his son,

nor indeed did he hurl forth a word that fell to the   Str. 5
    ground:
that godlike man took a stand right there
and bought his father's rescue with his own death,
and, for doing that awesome deed, he was deemed   40
by the young men of that ancient generation
to be foremost in virtuous behavior toward parents.
Those things are past:
but of men now, Thrasybulus
has come closest to the standard of filial devotion,   45

while approaching his uncle[8] in all manner of splendor.   Str. 6
He uses his wealth with intelligence,
he enjoys a youth without injustice or insolence,
and culls wisdom in the haunts of the Pierians.
And to you, Earthshaker, who rule the paths to horse   50
    racing,
he keeps close, Poseidon, with a mind you greatly favor.
And his sweet spirit,
in company with his drinking companions,[9]
surpasses the perforated labor of bees.[10]

[8] Theron.

[9] For another portrait of a young nobleman, see *Pyth.* 4.294–297. *Fr.* 124 from an encomium to Thrasybulus was perhaps intended for such a party.

[10] A kenning for honeycomb (cf. *Ol.* 6.47).

PYTHIAN 7

Although this is the shortest ode in the collection, it is to an important man, Megacles, son of Hippocrates, nephew and son-in-law of the legislator Cleisthenes, and uncle of Pericles, all members of a prominent Athenian family, the Alcmaeonidae. Megacles' great-grandfather Alcmaeon had won an Olympic chariot victory in 592 B.C. (alluded to in 14–15; cf. Hdt. 6.125). In 548 the Alcmaeonidae restored the burned temple of Apollo at Delphi with a bright façade of Parian marble (Hdt. 5.62). At the time of this ode, probably 486, Megacles was in exile after his ostracism from Athens the previous year (cf. Arist. *Ath. Pol.* 22.5).

Athens provides the best opening for an ode, because it and the Alcmaeonidae are the most celebrated city and family in Hellas (1–8). All Greece knows of their reconstruction of Apollo's temple (9–12). The family boasts five Isthmian, one Olympic, and two Pythian victories (13–17a). Although the poet rejoices in the family's success, he is saddened by the envy that has been directed against Megacles and consoles him by pointing out that abiding prosperity is subject to vicissitudes (18–21).

7. ΜΕΓΑΚΛΕΙ ΑΘΗΝΑΙΩΙ

ΤΕΘΡΙΠΠΩΙ

Κάλλιστον αἱ μεγαλοπόλιες Ἀθᾶναι
προοίμιον Ἀλκμανιδᾶν εὐρυσθενεῖ
3/4   γενεᾷ κρηπῖδ᾽ ἀοιδᾶν ἵπποισι βαλέσθαι.
5/6   ἐπεὶ τίνα πάτραν, τίνα οἶκον ναίων ὀνυμάξεαι
ἐπιφανέστερον
Ἑλλάδι πυθέσθαι;

πάσαισι γὰρ πολίεσι λόγος ὁμιλεῖ
10   Ἐρεχθέος ἀστῶν, Ἄπολλον, οἳ τεόν
11/12   δόμον Πυθῶνι δίᾳ θαητὸν ἔτευξαν.
13/14   ἄγοντι δέ με πέντε μὲν Ἰσθμοῖ νῖκαι, μία δ᾽
       ἐκπρεπής
15   Διὸς Ὀλυμπιάς,
δύο δ᾽ ἀπὸ Κίρρας,

5 τίνα οἶκον Boeckh: τίνα τ᾽ οἶκον Vv: τίν᾽ οἶκον γ¹
6 ναίων codd.: ναίοντ᾽ vel τ᾽ ἀίων (= ἀκούων) vel αἰῶν(ι)
schol. | ὀνυμάξεαι Boeckh: ὀνυμάξαι Vv (ὀνυμάξω v.l. in β e
paraphr.): ὀνυμάξομαι Didymus(?), Byz.
10–11 τεὸν δόμον V: τέον τε δόμον v: τέον γε δόμον
Moschopulus: τεὸν πρόδομον Schroeder

332

7. FOR MEGACLES OF ATHENS

WINNER, CHARIOT RACE, 486 B.C.

The great city of Athens is the fairest prelude	Str.
to lay down as a foundation for songs to honor	
the mighty race of the Alcmaeonidae for their horses.	3/4
For what fatherland, what house can you inhabit and	5/6
name	
with a more illustrious	
reputation in Hellas?	

None, for among all cities travels the report	Ant.
about Erechtheus' citizens,[1] Apollo, who made	10
your temple in divine Pytho splendid to behold.	11/12
Five victories at the Isthmus prompt me, as does one	13/14
outstanding Olympic festival of Zeus	15
and two victories at Cirrha,[2]	

[1] The Alcmaeonidae. Erechtheus was an early king of Athens.
[2] The city below Delphi where the equestrian events were held.

ὦ Μεγάκλεες,
17a ὑμαί τε καὶ προγόνων.
νέᾳ δ' εὐπραγίᾳ χαίρω τι· τὸ δ' ἄχνυμαι,
φθόνον ἀμειβόμενον τὰ καλὰ ἔργα. φαντί γε μάν
20 οὕτω κ' ἀνδρὶ παρμονίμαν
θάλλοισαν εὐδαιμονίαν τὰ καὶ τὰ φέρεσθαι.

20 κ' Wilamowitz: κεν codd.

O Megacles,   Ep.
belonging to your family and forebears.   17a
I rejoice greatly at your recent success, but this grieves
        me,
that envy[3] requites your noble deeds. Yet they say
that in this way happiness which abides   20
and flourishes brings a man now this, now that.[4]

---

[3] Megacles' ostracism.

[4] For the contrast of a family's long-term prosperity with the vicissitudes of an individual, see *Pyth.* 5.54–55.

PYTHIAN 8

If the scholiastic headnote is correct, the date of Aristomenes' victory is 446, making this the latest ode in the collection. There has been much speculation on the ode's historical circumstances, especially the troubled relations between Aegina and Athens, but it must remain mere speculation, since the poem contains no overt reference to Athens.

A puzzling feature is the poet's statement that Alcman was his neighbor, the guardian of his possessions, and had prophesied to him as he traveled to Delphi (58–60). From the time of the scholia questions have arisen about the content of the prophecy (was it a prediction of Aristomenes' victory?) and, more importantly, whether the poet is speaking in his own person or for the chorus. Either choice involves difficulties; on balance a slightly stronger case can be made for the poet as speaker.

A recurrent theme in the ode is the alternation of failure and success, evident in the narrative, in which the disaster of Adrastus' first expedition against Thebes is followed by the success ten years later of a second, though at the cost of his son's life; in the description of the four defeated athletes' homecoming; and in the famous concluding lines on the fragility of the human condition ("a dream of a shadow"). The address, ὦ παῖ (33), and the reference

336

to "mother" (85) point to Aristomenes' youthfulness, but there is no clear indication that his victory was in the boys' division.

The ode opens with a hymn to Hesychia (Peace, Concord) (1–5). She fosters gentleness, but when provoked, she is a formidable adversary, as Porphyrion and Typhos discovered (6–20).

The island of Aegina is celebrated for its heroes, the Aeacidae, and for its men (21–28), but the poet declines to go into detail about them (29–32). Instead, he praises Aristomenes, who, by imitating his uncles' success in athletics, merits what Amphiaraus prophesied as the Epigoni were fighting before Thebes (32–42). After noting that sons inherit their fathers' determination, as in the case of his own son Alcman, Amphiaraus predicted that Adrastus would be victorious, but would lose his son (43–55). Alcman is praised for prophesying to the poet on his way to Delphi (56–60).

Pindar mentions victories granted to Aristomenes by Apollo in his festivals at Pytho and on Aegina, and asks for the gods' continued favor (61–72). If men are successful without great effort, many think them wise, but in fact the gods determine who prevails (73–77).

After listing Aristomenes' victories at Megara, Marathon, and Aegina, the poet depicts the unhappy homecoming of the four opponents he defeated at Delphi (78–87). Unlike them, the victor is soaring because of his recent accomplishment and has high aspirations (88–92). But joy is transitory, and man's existence is insubstantial; nevertheless, when the gods grant success, life is gentle (93–97). The poem concludes with a prayer for Zeus and the Aeacidae to preserve Aegina's freedom (98–100).

8. ΑΡΙΣΤΟΜΕΝΕΙ
ΑΙΓΙΝΗΤΗΙ
ΠΑΛΑΙΣΤΗΙ

Α΄   Φιλόφρον Ἡσυχία, Δίκας
    ὦ μεγιστόπολι θύγατερ,
    βουλᾶν τε καὶ πολέμων
    ἔχοισα κλαῖδας ὑπερτάτας
5   Πυθιόνικον τιμὰν Ἀριστομένει δέκευ.
    τὺ γὰρ τὸ μαλθακὸν ἔρξαι τε καὶ παθεῖν ὁμῶς
    ἐπίστασαι καιρῷ σὺν ἀτρεκεῖ·

    τὺ δ᾽ ὁπόταν τις ἀμείλιχον
    καρδίᾳ κότον ἐνελάσῃ,
10 τραχεῖα δυσμενέων
    ὑπαντιάξαισα κράτει τιθεῖς
    ὕβριν ἐν ἄντλῳ, τὰν οὐδὲ Πορφυρίων μάθεν
    παρ᾽ αἶσαν ἐξερεθίζων. κέρδος δὲ φίλτατον,
    ἑκόντος εἴ τις ἐκ δόμων φέροι.

    6 ἄρξαι V

338

8. FOR ARISTOMENES
OF AEGINA

WINNER, WRESTLING, 446 B.C.

Kindly Peace,[1] O maker of greatest cities   Str. 1
and daughter of Justice,
you who hold the supreme keys
of counsels and wars,
accept this honor for a Pythian victory from Aristomenes.   5
For you know how to bestow gentleness and likewise
to receive it with unerring appropriateness;

but, whenever someone fixes implacable   Ant. 1
hatred in his heart,
you roughly oppose the might   10
of enemies and put their insolence
in the bilge. Porphyrion[2] did not know your power
when he unduly provoked you. Gain is most precious
if one takes it from the home of a willing giver.

---

[1] Hesychia, peace within the polis, is the daughter of Justice.

[2] King of the Giants, slain by Apollo according to Pindar (18),
but by Heracles' arrows according to Apollod. 1.6.2.

15 βία δὲ καὶ μεγάλαυχον ἔσφαλεν ἐν χρόνῳ.
Τυφὼς Κίλιξ ἑκατόγκρανος οὔ νιν ἄλυξεν,
οὐδὲ μὰν βασιλεὺς Γιγάντων· δμᾶθεν δὲ κεραυνῷ
τόξοισί τ' Ἀπόλλωνος· ὃς εὐμενεῖ νόῳ
Ξενάρκειον ἔδεκτο Κίρραθεν ἐστεφανωμένον
20 υἱὸν ποίᾳ Παρνασσίδι Δωριεῖ τε κώμῳ.

Β΄ ἔπεσε δ' οὐ Χαρίτων ἑκάς
ἁ δικαιόπολις ἀρεταῖς
κλειναῖσιν Αἰακιδᾶν
θιγοῖσα νᾶσος· τελέαν δ' ἔχει
25 δόξαν ἀπ' ἀρχᾶς. πολλοῖσι μὲν γὰρ ἀείδεται
νικαφόροις ἐν ἀέθλοις θρέψαισα καὶ θοαῖς
ὑπερτάτους ἥρωας ἐν μάχαις·

τὰ δὲ καὶ ἀνδράσιν ἐμπρέπει.
εἰμὶ δ' ἄσχολος ἀναθέμεν
30 πᾶσαν μακραγορίαν
λύρᾳ τε καὶ φθέγματι μαλθακῷ,
μὴ κόρος ἐλθὼν κνίσῃ. τὸ δ' ἐν ποσί μοι τράχον
ἴτω τεὸν χρέος, ὦ παῖ, νεώτατον καλῶν,
ἐμᾷ ποτανὸν ἀμφὶ μαχανᾷ.

35 παλαισμάτεσσι γὰρ ἰχνεύων ματραδελφεούς
Οὐλυμπίᾳ τε Θεόγνητον οὐ κατελέγχεις,

20 Παρνασσσίδι Boeckh: Παρνασίᾳ codd.

340

But force brings down even the proud boaster in the end.   Ep. 1
Hundred-headed Typhos from Cilicia did not escape it,[3]   16
nor indeed the king of the Giants, for they were overcome
by a thunderbolt and the arrows of Apollo, who graciously
welcomed the son of Xenarces[4] from Cirrha, crowned
with Parnassian foliage[5] and with a Doric victory revel.   20

Not far from the Graces has the lot   Str. 2
of this just island city fallen,
which has attained the renowned achievements
of the Aeacidae; and it possesses consummate
fame from the beginning: it is sung for rearing   25
heroes who were supreme in many victorious contests
and in swift battles,

and it is distinguished for its men as well.   Ant. 2
But I am not at leisure to dedicate
the whole long story   30
to the lyre and gentle voice,
lest tedious excess come and vex us. But that debt owed
to you, my boy, which runs at my feet, the latest of glories,
let it take flight through my art.

For, following the trail of your maternal uncles in   Ep. 2
    wrestling,
you do not disgrace Theognetus at Olympia[6]   36

---

[3] Hesychia's force. For the suppression of Typhos, see Hes.
Th. 820–868 and *Pyth.* 1.15–28.   [4] Aristomenes.
[5] Laurel.   [6] For Theognetus' Olympic victory in wres-
tling, see *A.P.* 16.2 (attributed to Simonides) and Paus. 6.9.1.
Clitomachus is otherwise unknown.

οὐδὲ Κλειτομάχοιο νίκαν Ἰσθμοῖ θρασύγυιον·
αὔξων δὲ πάτραν Μειδυλιδᾶν λόγον φέρεις,
τὸν ὅνπερ ποτ' Ὀικλέος παῖς ἐν ἑπταπύλοις ἰδών
40 υἱοὺς Θήβαις αἰνίξατο παρμένοντας αἰχμᾷ,

Γ′ ὁπότ' ἀπ' Ἄργεος ἤλυθον
δευτέραν ὁδὸν Ἐπίγονοι.
ὧδ' εἶπε μαρναμένων·
"φυᾷ τὸ γενναῖον ἐπιπρέπει
45 ἐκ πατέρων παισὶ λῆμα. θαέομαι σαφές
δράκοντα ποικίλον αἴθας Ἀλκμᾶν' ἐπ' ἀσπίδος
νωμῶντα πρῶτον ἐν Κάδμου πύλαις.

ὁ δὲ καμὼν προτέρᾳ πάθᾳ
νῦν ἀρείονος ἐνέχεται
50 ὄρνιχος ἀγγελίᾳ
Ἄδραστος ἥρως· τὸ δὲ οἴκοθεν
ἀντία πράξει. μόνος γὰρ ἐκ Δαναῶν στρατοῦ
θανόντος ὀστέα λέξαις υἱοῦ, τύχᾳ θεῶν
ἀφίξεται λαῷ σὺν ἀβλαβεῖ

55 Ἄβαντος εὐρυχόρους ἀγυιάς." τοιαῦτα μέν
ἐφθέγξατ' Ἀμφιάρηος. χαίρων δὲ καὶ αὐτός
Ἀλκμᾶνα στεφάνοισι βάλλω, ῥαίνω δὲ καὶ ὕμνῳ,
γείτων ὅτι μοι καὶ κτεάνων φύλαξ ἐμῶν

37 Κλειτομάχον V   44 ἐπιτρέπει VE^{ac} et cod. Plut. L^l

or Clitomachus' bold-limbed victory at the Isthmus,
but exalting the clan of the Meidylidae you earn the very
    words
which Oecles' son[7] once spoke in riddles as he beheld
the sons standing firm in battle at seven-gated Thebes,   40

when the Epigoni came from Argos   Str. 3
on a second expedition.
Thus he spoke as they fought:
"By nature the noble resolve from fathers
shines forth in their sons. I clearly see   45
Alcman wielding the dappled serpent on his flashing
shield in the forefront at the gates of Cadmus.[8]

But he who suffered in a former defeat,   Ant. 3
the hero Adrastus,
is now met with news   50
of better omen, but in his own household
he will fare otherwise: for he alone from the Danaan army
will gather the bones of his dead son and with the favor
of the gods will come with his host unharmed

to the spacious streets of Abas."[9] Such were   Ep. 3
the pronouncements of Amphiaraus, and I too am glad   56
to pelt Alcman with wreaths and sprinkle him with song,
because as my neighbor and guardian of my possessions,

    [7] Amphiaraus.
    [8] Amphiaraus was both a seer and a fighter (cf. *Ol.* 6.16–17);
the snake on Alcman's shield symbolizes his own prophetic powers
(schol.).   [9] Twelfth king of Argos.

ὑπάντασεν ἰόντι γᾶς ὀμφαλὸν παρ' ἀοίδιμον,
60 μαντευμάτων τ' ἐφάψατο συγγόνοισι τέχναις.

Δ΄ τὺ δ', Ἑκαταβόλε, πάνδοκον
ναὸν εὐκλέα διανέμων
Πυθῶνος ἐν γυάλοις,
τὸ μὲν μέγιστον τόθι χαρμάτων
65 ὤπασας, οἴκοι δὲ πρόσθεν ἁρπαλέαν δόσιν
πενταεθλίου σὺν ἑορταῖς ὑμαῖς ἐπάγαγες·
ὦναξ, ἑκόντι δ' εὔχομαι νόῳ

κατά τιν' ἁρμονίαν βλέπειν
ἀμφ' ἕκαστον, ὅσα νέομαι.
70 κώμῳ μὲν ἁδυμελεῖ
Δίκα παρέστακε· θεῶν δ' ὄπιν
ἄφθονον αἰτέω, Ξέναρκες, ὑμετέραις τύχαις.
εἰ γάρ τις ἐσλὰ πέπαται μὴ σὺν μακρῷ πόνῳ,
πολλοῖς σοφὸς δοκεῖ πεδ' ἀφρόνων

75 βίον κορυσσέμεν ὀρθοβούλοισι μαχαναῖς·
τὰ δ' οὐκ ἐπ' ἀνδράσι κεῖται· δαίμων δὲ παρίσχει,
ἄλλοτ' ἄλλον ὕπερθε βάλλων, ἄλλον δ' ὑπὸ χειρῶν.
μέτρῳ κατάβαιν'· ἐν Μεγάροις δ' ἔχεις γέρας,
μυχῷ τ' ἐν Μαραθῶνος, Ἥρας τ' ἀγῶν' ἐπιχώριον

72 ἄφθονον γ^γρ (ἀνεπίφθονον paraphr.): ἄφθιτον Vv
78 μέτρον VEG⁸H^γρ: μέτρῳ(ω) rell. | κατάβαιν'· ἐν Bergk²:
καταβαίνει Byz.: καταβαίνει ἐν vett.

344

he met me on my way to the earth's famed navel
and employed his inherited skills in prophecy.   60

And you, Far-shooter, who govern   Str. 4
the all-welcoming[10] famous temple
in the vales of Pytho,
it was there that you granted the greatest
of joys, and earlier at home you bestowed the coveted gift   65
of the pentathlon during the festivities for you both.[11]
O lord, I pray that with a willing mind

you look with harmonious favor   Ant. 4
on each step that I take.
Beside the sweetly singing revel band   70
Justice has taken her stand; and I request the gods'
ungrudging favor, Xenarces, upon your family's good
        fortune;
for if someone has gained success without long labor,
he seems to many to be a wise man among fools

and to arm his life with effective good planning.   Ep. 4
But those things do not rest with men; a god grants them,   76
exalting now one man, but throwing another beneath the
        hands.[12]
Enter the contest in due measure.[13] At Megara you hold
        the prize
and in the plain of Marathon; and with three victories you

[10] I.e. Panhellenic.   [11] The Aeginetan Delphinia (schol.);
Apollo's sister Artemis is included in the plural ὑμαῖς.
[12] The example is from wrestling, where the object is to stay on
top while throwing the opponent under one's hands.
[13] Addressed to Aristomenes.

80   νίκαις τρισσαῖς, ὦ Ἀριστόμενες, δάμασσας ἔργῳ·

Ε΄   τέτρασι δ᾽ ἔμπετες ὑψόθεν
     σωμάτεσσι κακὰ φρονέων,
     τοῖς οὔτε νόστος ὁμῶς
     ἔπαλπνος ἐν Πυθιάδι κρίθη,
85   οὐδὲ μολόντων πὰρ ματέρ᾽ ἀμφὶ γέλως γλυκύς
     ὦρσεν χάριν· κατὰ λαύρας δ᾽ ἐχθρῶν ἀπάοροι
     πτώσσοντι, συμφορᾷ δεδαγμένοι.

     ὁ δὲ καλόν τι νέον λαχὼν
     ἁβρότατος ἔπι μεγάλας
90   ἐξ ἐλπίδος πέταται
     ὑποπτέροις ἀνορέαις, ἔχων
     κρέσσονα πλούτου μέριμναν. ἐν δ᾽ ὀλίγῳ βροτῶν
     τὸ τερπνὸν αὔξεται· οὕτω δὲ καὶ πίτνει χαμαί,
     ἀποτρόπῳ γνώμᾳ σεσεισμένον.

95   ἐπάμεροι· τί δέ τις; τί δ᾽ οὔ τις; σκιᾶς ὄναρ
     ἄνθρωπος. ἀλλ᾽ ὅταν αἴγλα διόσδοτος ἔλθῃ,
     λαμπρὸν φέγγος ἔπεστιν ἀνδρῶν καὶ μείλιχος αἰών.
     Αἴγινα φίλα μᾶτερ, ἐλευθέρῳ στόλῳ
     πόλιν τάνδε κόμιζε Δὶ καὶ κρέοντι σὺν Αἰακῷ
100   Πηλεῖ τε κἀγαθῷ Τελαμῶνι σύν τ᾽ Ἀχιλλεῖ.

87 δεδαγμένοι Boeckh (δακνόμενοι paraphr.): δεδαϊγμένοι
codd.   96 ἄνθρωπος (e schol. ad Nem. 6.4) Boeckh (cf.
Plut., Eustath.): ἄνθρωποι codd.
    97 φέγγος ἔπεστιν Heyne: ἔπεστι φέγγος codd.

PYTHIAN 8

mastered Hera's local contest,[14] O Aristomenes, by your   80
    effort.

And upon four bodies you fell from above   Str. 5
with hostile intent,[15]
for whom no homecoming as happy as yours
was decided at the Pythian festival,
nor upon returning to their mothers did sweet laughter   85
arouse joy all around; but staying clear of their enemies
they shrink down alleyways, bitten by failure.

But he who has been allotted a new success   Ant. 5
is inspired by hope at his great splendor
and takes flight   90
on the wings of manly deeds, having
aspirations superior to wealth. In a short time the delight
of mortals burgeons, but so too does it fall to the ground
when shaken by a hostile purpose.[16]

Creatures of a day! What is someone? What is no one?[17]   Ep. 5
    A dream of a shadow
is man. But whenever Zeus-given brightness comes,   96
a shining light rests upon men, and a gentle life.
Dear mother Aegina, on its voyage of freedom
safeguard this city, together with Zeus and king Aeacus,
Peleus and noble Telamon, and with Achilles.   100

[14] The Aeginetan Heraea, established in imitation of the Argive games (schol.).   [15] For a similar example of defeating four successive opponents, see *Ol.* 8.67–69.

[16] Or *decree* (i.e. of a god). One scholion (133) proposes "contrary to expectation" for ἀποτρόπῳ γνώμᾳ.

[17] Or *what is a man, what is he not?* (schol.).

347

PYTHIAN 9

Probably performed in 474, this is the only ode to a victor of the race in armor. Because of the future δέξεται (73), many commentators have supposed that the ode was performed in Thebes, but the future cannot be taken so literally (cf. κωμάσομαι at 89, "I shall [now] celebrate"). The main narrative, which tells of Apollo's love for the huntress Cyrene, whom he takes from Thessaly to become queen of the foremost city in Libya, is structured by ring composition. The critical moment of Apollo's decision is dramatized in a dialogue with Chiron.

After cataloguing Telesicrates' victories, Pindar concludes the poem with a second narrative, ostensibly requested by the victor, telling how Telesicrates' ancestor won his wife in a foot race arranged by her father Antaeus in imitation of Danaus' marriage of his daughters. This account brings together two prominent themes in the ode, athletics and marriage.

Upon announcing his intention to praise Telesicrates and Cyrene (1–4), the poet moves immediately into a summary of the forthcoming narrative: Apollo took Cyrene from Pelion in Thessaly to be queen of Libya, where Aphrodite joined them in marriage (5–13). She, the daughter of Hypseus, king of the Lapithae, disliked the typical activities of girls, preferring instead to protect her father's

348

herds from wild predators (14–25). When Apollo saw her wrestling with a lion, he called Chiron from his cave to inquire about the girl's identity and to ask if he should make love to her (26–37).

Chiron answers playfully that first loves must be consummated in private and chides Apollo for asking questions to which he, the all-knowing god, already knows the answers (38–49). Nonetheless, he predicts that Apollo will establish Cyrene in Libya, where she will reign and bear a son, Aristaeus, who will protect the flocks (50–65). His prediction is swiftly fulfilled; on that very day she is installed as queen of a city famous for athletics (66–70). She will welcome Telesicrates, who was victorious at Pytho (71–75).

The poet has much to say in praise of the victor, but chooses to elaborate a few well-chosen themes (76–79). As he recalls Telesicrates' victory in the Theban Iolaea, he tells briefly of the Theban heroes Iolaus, Heracles, and Iphicles (79–89a). After praying for the Graces' continued inspiration, he extends the catalogue with three victories at Aegina and Megara (89a–92) and exhorts Telesicrates' townsmen to praise him for his many victories in the local games (93–103).

The poet is asked to tell of the victor's ancestor Alexidamus, who won his bride in a foot race (103–125).

9. ΤΕΛΕΣΙΚΡΑΤΕΙ
ΚΥΡΗΝΑΙΩΙ
ΟΠΛΙΤΟΔΡΟΜΩΙ

Α΄ Ἐθέλω χαλκάσπιδα Πυθιονίκαν
    σὺν βαθυζώνοισιν ἀγγέλλων
    Τελεσικράτη Χαρίτεσσι γεγωνεῖν
    ὄλβιον ἄνδρα διωξίππου στεφάνωμα Κυράνας·
5 τὰν ὁ χαιτάεις ἀνεμοσφαράγων
      ἐκ Παλίου κόλπων ποτὲ Λατοΐδας
    ἅρπασ᾽, ἔνεικέ τε χρυσέῳ παρθένον ἀγροτέραν
6a δίφρῳ, τόθι νιν πολυμήλου
    καὶ πολυκαρποτάτας θῆκε δέσποιναν χθονός
    ῥίζαν ἀπείρου τρίταν εὐ-
      ήρατον θάλλοισαν οἰκεῖν.

    ὑπέδεκτο δ᾽ ἀργυρόπεζ᾽ Ἀφροδίτα
10 Δάλιον ξεῖνον θεοδμάτων
    ὀχέων ἐφαπτομένα χερὶ κούφᾳ·
    καί σφιν ἐπὶ γλυκεραῖς εὐναῖς ἐρατὰν βάλεν αἰδῶ,

350

9. FOR TELESICRATES
OF CYRENE

WINNER, RACE IN ARMOR, 474 B.C.

I wish, in announcing that fortunate man Telesicrates   Str. 1
as a bronze-shielded Pythian victor,
to proclaim with the aid of the deep-bosomed Graces
a crowning song for chariot-driving Cyrene,
whom the long-haired son of Leto[1]   5
    once seized from the wind-echoing folds of Pelion,
and brought the virgin huntress in his golden
chariot to a place where he made her mistress   6a
of a land rich in flocks and abounding in fruit,
to inhabit the lovely and flourishing
    root of the third continent.[2]

Silver-footed Aphrodite welcomed   Ant. 1
her Delian-born guest   10
as she laid a gentle hand on his divinely wrought chariot,
and shed loving reverence over their sweet acts of love,

---

[1] Apollo.
[2] I.e. Africa, one of the three known continents.

ξυνὸν ἁρμόζοισα θεῷ τε γάμον
    μιχθέντα κούρᾳ θ' Ὑψέος εὐρυβία·
ὃς Λαπιθᾶν ὑπερόπλων τουτάκις ἦν βασιλεύς,
14a ἐξ Ὠκεανοῦ γένος ἥρως
15 δεύτερος· ὅν ποτε Πίνδου κλεενναῖς ἐν πτυχαῖς
    Ναῒς εὐφρανθεῖσα Πηνει-
      οῦ λέχει Κρέοισ' ἔτικτεν,

Γαίας θυγάτηρ. ὁ δὲ τὰν εὐώλενον
    θρέψατο παῖδα Κυράναν· ἁ μὲν οὔθ' ἱ-
    στῶν παλιμβάμους ἐφίλησεν ὁδούς,
οὔτε δείπνων †οἰκουριᾶν μεθ' ἑταιρᾶν τέρψιας,
20 ἀλλ' ἀκόντεσσίν τε χαλκέοις
    φασγάνῳ τε μαρναμένα κεράιζεν ἀγρίους
θῆρας, ἦ πολλάν τε καὶ ἡσύχιον
βουσὶν εἰρήναν παρέχοισα πατρῴαις,
    τὸν δὲ σύγκοιτον γλυκύν
    παῦρον ἐπὶ γλεφάροις
25 ὕπνον ἀναλίσκοισα ῥέποντα πρὸς ἀῶ.

Β΄ κίχε νιν λέοντί ποτ' εὐρυφαρέτρας
    ὀβρίμῳ μούναν παλαίοισαν
ἄτερ ἐγχέων ἑκάεργος Ἀπόλλων.
αὐτίκα δ' ἐκ μεγάρων Χείρωνα προσήνεπε φωνᾷ·

13 μιχθέντα BEFˢ(schol.): μιχθέντι VFⁱγ
19 δεῖπνον VᶠFᵃᶜGˢΣγρ | οἰκουριᾶν Vβ: οἰκουριῶν BFˡGˡ:
οἰκοριᾶν Moschopulus: ϝοικοϝορᾶν Schroeder: οἰκοαρᾶν Wila-
mowitz

352

joining together in a marriage of mutual consent
    the god and the daughter of mighty Hypseus,
who at that time was king of the overbearing Lapithae,
a hero, second in descent from Oceanus,[3]   14a
whom once in the famous glens of Pindus   15
Creusa, the Naid daughter of Gaea,[4] bore
    after finding joy in the bed of Peneius.

He raised his fair-armed   Ep. 1
child Cyrene. She, however, did not care
    for pacing back and forth at the loom
nor for the delights of meals with companions at home,
but with bronze javelins   20
and a sword she would fight and slay the wild
beasts, and truly she provided much peaceful
security for her father's cattle,
    while only briefly expending upon her eyelids
that sweet bed-mate,
the sleep that descends upon them toward dawn.[5]   25

Apollo, the far-shooting god with the broad quiver,   Str. 2
once came upon her as she was wrestling with
a mighty lion, alone and unarmed.
At once he called Chiron from his halls and said,

[3] The line of descent is Oceanus–Peneius (the main river in Thessaly)–Hypseus.

[4] Earth.

[5] I.e. she stayed up all night and only caught a nap before dawn (cf. *Od.* 14.528–533, where Eumaeus guards his swine at night). Others infer that she rose before dawn to hunt.

30 "σεμνὸν ἄντρον, Φιλλυρίδα, προλιπὼν
     θυμὸν γυναικὸς καὶ μεγάλαν δύνασιν
     θαύμασον, οἷον ἀταρβεῖ νεῖκος ἄγει κεφαλᾷ,
31a μόχθου καθύπερθε νεᾶνις
     ἦτορ ἔχοισα· φόβῳ δ' οὐ κεχείμανται φρένες.
     τίς νιν ἀνθρώπων τέκεν; ποί-
         ας δ' ἀποσπασθεῖσα φύτλας

     ὀρέων κευθμῶνας ἔχει σκιοέντων,
35 γεύεται δ' ἀλκᾶς ἀπειράντου;
     ὁσία κλυτὰν χέρα οἱ προσενεγκεῖν
     ἦρα καὶ ἐκ λεχέων κεῖραι μελιαδέα ποίαν;"
     τὸν δὲ Κένταυρος ζαμενής, ἀγανᾷ
         χλοαρὸν γελάσσαις ὀφρύι, μῆτιν ἑάν
     εὐθὺς ἀμείβετο· "κρυπταὶ κλαΐδες ἐντὶ σοφᾶς
39a Πειθοῦς ἱερᾶν φιλοτάτων,
40 Φοῖβε, καὶ ἔν τε θεοῖς τοῦτο κἀνθρώποις ὁμῶς
     αἰδέοντ', ἀμφανδὸν ἀδεί-
         ας τυχεῖν τὸ πρῶτον εὐνᾶς.

     καὶ γὰρ σέ, τὸν οὐ θεμιτὸν ψεύδει θιγεῖν,
     ἔτραπε μείλιχος ὀργὰ παρφάμεν τοῦ-
         τον λόγον. κούρας δ' ὁπόθεν γενεὰν
     ἐξερωτᾷς, ὦ ἄνα; κύριον ὃς πάντων τέλος
45 οἶσθα καὶ πάσας κελεύθους·
     ὅσσα τε χθὼν ἠρινὰ φύλλ' ἀναπέμπει, χὠπόσαι
     ἐν θαλάσσᾳ καὶ ποταμοῖς ψάμαθοι

354

"Come forth from your sacred cave, son of Philyra,   30
    and marvel at this woman's courage and great power
and at what a fight she is waging with unflinching head,
a girl whose heart is superior to toil   31a
and whose mind remains unshaken by storms of fear.
What mortal bore her? From what stock
    has she been severed

that she lives in the glens of the shadowy mountains   Ant. 2
and puts to the test her unbounded valor?   35
Is it right to lay my famous hand upon her
and indeed to reap the honey-sweet flower from the bed
    of love?"
The high-spirited Centaur smiled warmly
    with his gentle brow and at once answered him
with his advice: "Hidden are the keys to sacred
lovemaking that belong to wise Persuasion,   39a
Phoebus, and both gods and humans alike   40
shy from engaging openly for the first time
    in sweet love.

And so your amorous impulse prompted you,   Ep. 2
for whom it is not right to touch upon a lie, to make
    that misleading speech. Do you ask from where
the girl's lineage comes, O lord? And yet you know
the appointed end of all things and all the ways to them,   45
and how many leaves the earth puts forth in spring,
and how many grains of sand in the sea and rivers

---

38 χλοαρὸν Schroeder: χλιαρὸν Vv: χλαρὸν schol.

κύμασιν ῥιπαῖς τ' ἀνέμων κλονέονται,
   χὤ τι μέλλει, χὠπόθεν
ἔσσεται, εὖ καθορᾷς.
50 εἰ δὲ χρὴ καὶ πὰρ σοφὸν ἀντιφερίξαι,

Γ´ ἐρέω· ταύτᾳ πόσις ἵκεο βᾶσσαν
τάνδε, καὶ μέλλεις ὑπὲρ πόντου
Διὸς ἔξοχον ποτὶ κᾶπον ἐνεῖκαι·
ἔνθα νιν ἀρχέπολιν θήσεις, ἐπὶ λαὸν ἀγείραις
55 νασιώταν ὄχθον ἐς ἀμφίπεδον·
   νῦν δ' εὐρυλείμων πότνιά σοι Λιβύα
δέξεται εὐκλέα νύμφαν δώμασιν ἐν χρυσέοις
56a πρόφρων· ἵνα οἱ χθονὸς αἶσαν
αὐτίκα συντελέθειν ἔννομον δωρήσεται,
οὔτε παγκάρπων φυτῶν νά-
   ποινον οὔτ' ἀγνῶτα θηρῶν.

τόθι παῖδα τέξεται, ὃν κλυτὸς Ἑρμᾶς
60 εὐθρόνοις Ὥραισι καὶ Γαίᾳ
ἀνελὼν φίλας ὑπὸ ματέρος οἴσει.
ταὶ δ' ἐπιγουνίδιον θαησάμεναι βρέφος αὐταῖς,
νέκταρ ἐν χείλεσσι καὶ ἀμβροσίαν
   στάξοισι, θήσονταί τέ νιν ἀθάνατον,
Ζῆνα καὶ ἁγνὸν Ἀπόλλων', ἀνδράσι χάρμα φίλοις
64a ἄγχιστον ὀπάονα μήλων,

62 θαησάμεναι Bergk (θαυμάσασαι paraphr.): θηκάμεναι
Vγ^{γρ}: θακάμεναι B: θησάμεναι β (v.l. ?)

356

are beaten by the waves and blasts of wind,
   and what will happen and whence
it will come—all this you discern clearly.
But if I must match wits with one who is wise,   50

I will speak. You have come to this glen to be her   Str. 3
husband, and you are about to take her over the sea
to the finest garden of Zeus,
where you will make her ruler of a city, after gathering
an island people to the hill on the plain.[6]   55
   But as for now, Libya, mistress of broad meadows,
will welcome your famous bride in her golden palace
with gladness, and there at once she will grant her   56a
a portion of land to hold as her lawful possession,
one neither devoid of plants rich in every fruit,
   nor unacquainted with wild animals.

There she will give birth to a son, whom famous Hermes   Ant. 3
will take from under his dear mother and bear   60
to the fair-throned Horae[7] and to Gaea.
And when they behold the infant on their knees,
they shall drip nectar and ambrosia on his lips
   and shall make him immortal,
a Zeus or a holy Apollo, a delight to men dear to him
and ever-near guardian of flocks,   64a

[6] I.e. the people led by Battus from Thera (cf. *Pyth.* 4.6–8).
[7] The Seasons. Cyrene is descended from Gaea (cf. 16 and 102, where she is called Ga).

PINDAR

65 Ἀγρέα καὶ Νόμιον, τοῖς δ' Ἀρισταῖον καλεῖν."
ὡς ἄρ' εἰπὼν ἔντυεν τερ-
πνὰν γάμου κραίνειν τελευτάν.

ὠκεῖα δ' ἐπειγομένων ἤδη θεῶν
πρᾶξις ὁδοί τε βραχεῖαι. κεῖνο κεῖν' ἁ-
μαρ διαίτασεν· θαλάμῳ δὲ μίγεν
ἐν πολυχρύσῳ Λιβύας· ἵνα καλλίσταν πόλιν
70 ἀμφέπει κλεινάν τ' ἀέθλοις.
καί νυν ἐν Πυθῶνί νιν ἀγαθέᾳ Καρνειάδα
υἱὸς εὐθαλεῖ συνέμειξε τύχᾳ·
ἔνθα νικάσαις ἀνέφανε Κυράναν,
ἅ νιν εὔφρων δέξεται
καλλιγύναικι πάτρᾳ
75 δόξαν ἱμερτὰν ἀγαγόντ' ἀπὸ Δελφῶν.

Δ΄ ἀρεταὶ δ' αἰεὶ μεγάλαι πολύμυθοι·
βαιὰ δ' ἐν μακροῖσι ποικίλλειν
ἀκοὰ σοφοῖς· ὁ δὲ καιρὸς ὁμοίως
παντὸς ἔχει κορυφάν. ἔγνον ποτὲ καὶ Ἰόλαον
80 οὐκ ἀτιμάσαντά νιν ἑπτάπυλοι
Θῆβαι· τόν, Εὐρυσθῆος ἐπεὶ κεφαλάν
ἔπραθε φασγάνου ἀκμᾷ, κρύψαν ἔνερθ' ὑπὸ γᾶν
81a διφρηλάτα Ἀμφιτρύωνος

79 ἔγνον Ahrens: ἔγνων codd.

8 For Apollo Agreus (as hunter), Apollo Nomius (as shep-

358

called Agreus and Nomius by some, Aristaeus by others."[8] 65
Thus he spoke and encouraged him to consummate
   the sweet fulfillment of marriage.

Swift is the accomplishment once gods are in haste, Ep. 3
and short are the ways. That very day
   settled the matter. They joined together in love
in the gold-rich chamber of Libya, where she rules her
       city,
one most beautiful and famous for prizes in the games. 70
And now in holy Pytho the son of Carneiadas
has joined her to flourishing good fortune,
for by his victory there he made Cyrene glorious,
   and she will welcome him gladly
to his country of beautiful women,
having brought delightful fame from Delphi. 75

Great achievements are always worthy of many words, Str. 4
but elaboration of a few themes amid lengthy ones
is what wise men like to hear, for deft selection conveys
the essence of the whole just as well.[9] Seven-gated
       Thebes
once recognized that Iolaus too did not dishonor him.[10] 80
   After he cut off Eurystheus' head with the edge
of his sword, they buried Iolaus beneath the earth
in the tomb where his father's father lay, the charioteer 81a

herd), and Zeus Aristaeus, see Hes. *frr.* 215–217, Ap. Rhod.
2.506–507, and Diod. Sic. 4.81.2.   [9] Others interpret this
to mean: *for due proportion is supreme in everything alike.*

[10] I.e. Telesicrates was granted victory by Iolaus in the Theban
Iolaea.

σάματι, πατροπάτωρ ἔνθα οἱ Σπαρτῶν ξένος
κεῖτο, λευκίπποισι Καδμείων μετοικήσαις ἀγυιαῖς.

τέκε οἱ καὶ Ζηνὶ μιγεῖσα δαΐφρων
85 ἐν μόναις ὠδῖσιν Ἀλκμήνα
διδύμων κρατησίμαχον σθένος υἱῶν.
κωφὸς ἀνήρ τις, ὃς Ἡρακλεῖ στόμα μὴ περιβάλλει,
μηδὲ Διρκαίων ὑδάτων ἀὲ μέ-
μναται, τά νιν θρέψαντο καὶ Ἰφικλέα·
τοῖσι τέλειον ἐπ' εὐχᾷ κωμάσομαί τι παθών
89a ἐσλόν. Χαρίτων κελαδεννᾶν
90 μή με λίποι καθαρὸν φέγγος. Αἰγίνᾳ τε γάρ
φαμὶ Νίσου τ' ἐν λόφῳ τρὶς
δὴ πόλιν τάνδ' εὐκλέιξας,

σιγαλὸν ἀμαχανίαν ἔργῳ φυγών·
οὔνεκεν, εἰ φίλος ἀστῶν, εἴ τις ἀντά-
εις, τό γ' ἐν ξυνῷ πεπονημένον εὖ
μὴ λόγον βλάπτων ἁλίοιο γέροντος κρυπτέτω·
95 κεῖνος αἰνεῖν καὶ τὸν ἐχθρόν
παντὶ θυμῷ σύν τε δίκᾳ καλὰ ῥέζοντ' ἔννεπεν.
πλεῖστα νικάσαντά σε καὶ τελεταῖς

91 εὐκλέιξας Hermann (cf. Bacch. 6.16): εὐκλείξαι codd.

---

11 Amphitryon, father of Iphicles and grandfather of Iolaus,
was exiled from Tiryns (where Eurystheus ruled) and welcomed
in Thebes by the Spartoi ("Sown Men"), so-called because they
sprang from the dragon's teeth sown by Cadmus.

PYTHIAN 9

Amphitryon, a guest of the Spartoi after migrating
to the streets of the Cadmeans with the white horses.[11]

Wise Alcmene lay with him[12] and Zeus,
and in a single labor bore
twin sons,[13] mighty and victorious in battle.
Any man is dumb who does not embrace Heracles with
    his speech,
and does not continually remember Dirce's waters,
   which nourished him and Iphicles.
I shall celebrate them for the great good I enjoyed
when my wish was fulfilled. May the clear light
of the resounding Graces not leave me, for at Aegina
and at the hill of Nisus[14] full three times, I avow,
   you glorified this city

by escaping silent helplessness through your effort.[15]
Therefore, let no citizen, whether friendly or hostile,
   keep hidden a labor nobly borne on behalf of all,
thereby violating the command of the Old Man of the
    Sea,[16]
who said to praise even one's enemy
wholeheartedly and justly when he performs noble deeds.
When they saw you so often victorious as well

Ant. 4
85

89a
90

Ep. 4

95

---

[12] Amphitryon.
[13] Heracles and Iphicles.
[14] A mythical king of Megara.
[15] Or, reading the MSS's εὐκλείξαι: *I declare that I have glorified this city full three times at Aegina and at the hill of Nisus, by escaping silent helplessness through my effort.*
[16] Nereus, proverbial for wisdom and good advice.

ὡρίαις ἐν Παλλάδος εἶδον ἄφωνοί
   θ' ὡς ἕκασται φίλτατον
παρθενικαὶ πόσιν ἤ

100 υἱὸν εὔχοντ', ὦ Τελεσίκρατες, ἔμμεν,

Ε΄ ἐν Ὀλυμπίοισί τε καὶ βαθυκόλπου
   Γᾶς ἀέθλοις ἔν τε καὶ πᾶσιν
ἐπιχωρίοις. ἐμὲ δ' οὖν τις ἀοιδᾶν
   δίψαν ἀκειόμενον πράσσει χρέος, αὖτις ἐγεῖραι

105 καὶ παλαιὰν δόξαν ἑῶν προγόνων·
   οἷοι Λιβύσσας ἀμφὶ γυναικὸς ἔβαν
Ἴρασα πρὸς πόλιν, Ἀνταίου μετὰ καλλίκομον

106a μναστῆρες ἀγακλέα κούραν·
   τὰν μάλα πολλοὶ ἀριστῆες ἀνδρῶν αἴτεον
σύγγονοι, πολλοὶ δὲ καὶ ξεί-
   νων. ἐπεὶ θαητὸν εἶδος

ἔπλετο· χρυσοστεφάνου δέ οἱ Ἥβας

110 καρπὸν ἀνθήσαντ' ἀποδρέψαι
ἔθελον. πατὴρ δὲ θυγατρὶ φυτεύων
   κλεινότερον γάμον, ἄκουσεν Δαναόν ποτ' ἐν Ἄργει
οἷον εὗρεν τεσσαράκοντα καὶ ὀκ-
   τὼ παρθένοισι, πρὶν μέσον ἆμαρ, ἑλεῖν
ὠκύτατον γάμον· ἔστασεν γὰρ ἄπαντα χορόν

98 ἕκασται Εᵖᶜ: ἑκάστα V: ἑκάσται BG: ἕκαστα ΕᵃᶜF¹H
101 ἐν Byz.: ἐν τ' vett.
105 παλαιὰν δόξαν V: παλαιῶν δόξαν v: παλαιὰ δόξα Ε.
Schmid | ἑῶν Moschopulus: τεῶν vett.

in the seasonal festivals for Pallas,
    each of the maidens wished in silence
that you, O Telesicrates, were
her dearest husband or her son—   100

also in the Olympic games[17] and in those for   Str. 5
deep-bosomed Earth, and in all the local
ones. But as I slake my thirst
for songs, someone[18] exacts a debt from me to reawaken
as well the ancient glory of his ancestors, such as they   105
    were when they came for the sake of a Libyan woman
to the city of Irasa, as suitors
for the hand of Antaeus' famous fair-haired daughter,   106a
whom so many of her noblest kinsmen
were wooing, and many foreigners as well,
    because her beauty

was splendid and they were eager to cull   Ant. 5
the blooming fruit of golden-crowned Hebe.[19]   110
But her father, planning a more glorious
marriage for his daughter, had heard how in Argos
Danaus in his day had devised a means to gain
    a most speedy marriage for his forty-eight
unwed daughters[20] before noon: at once he placed

[17] The local Olympic games referred to here, as well as those
for Pallas and Earth, were all held in Cyrene.
[18] Telesicrates.   [19] Youth.
[20] Two of the fifty, Hypermestra and Amymone, already had
husbands (cf. Apollod. 2.1.5).

---

106 Ἴρασα Heyne: ἴρασαν codd.
113 ἑλεῖν GH^{pc} (e schol.?): ἐλθεῖν VBEFH^{ac}

114a ἐν τέρμασιν αὐτίκ᾽ ἀγῶνος·
115 σὺν δ᾽ ἀέθλοις ἐκέλευσεν διακρῖναι ποδῶν,
ἄντινα σχήσοι τις ἡρώ-
ων, ὅσοι γαμβροί σφιν ἦλθον.

οὕτω δ᾽ ἐδίδου Λίβυς ἁρμόζων κόρᾳ
νυμφίον ἄνδρα· ποτὶ γραμμᾷ μὲν αὐτὰν
στᾶσε κοσμήσαις, τέλος ἔμμεν ἄκρον,
εἶπε δ᾽ ἐν μέσσοις ἀπάγεσθαι, ὃς ἂν πρῶτος θορών
120 ἀμφί οἱ ψαύσειε πέπλοις.
ἔνθ᾽ Ἀλεξίδαμος, ἐπεὶ φύγε λαιψηρὸν δρόμον,
παρθένον κεδνὰν χερὶ χειρὸς ἑλών
ἆγεν ἱππευτᾶν Νομάδων δι᾽ ὅμιλον.
πολλὰ μὲν κεῖνοι δίκον
φύλλ᾽ ἔπι καὶ στεφάνους·
125 πολλὰ δὲ πρόσθεν πτερὰ δέξατο νικᾶν.

116 σχήσοι BH: σχήσει VG: σχείση et σχοίση EF
125 νικᾶν V: νίκας v(paraphr.)

the whole throng at the finish line of the contest   114a
and gave orders to decide by the trials of a foot race   115
which daughter each hero would win, of those
    who came to betroth them.

The Libyan made a similar offer for matching   Ep. 5
a groom to his daughter. He adorned her
    and set her at the finish line as the grand prize
and declared in their midst that whoever first leapt
       forward
and touched her dress would take her away with him.   120
Then Alexidamus, after excelling in the swift race,
took the cherished maiden hand-in-hand
and led her through the throng of Nomad horsemen.
    Many were the leaves
and crowns they showered upon him—
and many the winged wreaths of victories he had won   125
       before.

PYTHIAN 10

If the date of 498 given by the scholia is correct, this is the earliest epinicion in the collection, and yet it contains most of the distinctive features of Pindar's style. The only ode to a Thessalian, it was apparently commissioned by Thorax, the leader of the Aleuadae of Larissa, located down the Peneius River from Pelinna, the victor's city. The central narrative, framed in ring composition, tells of Perseus' journey to the Hyperboreans, whose blessed life serves as a measure of the success enjoyed by the victor and his father.

After a grand opening that links Thessaly with Lacedaemon through Heracles, the poet abruptly turns to the occasion at hand, Hippocleas' Pythian victory in the boys' diaulos (1–9). Although Apollo surely aided him in his victory, he also inherited athletic ability from his father, who had twice won the race in armor at Olympia and once at Pytho (10–16).

The poet prays that the gods may continue to favor them both and declares that a man is blessed who is himself a great victor and lives to see his son win Pythian crowns (17–26). Such a one has reached the limits of human success, beyond which lies the inaccessible land of the Hyperboreans (27–30). Perseus once visited them while they were delighting Apollo with their sacrifices of asses

(31–36). The Muse resides with them as they enjoy music, poetry, and feasting, and they never become sick or grow old (37–44). The narrative section concludes with a brief mention of Perseus' famous exploit of slaying the Gorgon and turning his mother's captors into stone (44–48).

After marveling at the power of the gods, the poet suddenly suspends his song's progress and declares that encomia must vary their subjects (48–54). He hopes that his songs will make the victor more admired among his countrymen, especially the young girls (55–59). It is sweet to gain what one desires in the present, but the unforeseeable future looms ahead (59–63). The poet places his confidence in his friend Thorax, who commissioned the ode, and praises his brothers, good men who maintain the Thessalian state (64–72).

10. ΙΠΠΟΚΛΕΙ
ΘΕΣΣΑΛΩΙ
ΠΑΙΔΙ ΔΙΑΥΛΟΔΡΟΜΩΙ

Α΄ Ὀλβία Λακεδαίμων,
  μάκαιρα Θεσσαλία. πατρὸς δ᾽ ἀμφοτέραις ἐξ ἑνός
  ἀριστομάχου γένος Ἡρακλέος βασιλεύει.
  τί κομπέω παρὰ καιρόν; ἀλλά με Πυθώ
    τε καὶ τὸ Πελινναῖον ἀπύει
5 Ἀλεύα τε παῖδες, Ἱπποκλέᾳ θέλοντες
  ἀγαγεῖν ἐπικωμίαν ἀνδρῶν κλυτὰν ὄπα.

  γεύεται γὰρ ἀέθλων·
  στρατῷ τ᾽ ἀμφικτιόνων ὁ Παρνάσσιος αὐτὸν μυχός
  διαυλοδρομᾶν ὕπατον παίδων ἀνέειπεν.
10 Ἄπολλον, γλυκὺ δ᾽ ἀνθρώπων τέλος ἀρχά
    τε δαίμονος ὀρνύντος αὔξεται·
  ὁ μέν που τεοῖς τε μήδεσι τοῦτ᾽ ἔπραξεν,
  τὸ δὲ συγγενὲς ἐμβέβακεν ἴχνεσιν πατρός

10. FOR HIPPOCLEAS
OF THESSALY

WINNER, BOYS' DIAULOS, 498 B.C.

Fortunate is Lacedaemon,   Str. 1
blessed is Thessaly. Over both rule the descendants
of one father, Heracles, greatest in battle.
Why am I vaunting inappropriately? Rather, Pytho
    and Pelinna[1] are calling upon me,
and Aleuas' sons,[2] who are eager to bring to Hippocleas   5
men's glorious voices in revelry,

for he competes in the games,   Ant. 1
and the valley of Parnassus proclaimed him to the host
of neighboring people the best of the boys who ran the
    diaulos.
Apollo, sweet waxes the end and the beginning   10
    for men when a god is prompting.
He achieved this, I believe, through your designs,
but by inherited ability he has trod in the footsteps of his
    father,

[1] The victor's city in western Thessaly.
[2] The Aleuadae were a powerful Thessalian family, of whom
Thorax (64) was head.

369

Ὀλυμπιονίκα δὶς ἐν πολεμαδόκοις
Ἄρεος ὅπλοις·
15 ἔθηκε καὶ βαθυλείμων ὑπὸ Κίρρας πετρᾶν
ἀγὼν κρατησίποδα Φρικίαν.
ἔποιτο μοῖρα καὶ ὑστέραισιν
ἐν ἀμέραις ἀγάνορα πλοῦτον ἀνθεῖν σφίσιν·

Β΄ τῶν δ' ἐν Ἑλλάδι τερπνῶν
20 λαχόντες οὐκ ὀλίγαν δόσιν, μὴ φθονεραῖς ἐκ θεῶν
μετατροπίαις ἐπικύρσαιεν. θεὸς εἴη
ἀπήμων κέαρ. εὐδαίμων δὲ καὶ ὑμνη-
τὸς οὗτος ἀνὴρ γίνεται σοφοῖς,
ὃς ἂν χερσὶν ἢ ποδῶν ἀρετᾷ κρατήσαις
τὰ μέγιστ' ἀέθλων ἕλῃ τόλμᾳ τε καὶ σθένει,

25 καὶ ζώων ἔτι νεαρόν
κατ' αἶσαν υἱὸν ἴδῃ τυχόντα στεφάνων Πυθίων.
ὁ χάλκεος οὐρανὸς οὔ ποτ' ἀμβατὸς αὐτῷ·
ὅσαις δὲ βροτὸν ἔθνος ἀγλαΐαις ἁ-
πτόμεσθα, περαίνει πρὸς ἔσχατον
πλόον· ναυσὶ δ' οὔτε πεζὸς ἰὼν ‹κεν› εὕροις
30 ἐς Ὑπερβορέων ἀγῶνα θαυμαστὰν ὁδόν.

15–16 βαθυλείμων ὑπὸ Κίρρας πετρᾶν | ἀγὼν Christ Hartungio praeeunte: βαθυλείμωνα ἀγὼν ὑπὸ κίρρας πέτραν codd.   26 ἴδῃ Callierges: ἴδοι codd.
27 αὐτῷ Triclinius e schol.: αὐτοῖς vett.
29 ‹κεν› suppl. Hermann

twice an Olympic victor in Ares' armor   Ep. 1
that bears the shock of war;
the contest in the deep meadow beneath Cirrha's cliffs[3]   15
also made Phricias[4] a victorious runner.
May destiny attend them as well in coming
days to make lordly wealth blossom for them.

And having been granted no small share of delightful   Str. 2
successes in Hellas, may they encounter from the gods   20
no envious reversals. May the god
not be pained in heart.[5] But blessed and a worthy subject
    for song in wise men's eyes is that man,
who conquers with his hands or the excellence of his feet
and wins the greatest of prizes[6] with courage and
    strength,

and while still living sees his young son   Ant. 2
duly win Pythian crowns.   26
The bronze heaven is never his to scale,
but as for all the glories which our mortal race
    attains, he completes the furthest voyage.
And traveling neither by ships nor on foot could you find
the marvelous way to the assembly of the Hyperboreans.   30

[3] At Pytho.
[4] The name of Hippocleas' father, or, some think, that of his
horse, indicating that he won the horse race at Delphi.
[5] I.e. may no god take offense. Many interpret this to mean
"only a god may be free from pain at heart."
[6] I.e. an Olympic victory.

παρ᾽ οἷς ποτε Περσεὺς ἐδαίσατο λαγέτας,
δώματ᾽ ἐσελθών,
κλειτὰς ὄνων ἑκατόμβας ἐπιτόσσαις θεῷ
ῥέζοντας· ὧν θαλίαις ἔμπεδον
35 εὐφαμίαις τε μάλιστ᾽ Ἀπόλλων
χαίρει, γελᾷ θ᾽ ὁρῶν ὕβριν ὀρθίαν κνωδάλων.

Γ´ Μοῖσα δ᾽ οὐκ ἀποδαμεῖ
τρόποις ἐπὶ σφετέροισι· παντᾷ δὲ χοροὶ παρθένων
λυρᾶν τε βοαὶ καναχαί τ᾽ αὐλῶν δονέονται·
40 δάφνᾳ τε χρυσέᾳ κόμας ἀναδήσαν-
τες εἰλαπινάζοισιν εὐφρόνως.
νόσοι δ᾽ οὔτε γῆρας οὐλόμενον κέκραται
ἱερᾷ γενεᾷ· πόνων δὲ καὶ μαχᾶν ἄτερ

οἰκέοισι φυγόντες
ὑπέρδικον Νέμεσιν. θρασείᾳ δὲ πνέων καρδίᾳ
45 μόλεν Δανάας ποτὲ παῖς, ἁγεῖτο δ᾽ Ἀθάνα,
ἐς ἀνδρῶν μακάρων ὅμιλον· ἔπεφνέν
τε Γοργόνα, καὶ ποικίλον κάρα
δρακόντων φόβαισιν ἤλυθε νασιώταις
λίθινον θάνατον φέρων. ἐμοὶ δὲ θαυμάσαι

θεῶν τελεσάντων οὐδέν ποτε φαίνεται
50 ἔμμεν ἄπιστον.

---

7 Apollo traditionally spent three winter months with the
Hyperboreans. It is uncertain what amuses him here: the asses'

With them Perseus, the leader of people, once feasted,   Ep. 2
upon entering their halls,
when he came upon them sacrificing glorious hecatombs
of asses to the god. In their banquets
and praises Apollo ever finds greatest delight   35
and laughs to see the beasts' braying insolence.[7]

And the Muse is no stranger   Str. 3
to their ways, for everywhere choruses of maidens,
sounds of lyres, and pipes' shrill notes are stirring.
With golden laurel they crown their hair   40
      and feast joyfully.
Neither sickness nor accursed old age mingles
with that holy race, but without toils or battles

they dwell there, having escaped   Ant. 3
strictly judging Nemesis.[8] Breathing courage in his heart,
the son of Danaë once came—Athena led him—   45
to that throng of blessed men. He slew
      the Gorgon, and, bearing her head adorned
with locks of serpents, came to the islanders,[9]
bringing them stony death. But to me, no marvel,

if the gods bring it about, ever seems   Ep. 3
beyond belief.   50

leapings (schol.), their high-pitched braying (schol.), or their erect
phalluses (most modern scholars).

[8] Nemesis seems to represent retributive justice for wrong-
doing, which the Hyperboreans have avoided by their upright
conduct, thus living extremely long lives.   [9] Of Seriphus,
where Danaë was held captive (cf. *Pyth.* 12.11–15).

κώπαν σχάσον, ταχὺ δ' ἄγκυραν ἔρεισον χθονί
πρῴραθε, χοιράδος ἄλκαρ πέτρας.
ἐγκωμίων γὰρ ἄωτος ὕμνων
ἐπ' ἄλλοτ' ἄλλον ὧτε μέλισσα θύνει λόγον.

Δ′ ἔλπομαι δ' Ἐφυραίων
56 ὄπ' ἀμφὶ Πηνεϊὸν γλυκεῖαν προχεόντων ἐμάν
    τὸν Ἱπποκλέαν ἔτι καὶ μᾶλλον σὺν ἀοιδαῖς
    ἕκατι στεφάνων θαητὸν ἐν ἅλι-
        ξι θησέμεν ἐν καὶ παλαιτέροις,
    νέαισίν τε παρθένοισι μέλημα. καὶ γάρ
60 ἑτέροις ἑτέρων ἔρωτες ἔκνιξαν φρένας·

    τῶν δ' ἕκαστος ὀρούει,
    τυχών κεν ἁρπαλέαν σχέθοι φροντίδα τὰν πὰρ πο-
        δός·
    τὰ δ' εἰς ἐνιαυτὸν ἀτέκμαρτον προνοῆσαι.
    πέποιθα ξενίᾳ προσανέϊ Θώρα-
        κος, ὅσπερ ἐμὰν ποιπνύων χάριν
65 τόδ' ἔζευξεν ἅρμα Πιερίδων τετράορον,
    φιλέων φιλέοντ', ἄγων ἄγοντα προφρόνως.

    πειρῶντι δὲ καὶ χρυσὸς ἐν βασάνῳ πρέπει
    καὶ νόος ὀρθός.
    ἀδελφεοῖσί τ' ἐπαινήσομεν ἐσλοῖς, ὅτι

    60 ἔρωτες ἔκνιξαν Mair: ἔρως ἔκνιξε Vv

374

Hold the oar, quickly plant the anchor in the earth
from the prow as a safeguard against the jagged reef,
for the finest of victory hymns
flit like a bee from one theme to another.

I hope, when the Ephyraeans[10]   Str. 4
pour forth my sweet voice beside the Peneius,   56
that with my songs I may make Hippocleas
even more splendid for his crowns
    in the eyes of his comrades and his elders,
and the darling of unmarried girls. Indeed, desires
for various things stir the minds of various men,   60

and each one who wins what he strives for   Ant. 4
may gain the coveted object of his immediate concern,
but there is no sure sign to foresee what a year may bring.
I put my trust in the comforting hospitality
    of Thorax, who in his zeal to favor me
yoked this four-horse chariot of the Pierians,   65
as friend to friend and willing guide to guide.

When one tests it, gold shines forth on a touchstone   Ep. 4
as does an upright mind.
We shall praise as well his noble brothers[11]

[10] The city of Crannon (near Pelinna) was formerly called
Ephyra (schol.).

[11] Eurypylus and Thrasydaeus (cf. Hdt. 9.58).

---

69 ἀδελφεοῖσι τ᾿ . . . ἐσλοῖς Wilamowitz: ἀδελφεούς τ᾿ . . .
ἐσλούς codd.

70 ὑψοῦ φέροντι νόμον Θεσσαλῶν
    αὔξοντες· ἐν δ᾽ ἀγαθοῖσι κεῖται
    πατρώιαι κεδναὶ πολίων κυβερνάσιες.

71 κεῖται GᵃH(schol.): κεῖνται rell.

because they uphold and exalt the state　　　　　　　　70
of the Thessalians; with good men rests
the governance of cities as a cherished inheritance.

PYTHIAN 11

The centerpiece of this poem, sometimes called a "little *Oresteia*," is the story of Clytaemestra's murder of Agamemnon. It is narrated in ring composition and provides a striking contrast to the public-spirited success of the victor and his family, who strive for achievements in the tradition of the Theban hero Iolaus and the Tyndaridae. The poet's elaborate disclaimer in 38–42, in which he asks if he has strayed from his course, is meant to call attention to the discrepancy between the myth and the career of Thrasydaeus and his father. The scholia give conflicting dates and events for the victory: 474 in the boys' stadion and 454 in the men's diaulos (or stadion); the former is more likely.

The major heroines of Thebes are summoned to Apollo's Ismenian temple to celebrate Pytho, where Thrasydaeus has won a third victory for Thebes (1–16). The poet glides quickly into the story of Orestes, who was rescued by his nurse Arsinoa from Clytaemestra's designs on his life after she had killed Cassandra and Agamemnon (17–22). He ponders whether she was angered because of the sacrifice of Iphigeneia, or because of her adulterous love affair, a sin that becomes town gossip when it concerns the wealthy (22–30). Without giving an answer, he closes the ring by briefly relating the deaths of Agamemnon and

Cassandra after Troy's destruction, the escape of Orestes to Strophius, and his eventual return to slay his mother and Aegisthus (31–37).

The poet asks if he has taken a wrong turn or gotten off course (38–40) and reminds his Muse that she is under contract to praise Pythonicus and his son Thrasydaeus, both of whom won the foot race at Pytho (41–50). He states his preference for god-given success and for a moderate position in a city (as opposed to the tyrant's station), and praises accomplishments that promote the common good because they keep envy at bay (50–54). The best possession to bequeath at death is a good name, which is what Iolaus, Castor, and Polydeuces (all three athletes and patrons of games) enjoy in song (55–64).

11. ΘΡΑΣΥΔΑΙΩΙ
ΘΗΒΑΙΩΙ

ΠΑΙΔΙ ΣΤΑΔΙΕΙ

Α΄ Κάδμου κόραι, Σεμέλα μὲν Ὀλυμπιάδων ἀγυιᾶτι,
    Ἰνὼ δὲ Λευκοθέα
      ποντιᾶν ὁμοθάλαμε Νηρηΐδων,
    ἴτε σὺν Ἡρακλέος ἀριστογόνῳ
    ματρὶ πὰρ Μελίαν χρυσέων ἐς ἄδυτον τριπόδων
  5 θησαυρόν, ὃν περίαλλ᾽ ἐτίμασε Λοξίας,

    Ἰσμήνιον δ᾽ ὀνύμαξεν, ἀλαθέα μαντίων θῶκον,
    ὦ παῖδες Ἁρμονίας,
      ἔνθα καί νυν ἐπίνομον ἡρωίδων
    στρατὸν ὁμαγερέα καλεῖ συνίμεν,
    ὄφρα Θέμιν ἱερὰν Πυθῶνά τε καὶ ὀρθοδίκαν
 10 γᾶς ὀμφαλὸν κελαδήσετ᾽ ἄκρᾳ σὺν ἑσπέρᾳ

    1 ἀγυιᾶτι Christ: ἀγυιᾶτις codd.
    6 μαντίων Hermann: μαντείων v: μαντεῖον V
    8 ὁμαγερέα Mommsen: ὁμηγερέα BEF: ὁμηγυρέα γ:
    ὀμυγερέα V
    10 κελαδήσετ᾽ Heyne (ὑμνήσητε paraphr.): κελαδῆτε codd.

380

11. FOR THRASYDAEUS
OF THEBES

WINNER, BOYS' STADION

Daughters of Cadmus, you, Semele, neighbor	Str. 1
of the Olympian goddesses, and you, Ino Leucothea,[1]	
who share the chambers of the Nereid sea nymphs,	
go with the most nobly born mother[2] of Heracles	
and join Melia[3] at the treasury of the golden tripods,	
the sanctuary which Loxias[4] especially honored	5

and named the Ismenion,[5] the true seat of seers.	Ant. 1
O daughters of Harmonia,[6]	
there he now summons	
the local host of heroines to gather together,	
so that you may celebrate holy Themis,[7] Pytho,	
and the just-judging center of the earth at nightfall	10

[1] For Semele and Ino, see *Ol.* 2.25–30 and Appendix, genealogy of the Daughters of Cadmus.   [2] Alcmene.

[3] Mother by Apollo of Tenerus and Ismenus (cf. Paus. 9.10).

[4] Cult name of Apollo in his prophetic guise.

[5] The temple of Apollo, named for his son Ismenus, famous for rendering oracles.   [6] Harmonia, Cadmus' wife, bore Semele and Ino.   [7] Themis occupied the Delphic oracle before Apollo (cf. Aesch. *Eum.* 2–4). If lowercase, it means "ordinance."

PINDAR

ἑπταπύλοισι Θήβαις
χάριν ἀγῶνί τε Κίρρας,
ἐν τῷ Θρασυδᾷος ἔμνασεν ἑστίαν
τρίτον ἔπι στέφανον πατρῷαν βαλών,
15 ἐν ἀφνεαῖς ἀρούραισι Πυλάδα
νικῶν ξένου Λάκωνος Ὀρέστα.

Β′ τὸν δὴ φονευομένου πατρὸς Ἀρσινόα Κλυται-
μήστρας
χειρῶν ὕπο κρατερᾶν
ἐκ δόλου τροφὸς ἄνελε δυσπενθέος,
ὁπότε Δαρδανίδα κόραν Πριάμου
20 Κασσάνδραν πολιῷ χαλκῷ σὺν Ἀγαμεμνονίᾳ
ψυχᾷ πόρευ' Ἀχέροντος ἀκτὰν παρ' εὔσκιον

νηλὴς γυνά. πότερόν νιν ἄρ' Ἰφιγένει' ἐπ' Εὐρίπῳ
σφαχθεῖσα τῆλε πάτρας
ἔκνισεν βαρυπάλαμον ὄρσαι χόλον;
ἢ ἑτέρῳ λέχεϊ δαμαζομέναν
25 ἔννυχοι πάραγον κοῖται; τὸ δὲ νέαις ἀλόχοις
ἔχθιστον ἀμπλάκιον καλύψαι τ' ἀμάχανον

ἀλλοτρίαισι γλώσσαις·
κακολόγοι δὲ πολῖται.
ἴσχει τε γὰρ ὄλβος οὐ μείονα φθόνον·

21 πόρευ' VE^{pc}F: πόρευσ(εν) BE^{ac}γ

382

in honor of seven-gated Thebes	Ep. 1
and the contest at Cirrha,	
in which Thrasydaeus made famous the hearth	
of his fathers when he cast a third wreath upon it[8]	
as a victor in the rich fields of Pylades,	15
the host of Laconian Orestes,[9]	

who, indeed, at the slaughter of his father,[10] was rescued	Str. 2
by his nurse Arsinoa out from under the powerful hands	
of Clytaemestra and away from her grievous treachery,	
when with the gray bronze she dispatched Cassandra,	
Dardanian Priam's daughter, along with Agamemnon's	20
soul, to the shadowy shore of Acheron—	

that pitiless woman. Was it then the sacrificial slaying	Ant. 2
of Iphigeneia at Euripus[11] far from her homeland that	
provoked her to rouse up her heavy-handed anger?	
Or did nighttime lovemaking lead her astray	
by enthralling her to another's bed? That sin[12]	25
is most hateful in young wives and impossible to conceal	

because of others' tongues,	Ep. 2
for townsmen are scandalmongers.	
Then, too, prosperity sustains a matching envy,	

---

[8] Presumably the third Pythian victory of his family (cf. 43–50).   [9] Pindar, like Stesichorus, places Agamemnon's palace at Amyclae in Laconia (cf. Paus. 3.19.6); Homer located it in Mycenae, Aeschylus in Argos.   [10] Agamemnon.

[11] The strait between Attica and Euboea, where the Greek fleet assembled.

[12] Adultery.

30 ὁ δὲ χαμηλὰ πνέων ἄφαντον βρέμει.
θάνεν μὲν αὐτὸς ἥρως Ἀτρεΐδας
ἵκων χρόνῳ κλυταῖς ἐν Ἀμύκλαις,

Γ΄ μάντιν τ᾽ ὄλεσσε κόραν, ἐπεὶ ἀμφ᾽ Ἑλένᾳ πυρω-
θέντων
Τρώων ἔλυσε δόμους
ἁβρότατος. ὁ δ᾽ ἄρα γέροντα ξένον
35 Στροφίον ἐξίκετο, νέα κεφαλά,
Παρνασσοῦ πόδα ναίοντ᾽· ἀλλὰ χρονίῳ σὺν Ἄρει
πέφνεν τε ματέρα θῆκέ τ᾽ Αἴγισθον ἐν φοναῖς.

ἦρ᾽, ὦ φίλοι, κατ᾽ ἀμευσίπορον τρίοδον ἐδινάθην,
ὀρθὰν κέλευθον ἰὼν
τὸ πρίν· ἤ μέ τις ἄνεμος ἔξω πλόου
40 ἔβαλεν, ὡς ὅτ᾽ ἄκατον ἐνναλίαν;
Μοῖσα, τὸ δὲ τεόν, εἰ μισθοῖο συνέθευ παρέχειν
φωνὰν ὑπάργυρον, ἄλλοτ᾽ ἄλλᾳ ταρασσέμεν

ἢ πατρὶ Πυθονίκῳ
τό γέ νυν ἢ Θρασυδαΐῳ,
45 τῶν εὐφροσύνα τε καὶ δόξ᾽ ἐπιφλέγει.
τὰ μὲν ⟨ἐν⟩ ἅρμασι καλλίνικοι πάλαι
Ὀλυμπίᾳ τ᾽ ἀγώνων πολυφάτων
ἔσχον θοὰν ἀκτῖνα σὺν ἵπποις,

33 πυρωθέντας Snell   38 ἀμευσιπόρους τριόδους
Hermann   41 μισθοῖο Christ (cf. paraphr.): μισθῷ codd.

whereas the din of a man of low ambition goes unnoticed. 30
Atreus' heroic son himself died
when at last he came to famous Amyclae,

and he brought death on the prophetic maiden,[13] after he   Str. 3
despoiled of their luxury the homes of the Trojans, who
   were visited by fire for the sake of Helen. The young
boy, though, went to his aged host Strophius,[14] who lived 35
at the foot of Parnassus. But, with Ares' eventual help,
he slew his mother and laid Aegisthus in gore.

Can it be, O my friends, that I got confused where the   Ant. 3
   way forked,
when before I was going on the straight road?
   Or did some wind throw me
off course, like a small boat at sea?   40
Muse, it is your duty, since you have contracted to hire
your voice for silver, to keep it moving this way and that,

either now to his father, Pythonicus,[15]   Ep. 3
or to Thrasydaeus,
for their celebration and glory are ablaze.   45
Not only were they victorious of old with chariots
and in the famous contests at Olympia
captured swift brilliance with their horses,

---

[13] Cassandra.   [14] Pylades' father, king of Phocis.
[15] Some take Πυθονίκῳ as an epithet: *a Pythian victor*.

---

42 ταρασσέμεν E. Schmid (χρὴ non leg. schol.): χρὴ τα-
ρασσέμεν codd.   43 Πυθονίκῳ Triclinius: πυθιονίκω(ι) vett.
46 ⟨ἐν⟩ suppl. Triclinius

Δ´ Πυθοῖ τε γυμνὸν ἐπὶ στάδιον καταβάντες ἤλεγξαν
50 Ἑλλανίδα στρατιὰν
    ὠκύτατι. θεόθεν ἐραίμαν καλῶν,
    δυνατὰ μαιόμενος ἐν ἁλικίᾳ.
    τῶν γὰρ ἀνὰ πόλιν εὑρίσκων τὰ μέσα μακροτέρῳ
    ὄλβῳ τεθαλότα, μέμφομ᾽ αἶσαν τυραννίδων·

    ξυναῖσι δ᾽ ἀμφ᾽ ἀρεταῖς τέταμαι· φθονεροὶ δ᾽ ἀμύ-
        νονται.
55 ἀλλ᾽ εἴ τις ἄκρον ἑλὼν
    ἡσυχᾷ τε νεμόμενος αἰνὰν ὕβριν
    ἀπέφυγεν, μέλανος ἂν ἐσχατιάν
    καλλίονα θανάτου ⟨στείχοι⟩ γλυκυτάτᾳ γενεᾷ
    εὐώνυμον κτεάνων κρατίσταν χάριν πορών·

    ἅ τε τὸν Ἰφικλείδαν
60 διαφέρει Ἰόλαον
    ὑμνητὸν ἐόντα, καὶ Κάστορος βίαν,
    σέ τε, ἄναξ Πολύδευκες, υἱοὶ θεῶν,
    τὸ μὲν παρ᾽ ἆμαρ ἕδραισι Θεράπνας,
    τὸ δ᾽ οἰκέοντας ἔνδον Ὀλύμπου.

53 ὄλβῳ Triclinius: σὺν ὄλβῳ vett.
54 ἀμύνονται β¹: ἀμύνοντ᾽ rell.
55 ἀλλ᾽ εἴ τις Boeckh: ἄτα. εἴ τις codd.: ἄτᾳ· τίς . . .
ἀπέφυγεν; Hóman | ἡσυχᾷ Mommsen Hermanno praeeunte:
ἡσυχία(ι) codd.
56 μέλανος ἂν E. Schmid: μέλανος δ᾽ ἂν codd.

but also when they entered the naked foot race at Pytho   Str. 4
they put to shame the Hellenic host with their speed.   50
    May I desire blessings from the gods,
as I seek what is possible at my age, for within a city I find
the middle estate flourishing with more enduring
prosperity, and I censure the condition of tyrannies.

I strive for achievements others share in; for envious men   Ant. 4
    are warded off.
But if a man has won the peak   55
    and dwelling there in peace has avoided dire
insolence, he would go to a more noble bourne
of black death, having given his sweetest offspring
the best of possessions, the grace of a good name.[16]

That is what makes known Iolaus,   Ep. 4
Iphicles' son,   60
as a subject of hymns, and mighty Castor,
and you, lord Polydeuces, sons of the gods,
you who spend one day in your homes at Therapna,
and on the next dwell in Olympus.

[16] Lines 54–57 contain one of the most corrupt passages in the odes. The reading of Schroeder and Turyn of 54–56 is: φθονεροὶ δ᾽ ἀμύνονται | ἄτᾳ· τίς ἄκρον ἑλών | ἡσυχᾷ τε νεμόμενος αἰνὰν ὕβριν | ἀπέφυγεν· "Envious ones fight back in their delusion. Who, having won the peak and dwelling there in peace avoids (their) dread insolence?"

---

57 θανάτου B: θάνατον rell. (sed θανάτου gl. adscr. 56 E) | ⟨στείχοι⟩ suppl. Wilamowitz: ἐν Vv

PYTHIAN 12

From the time of its founding, the Pythian festival included musical contests. In 490 Midas of Acragas won the competition for the *aulos*, which I have translated by "pipe," but was in fact more like a modern clarinet or oboe and consisted of a bronze mouthpiece and reed body. Traditionally the invention of Athena, it was known for its expressive range (cf. πάμφωνον at 19 and *Ol.* 7.12) and especially for the "many headed tune," whose invention Pindar also attributes to Athena.

The story of Danaë, merely sketched by Pindar in ring composition, is as follows. King Acrisius of Argos, fearing that the child born to his daughter Danaë would supplant him, locked her up in a tower. Zeus came to her in a shower of gold and sired Perseus. When the king learned of it, he shut the mother and her baby in a chest and put them out to sea. They came ashore on the island of Seriphus, where King Polydectes kept them for many years, making Danaë his mistress. When he invited the leaders of Seriphus to come to a feast and bring him gifts, the young Perseus went off to acquire the head of the Gorgon Medusa as his present. By stealing the one eye belonging to the Graeae, Phorcus' daughters, he forced them to reveal the location of their three sisters, the Gorgons. With the help of

388

Athena, Perseus cut off Medusa's head, brought it to the banquet, and turned his enemies to stone.

The poem opens with an invocation of Acragas (as nymph and city) to accept this celebration of Midas for his victorious pipe playing at Pytho (1–6). Athena invented the art of pipe playing when she reproduced in music the Gorgons' dirge for their sister, Medusa, after Perseus carried off her head, with which he turned the people of Seriphus to stone (6–12). He blinded the Graeae and punished Polydectes for his enslavement of Danaë (13–18), after which Athena composed the "many-headed tune" in imitation of Euryale's lament for her sister, and gave it to mortals (18–23). It still serves to summon people to the games and to lead dances (24–27).

The ode closes with a series of gnomes stressing the hard work necessary for success and the unpredictability of divine gifts (28–32).

12. ΜΙΔΑΙ ΑΚΡΑΓΑΝΤΙΝΩΙ

ΑΥΛΗΤΗΙ

Α΄ Αἰτέω σε, φιλάγλαε, καλλίστα βροτεᾶν πολίων,
Φερσεφόνας ἕδος, ἅ τ᾽ ὄχθαις ἔπι μηλοβότου
ναίεις Ἀκράγαντος ἐΰδματον κολώναν, ὦ ἄνα,
ἵλαος ἀθανάτων ἀνδρῶν τε σὺν εὐμενίᾳ
5 δέξαι στεφάνωμα τόδ᾽ ἐκ Πυθῶνος εὐδόξῳ Μίδᾳ
αὐτόν τέ νιν Ἑλλάδα νικάσαντα τέχνᾳ, τάν ποτε
Παλλὰς ἐφεῦρε θρασειᾶν ⟨Γοργόνων⟩
οὔλιον θρῆνον διαπλέξαισ᾽ Ἀθάνα·

Β΄ τὸν παρθενίοις ὑπό τ᾽ ἀπλάτοις ὀφίων κεφαλαῖς
10 ἄιε λειβόμενον δυσπενθέι σὺν καμάτῳ,
Περσεὺς ὁπότε τρίτον ἄυσεν κασιγνητᾶν μέρος
ἐνναλίᾳ Σερίφῳ λαοῖσί τε μοῖραν ἄγων.

5 εὐδόξου μίδα EF(schol.)
7 ⟨Γοργόνων⟩ suppl. Triclinius e schol.
11 ἄυσε(ν) codd.: ἄνυσεν Σ^{γρ}: ἄνυσσεν Boeckh

---

[1] Acragas, both the city and its eponymous nymph.
[2] Of song (schol.) or the song as well as the wreath (Gilder-sleeve).

12. FOR MIDAS OF ACRAGAS

WINNER, PIPE PLAYING, 490 B.C.

I beseech you, lover of splendor, loveliest of mortals' Str. 1
    cities,[1]
abode of Persephone, you who dwell upon the well-built
    height
above the banks of the Acragas, where sheep graze, O
    queen,
along with the good will of gods and men graciously
receive this crown[2] from Pytho offered by famous Midas 5
and welcome the man himself, who defeated Hellas in the
    art
which Pallas Athena once invented
by weaving into music the fierce Gorgons' deathly dirge

that she heard pouring forth from under the Str. 2
    unapproachable
snaky heads of the maidens in their grievous toil, 10
when Perseus cried out in triumph as he carried the third
    of the sisters,[3]
bringing doom to wave-washed Seriphus and its people.

---

[3] Or, moving the comma in 10 after λειβόμενον: *that she
heard pouring forth . . . when in his grievous toil Perseus cried
out for help the third time as he carried a portion of the sisters*. Cf.

ἤτοι τό τε θεσπέσιον Φόρκοι᾿ ἀμαύρωσεν γένος,
λυγρόν τ᾿ ἔρανον Πολυδέκτᾳ θῆκε ματρός τ᾿
    ἔμπεδον
15 δουλοσύναν τό τ᾿ ἀναγκαῖον λέχος,
εὐπαράου κρᾶτα συλάσαις Μεδοίσας

Γ´ υἱὸς Δανάας, τὸν ἀπὸ χρυσοῦ φαμὲν αὐτορύτου
ἔμμεναι. ἀλλ᾿ ἐπεὶ ἐκ τούτων φίλον ἄνδρα πόνων
ἐρρύσατο παρθένος αὐλῶν τεῦχε πάμφωνον μέλος,
20 ὄφρα τὸν Εὐρυάλας ἐκ καρπαλιμᾶν γενύων
χριμφθέντα σὺν ἔντεσι μιμήσαιτ᾿ ἐρικλάγκταν
    γόον.
εὗρεν θεός· ἀλλά νιν εὑροῖσ᾿ ἀνδράσι θνατοῖς ἔχειν,
ὠνύμασεν κεφαλᾶν πολλᾶν νόμον,
εὐκλεᾶ λαοσσόων μναστῆρ᾿ ἀγώνων,

Δ´ λεπτοῦ διανισόμενον χαλκοῦ θαμὰ καὶ δονάκων,
26 τοὶ παρὰ καλλίχορον ναίοισι πόλιν Χαρίτων
Καφισίδος ἐν τεμένει, πιστοὶ χορευτᾶν μάρτυρες.
εἰ δέ τις ὄλβος ἐν ἀνθρώποισιν, ἄνευ καμάτου
οὐ φαίνεται· ἐκ δὲ τελευτάσει νιν ἤτοι σάμερον

25 θαμὰ ν (ἔνιοι θαμὰ Π⁴²): θ᾿ ἅμα VΠ⁴²
26 καλλίχορον Π⁴²: καλλιχόρῳ ν: καλλιχώρῳ V | πόλει V

A. Köhnken, "Two Notes on Pindar," *Bulletin of the Institute of Classical Studies* 25 (1978) 92–95.

Yes, he blinded the awesome race of Phorcus[4]
and he made painful for Polydectes his feast, the
    enforced
bondage of his mother, and her bed of compulsion,   15
after severing the head of beautiful-cheeked Medusa—

the son of Danaë, who, we tell, was born of free-flowing   Str. 3
gold. But when she[5] had rescued her beloved hero from
those toils, the maiden composed a melody with every
    sound for pipes,
so that she might imitate with instruments the echoing   20
    wail
that was forced from the gnashing jaws of Euryale.
The goddess invented it, but invented it for mortals
to have, and she called it the tune of many heads,
famous reminder of contests where people flock,

the tune that often passes through the thin bronze and   Str. 4
    the reeds
which grow by the Graces' city[6] of beautiful dancing   26
    places
in the precinct of Cephisus' daughter,[7] faithful witnesses
    of dancers.
If there is any happiness among men, it does not appear
without toil. A god will bring it to fulfillment either
    today—

[4] The three Graeae, daughters of Phorcus as were the Gorgons, had only one eye among them, which Perseus took, refusing to return it until they told him how to find their sisters.
[5] Athena.   [6] Orchomenus (cf. *Ol.* 14.1–4).
[7] The nymph Copaïs.

30 δαίμων—τὸ δὲ μόρσιμον οὐ παρφυκτόν—ἀλλ᾽ ἔσται
        χρόνος
    οὗτος, ὃ καί τιν᾽ ἀελπτίᾳ βαλών
    ἔμπαλιν γνώμας τὸ μὲν δώσει, τὸ δ᾽ οὔπω.

30 τὸ δὲ Triclinius: τό γε vett. | οὐ παρφυκτόν v (γρ[άφε-
τ(αι)] κ(αὶ) οὐ παρφυκτόν Π⁴²: οὖ πα φυκτόν VΠ⁴²
   31 ἀελπτίᾳ edd.: ἀελπτία Vβ: ἀελπία B: ἀελπείᾳ Mommsen

what is fated cannot be avoided—but there will come   30
that time which, striking a person with surprise,
will unexpectedly give one thing, but defer another.

APPENDIX

GENEALOGIES

The line of Laius (*Ol.* 2)

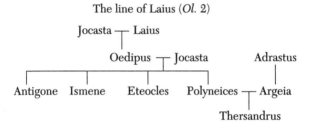

The Daughters of Cadmus (*Ol.* 2, *Pyth.* 3, 11)

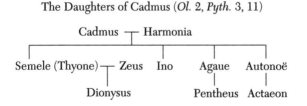

APPENDIX

Tlapolemus (*Ol.* 7)

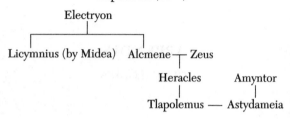

Aeacus and the Aeacidae (*Ol.* 8, *Nem.* 3, etc.)

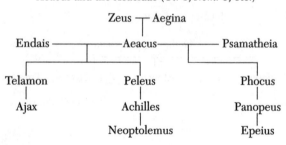

APPENDIX

Deucalion and Pyrrha (*Ol.* 9)

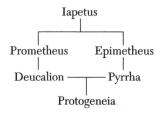

Aeolus and the Aeolidae (*Pyth.* 4)

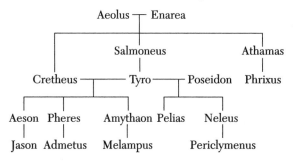